Upstaging
the
Cold War

A volume in the series
Culture, Politics, and the Cold War
Edited by Christian G. Appy

Upstaging the Cold War

American Dissent and Cultural Diplomacy, 1940–1960

Andrew J. Falk

University of Massachusetts Press

AMHERST AND BOSTON

LC 2009045170
ISBN 978-1-55849-728-3

Designed by Dennis Anderson
Set in Trump Mediaeval
Printed and bound by Thomson-Shore, Inc

Library of Congress Cataloging-in-Publication Data

Falk, Andrew Justin, 1969–
Upstaging the Cold War : American dissent and cultural diplomacy, 1940–1960 /
Andrew J. Falk.
p. cm. — (Culture, politics, and the Cold War)
Includes bibliographical references and index.
ISBN 978-1-55849-728-3 (cloth: alk. paper)
  1. Motion picture industry—Political aspects—United States—History—20th
century.   2. Motion pictures—Political aspects—United States—History—20th
century.   3. Screenwriters—United States—Political activity.   4. Blacklisting of
authors—United States—History—20th century.   5. Television and politics—
United States—History—20th century.   6. Communism and motion pictures—
United States.   7. Cold War—Influence.   I. Title.
PN1993.5.U6F34 2010
302.2'343097309045—dc22
2009045170

British Library Cataloguing in Publication data are available.

For Kristen
another book for her collection

That is a mystery that has disturbed rulers all over the world—
how the people know . . . how news runs through censorships,
how the truth of things fights free of control. It is a great mystery.

—John Steinbeck, *The Moon Is Down*

Contents

Illustrations

Acknowledgments

ONE OF THE great joys in being a historian is the ability to spend time with interesting people from the past. This book allowed me access to the private thoughts and correspondence of many gifted diplomats, moguls, and screenwriters of the period. I suspect, and my family will probably agree, that I would have completed this book sooner had I not found myself drawn into reading some of the most intellectually intoxicating letters and scripts I have ever seen. And yet, for all their notoriety, policymakers and playwrights understood that their work relied on a crowd of others: presidents and producers, investigators and performers, speechwriters and copyeditors, columnists and critics, voters and audiences. Like the texts it analyzes, this book itself is the product of collaboration.

Many archivists and librarians oriented me to their collections and pointed me toward relevant documents. I received valuable assistance at the National Archives in Washington, D.C., and at College Park, Maryland, in several divisions of the Library of Congress; the Harry Truman Presidential Library in Independence, Missouri; the Dwight D. Eisenhower Presidential Library in Abilene, Kansas; the Wisconsin Historical Society in Madison, and the Harry Ransom Humanities Research Center and the Perry-Castañeda Library in Austin, Texas.

Janet Davis, Roderick Hart, Gunther Peck, Jim Sidbury, and Penny Von Eschen challenged me as I formed my thoughts on the connections between nationalism, politics, and popular culture. Stephen Berrey, Rebecca Montes-Donovan, Clint Starr, and John Troutman—the esteemed *Writer's Bloc*—brought fresh perspectives, critical eyes, and much camaraderie. Nick Cull, Chris Endy, Robert Griffith, Laura McInaney, Chester Pach, Richard Pells, and Marilyn Young read portions of rough text, and their comments helped refine the argument. Bob Schulzinger and Tom Zeiler, the editors of *Diplomatic History*, granted me permission to use portions of my article from that journal and stimulated me with each issue. Frank Costigliola advised on the themes early on and later steered me toward the University of Massachusetts Press. Robert Abzug, Sally Clarke, Wm. Roger Louis, and Thomas Schatz read the entire manuscript and offered constructive criticism from their diverse perspectives. Michael Stoff, a master writer and teacher, balanced incisive criticism with compassion in his valuable feedback. Mark Lawrence is too modest to appreciate how indispensable he has been in helping me conceptualize the book and providing wise professional advice.

The Department of History at the University of Texas at Austin provided generous support in the form of a Eugene and Dora Bonham research grant and the Centennial Travel Grant. A postdoctoral fellowship at the University of Georgia provided time for reflection, revision, and a chance to meet with Bill Stueck on a regular basis. Travel funds and a dean's grant from the College of Liberal Arts and Sciences at Christopher Newport University helped in the later stages of editing and publication; my colleagues in the history department provide a collegial and stimulating professional home. In particular, I have benefited from the counsel of Phil Hamilton, Brian Puaca, Sheri Shuck-Hall, and Xiaoqun Xu.

Chris Appy, the general editor of the series Culture, Politics, and the Cold War, inspired me by producing and supporting scholarship that broadens our collective understanding of the Cold War era. His comments, and those of the anonymous reviewers, strengthened the final work and helped me fit it into the larger series. I am indebted to Clark Dougan, senior editor at the University of Massachusetts Press, who encouraged me and demystified the publication process. I thank them for supporting my manuscript at various stages and, along with the fine staff at the press, for seeing it through to publication.

Though this book is the product of collaboration, of course, I alone carry the responsibility for any shortcomings.

I owe special thanks to my friends and family. George Bouza and Megan and Justin Booth graciously opened their homes for extended research trips. Other relatives and friends offered helpful suggestions, expressed interest often, and celebrated milestones along the way. In particular, I wish to acknowledge Cindy Falk and Charles Rahm, Debra and Mark Gojer, Margaret Karns, Liz and Ted Karns, Scott Karns, Bud Colgan, Susan Falk, and Jean McFaddin.

It is no overstatement to say that much of what appears on these pages is there because of my parents, Janis and Byron Falk. They fostered a love of learning and of history, and they instilled in me the value of persistence, qualities crucial to completing this book. Always quick to express pride in my achievements to anyone who will listen, they assisted me in many ways but especially by providing their respect and love.

My children, Noah and Lauren, have added much-needed perspective and have brought me immense pride and joy. Perhaps as adults they'll read this story at a bedtime in the future and recall how we shared a curiosity about the world around us. They and Ben delight me and remind me that my domestic affairs are more important than old foreign affairs.

My wife, Kristen, shared so many of the trials and triumphs associated with this book that I cannot possibly list them all. During the research process she spent long days in archives and many weeks away from home. More than once I found my files filled with her marginalia on Dean Acheson or Dore Schary. During the writing process she spent countless nights reading drafts and editing chapters. She also managed her own career and cared for our children. Through it all, I benefited from Kristen's intelligence, good humor, patience, and love. It's a rare pleasure to dedicate a book to someone who enjoys reading so many of them.

Upstaging
the
Cold War

Introduction

The New Negotiators

Scene One: 1939

A FEW MINUTES past three on the sunny afternoon of April 30, 1939, President Franklin Roosevelt officially opened the New York World's Fair. For the next six months, Depression-weary Americans happily shelled out money all day long to enjoy the many attractions there. Thematically, the fair offered a look at peace and progress by focusing on worlds of tomorrow where problems of the present day—traffic, pollution, poverty—had been solved. There was little to suggest that much of the rest of the world had been swallowed by fascism, militarism, and dictatorship. The peace and progress represented here were general, platitudinous, and apolitical. By incorporating these themes, the fair said more about Depression-era anxiety and optimism than anything else. Indeed, few visitors believed such idyllic visions were part of any American-led program for the world. Americans at that time generally preferred to look inward, and fairgoers marveled at the city, not at the world beyond its borders. As one observer of the fair noted, "New York in 1939 had its own style of life, and the nation as a whole admired, copied and enjoyed it."[1] The local mattered more than the national in many ways.

That year was hailed as Hollywood's greatest, not just in box office receipts but also by critics. Many fine motion pictures lit up the big screen: *The Wizard of Oz, Stagecoach, Ninotchka,* Frank Capra's *Mr. Smith Goes to Washington,* and David O. Selznick's *Gone with the Wind.* At the fair a copy of Margaret Mitchell's classic novel was placed inside a time capsule along with a newsreel. Screenwriter Dalton Trumbo wrote at least six scripts that year and also openly engaged in leftist politics as part of the Popular Front in Hollywood. Playwright Lillian Hellman was the toast of Broadway when she earned a Pulitzer Prize for *The Little Foxes.*

1

Americans gather around a television set at the RCA exhibit at the New York World's Fair, 1939. Courtesy Library of Congress, Prints & Photographs Division, LC-USZ62-116255.

Those attending the fair, though, were most intrigued by a new medium on the horizon: television. At the RCA pavilion, on the Avenue of Progress near the Court of Peace, twelve television receivers were put on display for the public to inspect. *Amos & Andy* sparred in blackface during the experimental demonstrations. The young teenager Rod Serling was there, and probably passed without noticing the DuMont advertisement proclaiming, "Sooner than you think, television will play a vital part in the life of the average American."[2] David Sarnoff, chairman of RCA, announced the birth of television with "a feeling of humbleness." Sarnoff had reason for humility, for television would not overtake motion pictures for many years to come. The fair closed its gates in October 1940, at which time war gripped Europe and the Pacific and forced Americans to come to terms with its ambiguous role in world affairs.

Though Selznick, Trumbo, Hellman, Serling, and Sarnoff could not have anticipated it, their lives would mingle in national and international affairs in the coming years. Each would seek to construct an American national identity for global consumption through the media. During and after the Second World War—a seminal period in all their lives and in the national experience—individuals within culture industries helped shape American foreign relations in supportive and critical ways, in the content of their scripts and from behind the scenes, at home and abroad.

Scene Two: 1950

A few years later and a political eon away, during the summer of 1950 another world's fair was held, this time in Chicago under the banner "Frontiers of Freedom." It reflected a world remarkably different from the one that had existed in 1939. Ten minutes from the downtown Loop, patrons strolled through sixty acres of parks devoted to showing the best of Cold War America. As Robert Haddow explains, "The fair trumpeted American superiority with its displays of new technologies and their ability to transform age-old problems into a modern utopia."[3] It showcased fashionable clothing, kitchen appliances, and television, which was quickly becoming a symbol of postwar capitalist abundance. Planners hoped the Chicago fair would promote American business, but the primary product they sold was America itself. This was especially, evident when, the day after the fair opened, President Harry Truman learned that communist North Korea had ignited the Korean War. Men in uniform were admitted free to see, in the words of the fair's president, "what we are fighting for."[4]

Although the nation was portrayed as a dynamo of economic and technological progress much as the New York fair had done in 1939, now a decade later in Chicago, the United States was portrayed as a beacon of political· progress as well. Guests consumed a sanitized and idealized past. Three times a day audiences crammed in to see "the American story" of pioneers who had made peace with Natives, had triumphed over the elements, "had thrown off the yoke of oppressive aristocracy in favor of representative government," and had been reunited by common purpose after civil war. Following that show, audiences took a train to the Showboat Theater and viewed "Dixieland" exhibits that implied racial harmony and unity.

In 1950 the "titans of industry" promised to continue the nation's progress by domesticating the atom for postwar families. Just a few months after the Soviets detonated their atomic device, American policymakers told nervous citizens about peaceful uses for the atom. Representatives from Westinghouse encouraged suburbanites to enter the Theater of the Atom and "learn how atomic power may someday cure cancer . . . and, perhaps, carry rockets to the moon." In the short term, though, Westinghouse could only demonstrate its "atomic exploding mousetraps."[5] Also in 1950, Paul Hoffman, head of the Economic Cooperation Administration and the Marshall Plan, explained that Americans must wage a Cold War on four fronts: military, economic, political, and cultural. "Set the Marshall Plan's bread and butter" against "the hollow cake of the Big Lie," Hoffman wrote that year in a book titled *Peace Can Be Won*. That American culture could influence world opinion was not a new concept in 1950, but policymakers more consciously than ever before crafted and censored a panoply of political programs.

The year also witnessed both the rise to prominence of Joseph McCarthy and the State Department's new, global containment policy, which encompassed a cultural dimension. This environment led to more purges of perceived radicals in the artistic community. Ardent Cold Warriors hoped to root out artists who challenged anticommunism, expressed anxiety over atomic testing, distrusted expansive capitalism, criticized Red hysteria, promoted pacifism, encouraged anticolonialism and civil rights, and generally contested notions of American exceptionalism—opposing in many ways all that the Chicago world's fair heartily endorsed. In 1950 the most well-known leftist purveyors of "subversive" propaganda— Dalton Trumbo and the rest of the Hollywood Ten—exhausted their appeals and went to prison for refusing to "name names." Many others, including the prominent playwright Lillian Hellman, found themselves blacklisted. Lesser-known talent, such as writers Rod Serling and Paddy Chayefsky, expressed sympathy for Cold War critics and brought similar views to the infant television industry. Despite the striking differences of opinion regarding American character which simmered under the surface, themes of national unity, middle-class domesticity, democratic-capitalism, progress, and anticommunism were on display for Americans and the world in Chicago during the summer of 1950.

Scene Three: 1959

Almost another decade passed, and the scene shifted to Moscow in 1959, where the Eisenhower administration oversaw an American exhibition in Sokolniki Park. On July 25, 1959, Vice President Richard Nixon opened this latest attempt to portray America to the world, especially to the Soviets. The pavilion exhibited many examples of modern art, hardly the Norman Rockwell paintings that the anticommunist Nixon preferred.[6] It included a sculpture by Jo Davidson, the blacklisted leader of a radical organization labeled by the government years before as "subversive." The screenwriter Paddy Chayefsky, who had earlier been under observation by suspicious FBI investigators for his unflattering portrayals of American antiheroes, like *Marty*, also went on tour to Moscow, this time representing the State Department. By exporting his censored scripts to the

BBC, Rod Serling had secured for himself an international reputation as a Cold War critic and advocate for nuclear disarmament. Such events annoyed some anticommunists in Congress who worried about how the nation was being represented to the world, but they could do little to change things. Their day of unencumbered influence had passed.

Nixon's famous "kitchen debate" with Soviet premier Nikita Khrushchev took place in front of David Sarnoff's then-prevalent RCA cameras. Instantaneous television transmission made it possible for the world to view the Cold War contest. *New York Times* reporter James "Scotty" Reston stood by, "wondering whatever became of diplomacy."[7] In fact, diplomacy had changed its meaning in the years since 1939. The impromptu debate may have appeared on the screen, but the icon of consumer economies that carried it to audiences—television—was almost as relevant to foreign policy as the epithets Nixon and Khrushchev pitched at each other. American culture, in terms of content and consumer product, provided a formidable weapon in the nation's arsenal. What appeared to be cultural exchanges intended to "further understanding" offered only a facade of real peace in 1959. Eisenhower and Khrushchev marketed a "spirit of Camp David," and they made gestures toward "peaceful coexistence," but both maintained bipolarity.

That same year, the screenwriter Dalton Trumbo, one of the most prominent blacklisted artists in America, wrote the screenplay for *Exodus* and adapted *Spartacus* for the screen. His name appeared on both motion pictures, and the blacklist effectively ended after a decade of ghost writing from expatriate havens in Europe and from behind false or borrowed names. But perhaps the more amazing event involving Trumbo took place with little fanfare: an agent representing Hollywood studios negotiated for the release of another Trumbo film, *The Brave One*, in the Soviet Union, and the USIA Motion Picture Service at the State Department endorsed the deal.[8] The Eisenhower administration had appropriated progressive talent and themes as a means to wage the Cold War and undermine the Soviet bloc. American public diplomacy programs had come to rely on dissident talent to promote America abroad.

A world's fair, such as the ones in these three instances, provides a good snapshot of the nation by capturing people and their values in time. America stood for different things in 1939, 1950, and 1959. The fairs also show the intersection where the domestic and the foreign meet, because the exhibitions are physical sites where nations introduce themselves to the world. These features—the shift in attitudes of citizens over time and the changing identity of the nation on the global stage—are intrinsic to this study of American politics, culture, and foreign relations during the period encapsulated in these three snapshots.[9]

Standard histories of the period 1940–1960, especially those that have focused on American policymakers as the key actors, have shown how Cold Warriors in government embraced anticommunism, unilateralism, bipolarity, global containment, and a belief in robust capitalism and American exceptionalism. Policymakers and their allies successfully marginalized, if not outright silenced, voices of dissent in the United States. As the ideological contest against communism solidified by 1950, American propagandists saw value in exporting a sanitized and idealized version of the national identity for global consumption, as encapsulated at the Chicago fair. While policymakers in Washington investigated private political activities, convened congressional hearings, and withheld passports, they relied on their partners in Hollywood, Broadway, and the television networks, among others, to police their industries, censor content, and employ a blacklist in support of national policy. To readers of this traditional narrative, the world's fair of 1950 looks familiar; but how can one explain the rehabilitation of the writers and performers who reappear in the final scene in 1959, when these influential Cold War critics found themselves working under the auspices of the United States government?[10]

This book argues that American cultural diplomacy was nurtured in a cradle of dissent. By shifting our attention toward people outside of government, by tracing dissent from one medium to another, and by turning the page of the traditional narrative, we see that Cold War critics continued to carve out cultural space for free expression and foreign policy dissent well into the 1950s. Further, they found outlets in the United States and abroad to reach mass audiences, many of whom welcomed more realistic portrayals of the superpower than Cold Warriors preferred. Eventually, propagandists became convinced that they could turn the export of American dissent into an asset in the Cold War contest for hearts and minds by selling American values and extending American influence. American dissenters persisted and helped feed the state's propaganda machine.

The New Negotiators

While policymakers tried to construct public information and propaganda campaigns for global consumption, individuals in culture industries— film, television, and theater—offered competing messages about American foreign policies. They addressed the developing conflict with the Soviet Union, control over nuclear weapons, participation in the United Nations, support for anticolonial movements, and other contentious issues. The critics' alternative ideology influenced their actions behind the scenes as well as the content of their scripts. Though they may not have thought of themselves in these terms, Cold War critics became America's new negotiators.[11]

Negotiators are politically active representatives of the nation who seek to influence policy and help define national interests for foreign audiences. American Cold War critics fit the description. They organized themselves into unions and joined other institutions and causes to express opinions and to affect policy. Artists such as Trumbo and Hellman formed ties between themselves and the nation by speaking on issues far removed from their local work and by communicating their views to audiences in Washington and around the country. Even the more circumspect writers, such as Serling and Chayefsky, believed they could use the medium of television to change attitudes on issues ranging from atomic testing to anticommunist hysteria to muscular Americanism. Popular culture became an avenue to earning money and to transporting ideological beliefs to the public.[12] Critics all shared some level of consciousness about their activities as influential political actors on the world stage. If they did not, the government made them aware of it. Government officials viewed cultural producers as influential activists in relation to American foreign policy. Once dissent reached foreign shores, Cold Warriors in Congress and in the State Department bureaucracy feared that critics—as new negotiators—would use film, television, and theater to undermine international perceptions of American unity and leadership. The state found ways to silence these voices and prevent them from "negotiating" on behalf of the United States. Only once it became apparent that foreign audiences had embraced American dissent did American policymakers incorporate that dissent into official public diplomacy. If few recognized Trumbo and Serling as new negotiators earlier, by 1959 many agreed that they were. Whether cultural producers worked in concert with the state or at cross-purposes with it, government officials agreed that cultural diplomacy could be used to unite Americans, to unite the "Free World" under American leadership, to undermine the communist bloc, and to win the hearts and minds of people in nonaligned regions of the world.

Incorporating the activities of new negotiators changes the way we view public diplomacy, an area of increasing scholarly interest.[13] I use the term "cultural diplomacy" to refer to the collaborative process that creates and sustains official and informal cultural interaction between nations. Although most historians agree that propaganda, psychological warfare, and other information campaigns involve the state, others note that the government often relies on nonstate actors, nongovernmental organizations, and private efforts to fulfill the national mission. In these studies, typically the state (as sponsor) and the nonstate actor (as client) mutually agree to form a partnership and, many times, fashion popular and sanitized "middlebrow" programs that complement American diplomatic initiatives.[14]

I attempt to build on these works by demonstrating three things. First, there has been much contention and volatility involved in the formation, execution, and reception of American cultural diplomacy programs in film, television, theater, and other public exhibitions. By moving away from the state, one can see that cultural diplomacy is a messy and mutable process of collaboration and adaptation involving a variety of media. The story I present is a history of the foundations of diplomacy, of ideas and organization. It sheds light on policy formation, bureaucratic developments, and the marketplace of ideas that influence those processes.

Second, policymakers and private citizens have concerned themselves with many issues related to American foreign policy: political, economic, strategic, racial, legal, and gendered. Other studies examine thoroughly a particular medium or genre, a specific theme or issue, or a few key works. This one tries to show the breadth of activity in cultural programming even when it examines a few important actors representing many others.[15] Ultimately, I seek to demonstrate the complexity of American cultural programming as the state's official message competes with the message offered by unofficial, influential, dissenting messengers.

Third, this book explores the roles played by foreign audiences in the late 1950s, when they helped dictate changes in American cultural diplomacy. Already several fine studies prove that Washington has struggled to control cultural diplomacy. This interpretation attempts to link foreign tastes with changes in American policy. Undoubtedly, future studies will rely more heavily on foreign sources to develop this argument, but evidence suggests that independent American cultural producers and European audiences were more active and the state more reactive than typically portrayed in triumphal histories of the Cold War.

While the narrative is important to any history, so too is the theoretical framework it employs. The many forms of popular culture under discussion represent the attitudes, values, and worldviews that made up ideologies at that time, which in turn constructed a Cold War–era national identity. In his groundbreaking work *Ideology and U.S. Foreign Policy*, Michael Hunt argues that "ideology is central, not incidental, to policymaking" and that such ideas "are closely intertwined with domestic political values and arrangements." Here I view ideology as a network of ideas closely associated with a "worldview"—a system of symbols and beliefs that individuals express with sincerity in what Hunt calls "public rhetoric." Such rhetoric is a form of communication widely disseminated and "easily understood by its audience" whether viewers agree with the message in whole, in part, or not at all.[16] As historian Frank Ninkovich has suggested, "ideology travels," and it may be expressed powerfully in popular culture.[17] Whereas the dominant or majority culture crafts programs to normalize its ideology, others outside traditional institutions of power—producers, playwrights, and performers, for example—often have sought to legitimize their ideology with no less enthusiasm.[18]

People expressing conflicting ideologies, therefore, seek to exert power over the production, distribution, and exhibition of popular culture. By doing so they indirectly help define the national identity that those forms of culture represent. One premise implied in this book is that power rests with all who use it, not just governments and armies. According to Michel Foucault, power is diffuse. Nobody has all the power; it just exists to be used—in this case, to define the national identity for domestic and foreign audiences.[19] Another premise is that nationalism is "primarily a principle which holds that the political and national unit should be congruent." The state uses its implied power to override other entities and individuals at home and abroad with the purpose of aligning the views of the state with representations of the nation. Power, then, so central to understanding traditional diplomacy, is at the core of the story contained in this book.[20]

Upstaging the Cold War traces the new negotiators across time and space, from 1940 to 1960, from Hollywood to television, from political activities to production content to audiences, from America to Europe. The first two chapters show that during the 1940s the motion picture industry confronted problems related to international affairs: anticommunism, anti-Semitism, interventionism, foreign trade, the Second World War, and "domestic fascism." Whereas executives emphasized their American identities and formed partnerships with the government, progressive talent sought to fashion a new world order based on other principles: universalism, anticolonialism, self-determination, humane capitalism, and impartiality in judging the actions of all nations. They used their influence in cultural affairs to enter political fights over the atomic bomb, foreign aid, Palestine, and the United Nations.

Chapters 3 and 4 demonstrate that progressive ideology also permeated film content. As superpower relations deteriorated, Cold Warriors cast the activities of the Hollywood Left as antithetical to American values. Anticommunists alienated radicals and opened foreign markets to friendly producers who silenced progressive voices in Hollywood.

Chapters 5 and 6 explain how, with traditional avenues of political protest closed to them, progressives used the utopian experiment of television as a megaphone for their dissent. Government officials, network executives, advertising agencies, the artistic community, and citizen groups believed that television held great promise as a democratizing medium. In particular, executives at the National Broadcasting Company (NBC) and the Columbia Broadcasting System (CBS) viewed themselves as stewards of the public interest and guarantors of quality television. The networks institutionalized censorship as a means to *promote* progressive themes rather than to excise them hastily. In the late 1940s and early 1950s, these individuals believed television should uplift and educate people, avoid racial stereotypes (especially of America's allies in the postcolonial world), and limit the excesses of capitalist influence. While the Hollywood Left buckled at this same moment, foreign policy dissent moved from motion pictures to television.

In the 1950s the Truman and Eisenhower administrations increasingly viewed the Cold War in ideological terms and emphasized American soft power. Policymakers constructed a cultural weapon to complement military and economic means of containing communism. The State Department exported "sanitized" images of America; anticommunists policed television; and networks redefined the "public interest." As the 1950s continued, progressive programs vanished, replaced by genres touting American exceptionalism.

The final chapter takes the story overseas, where progressives transported their dissent to outlets abroad. They presented Europeans with a perspective different from the cultural exports sponsored by the government, a view that European audiences embraced. When zealous anticommunists purged American exports of their progressive themes and sought to limit the activities of expatriates and dissidents, their methods appalled Europeans and embarrassed the Eisenhower administration, which learned that it was losing European support. By the late 1950s the administration had embraced progressive artists and their productions as cultural weapons. Both cultural critics and policymakers discovered new ways to stage the Cold War.

And like a good drama, this contest played itself out in darkened theaters and on television sets for audiences all over the world.

1

Hollywood in the Crucible of War

IN EARLY MAY 1940, Hollywood producer David O. Selznick spoke to an audience gathered at the University of Rochester. While his motion picture *Gone with the Wind* (1939) was playing in crowded movie houses around the country, Selznick had strutted through a season of awards ceremonies and speaking engagements. Hollywood's bespectacled "wunderkind"—at the very pinnacle of his storied career—gladly accepted critical praise and box office rewards that spring. But despite shepherding his production with an almost obsessive eye, Selznick had other things on his mind this night in Rochester. On the eve of Hitler's seizure of Paris, Selznick lectured students on "New Frontiers in American Life." At Hollywood's brightest moment and perhaps the world's darkest, Selznick stood at the intersection between foreign policy and popular culture.

That night, Selznick spoke of a new age dawning in world affairs as well as in cultural affairs. The man who produced what many regarded as Hollywood's greatest spectacular also understood that motion pictures reached beyond mere commercialism. "I am not insensitive to the importance of motion pictures upon the American way of living as a whole, and upon American thought, and indeed upon world thought," he told students eager to hear his message. With war on his and his listeners' minds, Selznick added, "As a propaganda medium, whether or not it is consciously so used, it has few if any equals." Of course, the political uses of cinema were well known already by 1940. "For better or for worse," Selznick told his audience, motion pictures affected the viewer's fundamental "ideals" and "behavior" by defining glamour, success, and even nationalism. American films constructed common values for "people of all races—white and yellow and brown—the whole world over" because audiences identified with Clark Gable, and "girls of six continents argue that they should

11

be allowed to behave differently than their mothers because of the screen behavior of Loretta Young." More broadly, "Democracy can find no more effective salesmen in the halls of a war-time Parliament than our Hollywood-created Hardy family." In sum, American films—acting as "this country's most fascinating ambassadors"—would project American power abroad.[1]

As powerful as the motion picture would be in the short term, a new frontier in television would go even further in the long term. Speaking months after David Sarnoff and Franklin Roosevelt introduced television at the New York World's Fair, Selznick implored his audience to envision a time in the future when Hollywood would broadcast motion pictures into "millions of homes throughout the world." Just imagine the prospects.[2]

Selznick, scion of an earlier generation of ethnic filmmakers, understood that the American motion picture industry was coming of age in the 1940s, with "a young generation taking over." Selznick was among them. Hollywood was populated by idealistic, ambitious, and influential individuals like him who infused their productions with political opinions. As much as the production process was the result of collaboration, individuals' ideas made their way to the screen. And in the 1940s, with little doubt, the film production process was enveloped in the most politically charged environment in its history. Political values, largely influenced by the changing world scene of the 1940s, affected motion picture content and the industry's production process itself. By looking at both industry development and cinematic content, one may see that a contest over American national identity took place during the 1940s, particularly in the crucible of the Second World War.

Rehearsal for War

Hollywood had changed dramatically since its founding almost fifty years earlier, from dusty desert to cultural showplace with a powerful, entrenched studio system. The "Big Eight" comprised the five "Major" studios—MGM, Paramount, Warner Bros., Twentieth Century-Fox, and RKO Pictures—and the three "Major Minor" studios: Universal, Columbia, and the important independent distributor United Artists.[3] Together, these eight studios accounted for 75 percent of American films and 65 percent of the world's films. All told, these eight studios controlled the domestic market by gathering 90 percent of the box office receipts.

Production was only one part of their operations in the 1940s. The five Majors also owned theater chains. Paramount alone controlled 1,250 theaters in forty-three states before the war. Others divided the country roughly into theater regions. The studio oligopoly thus dominated the motion picture process from production to distribution to exhibition. Such activities raised both studio profits and Justice Department eyebrows. New Dealers in the Justice Department recited a litany of allegations: studios bound talent to long-term contracts, forced theaters to rent films sight unseen in a practice called "blind bidding," attached shorts and newsreels to features, colluded to raise rental fees, and in a practice called "block-booking" demanded that theater owners showcase even the studios' mediocre output in order to exhibit the top-grossers as well.[4] As strong as its financial muscles were, the studio's true power lay in its ability to shape cultural images for Americans. Yet despite these indisputable signs of power, formidable problems already existed. In the years ahead, several forces—independent producers, talent guilds, and government regulators among them—would challenge studio authority.[5]

World events also would threaten long-standing practices and film content. Five significant issues preoccupied many segments of the Hollywood community before the Second World War: anticommunism, anti-Semitism, interventionism, foreign trade, and antitrust laws. In all cases these issues related to American foreign relations, to how the government and the American public viewed Hollywood, and to how the industry viewed itself. In no small part because of their struggles in these five areas, the studios became ardent supporters of, and eager partners with, the government's war effort.

One problem that preoccupied Hollywood before the war was the perceived spread of communism, especially as unions proliferated in southern California during the New Deal. Not everyone was aware of that preoccupation: in 1936 screenwriter Morrie Ryskind wrote about the lack of Hollywood "soap boxes" in an article for *The Nation*. "Hollywood is essentially a summer resort," he explained, where people "check their thinking caps and go in for some fun. They relax. Everybody relaxes," he concluded. "Even strict Marxists, I am reliably informed, relax at summer resorts."[6] Ryskind, the writer of Marx Brothers films, apparently knew more about Groucho than about Karl, for he was blind to Hollywood's boundless activism. At the very same time that Ryskind soaked up the California sun, prominent members of the film community attended lectures on the European situation, rallied against lynchings, collected money for political candidates, and organized labor into unions. Furthermore, a so-called Red Squad attacked "communistic" talent. In the eyes of many, Hollywood was not so much a "resort" as a powder keg.

While the Popular Front of leftist artists and activists enjoyed unprecedented freedom of expression during the 1930s, suspicious members of Congress investigated the social and political networks in Hollywood. At first Congress explored suspected communist connections in the Federal Writers Project and the Federal Theater Project but soon examined Hollywood when, in the mid-1930s, union leaders made efforts to organize the film community into separate trade guilds. These efforts proved controversial even though many political moderates signed membership cards. When the Screen Actors Guild (SAG) was formed in 1933, one *Variety* headline screamed, "Pinks Plan to Stalinize Studios," and studio recognition of SAG did not come for another four years.[7] Socialist Upton Sinclair's 1934 gubernatorial campaign in California further alarmed studio chiefs, some of whom smeared him in phony newsreels. Once the dust settled, a screenwriter proudly proclaimed in *The Nation*, "Hollywood is a union town."[8] Soon thereafter other guilds formed: the Screen Writers Guild (1938) and the Directors Guild of America (1939). Union activity brought new life to Hollywood activists. George Pepper, a violinist suffering with arthritis, found purpose as an organizer for musicians. Lillian Hellman and Lester Cole, frustrated by pay of $50 a week as readers at MGM, tried to organize their fellow workers. Even the waiters at the famous Brown Derby formed a union.

The calm did not last long. A prolonged battle between studio executives and the guilds took place when the guilds sought to affiliate with larger trade unions. In 1939 the International Alliance of Theatrical and Stage Employees (IATSE) sought to control all Hollywood labor under the American Federation of Labor (AFL), whereas studio executives favored the more amenable leadership of the United Studio Technicians Guild (USTG) under the Congress of Industrial Organizations (CIO). Eventually, IATSE and the AFL won the battle for union membership when an incredible 40,000 members in 849 individual locals (mostly the theater projectionists scattered around the country) joined a majority of Hollywood's workers under IATSE leadership. When this happened, frustrated studio executives found a way to alter the labor landscape.[9]

Hollywood's internal labor fight emerged just as Americans were changing their opinions regarding communism during the 1930s. Communism became identified less with the working class and the Depression-era difficulties and more with Stalinist brutality, purges, and show trials. Stalin's negotiation of his nonaggression pact with Hitler in 1939 further confused and embarrassed American communists. Some radicals merely accepted it. "I figured it was a temporary thing," actor Lionel Stander explained, "and that the reason for the Pact was the inability of the democracies to line up with the Soviet Union against Hitler." He added frankly, "I was never amazed or startled by the flip-flops of international diplomacy."[10] For most, though, it appeared that communism had shed its domestic economic applications and taken on a much darker and sinister international political meaning. To those Americans who had traditionally expressed misgivings with all things Red, Hollywood appeared to be among the most conspicuous places to find American communist activity. In truth, experts estimate there were no more than 300 party members in Hollywood at any time during the 1930s, but the perception overshadowed the reality.[11] And, at times, perceptions matter more.

In the face of the collapse of the leftist Popular Front by 1940, the ability to use the communist issue during an election year proved too tantalizing to resist for members of the Dies Committee of the House of Representatives. That year, charges of communist influence in the nation's sacred cultural institutions became common. Broadway, according to the *New York Mirror*, had become "the Great Red Way" as "parlor Reds" walked from their "pink penthouses" to "paint" the finest stages with red propaganda.[12] In February, Congressman Martin Dies targeted forty-three performers and suggested that they had ties to the Communist Party. Linking performers to communism was more than rhetorical growling that summer when the Smith Alien Registration Act became law. The Smith Act made it a crime to conspire to advocate the forcible overthrow of the government. By criminalizing leftist political meetings—and leftist ideology by extension—the government had declared war on cultural communists, both perceived and real. Many of those targeted looked for Dies to make a public declaration of their political purity in order to continue their careers, and in August, after meeting with such liberal actors as James Cagney, Humphrey Bogart, and Fredric March, Dies did "cleanse" them of any Red affiliation. But others were sacrificed.

Studio chiefs, backed by congressional activity, found IATSE's leaders more compliant in this anticommunist atmosphere. Once viewed by moguls and talent alike as a formidable labor organization, IATSE became a company union. Leftists viewed IATSE's leaders Willie Bioff and George Browne as corrupt sellouts. This transformation proved important when a rival labor organization emerged in 1941. Led by a ham-fisted former boxer, Herb Sorrell, the Conference of Studio Unions (CSU) sparred with IATSE for control over the Hollywood talent guilds. Studio moguls joined Bioff and Browne in a Red-baiting campaign to smear Sorrell and to alienate his membership. Charges of communist infiltration in Hollywood's unions raised more red flags in Washington. Rumors of more investigations spread in southern California. By 1941 one could say that all Hollywood talent had been efficiently unionized in just a few years' time, but that would ignore the internal divisions that remained well into the Cold War years.

On the eve of the Second World War, an uneasy calm settled on the combustible labor situation. But opposing camps would long remember how the volatile charges of communist activity played to a wider audience, especially as combatants sat under hot klieg lights in a Washington committee room. As Hollywood entered the war, labor strife and the public tarring of high-profile talent was an embarrassment for studio executives. Arguably, it led many of them to exhibit their citizenship credentials in the most overt ways during the years ahead.

Like anticommunism, Jewish "influence" was another problem related to world affairs which marred Hollywood's image in the prewar years. Jewish immigrants, hoping to make a better life for themselves by assimilating into America, in actuality became frustrated outsiders of mainstream society. The motion picture industry—seen as an institution catering to lowbrow culture—offered one of the few trades open to Jews in the early twentieth century, and many eventually prospered as moguls: Harry Cohn, William Fox, Samuel Goldwyn, Carl Laemmle, Louis B. Mayer, Nicholas Schenck, Jack and Harry Warner, Adolph Zuckor, and others. As these film czars bristled at their treatment beyond the borders of southern California, anti-Semites joined the fight. Congressman John Rankin of Mississippi, the spiritual leader of the Dies Committee, continually linked the "Jew Problem" with the "Negro Problem" as well as with communism. Congressman Gerald P. Nye went so far as to indict Jews for anti-Semitism when he said, "If anti-Semitism exists in America, the Jews have themselves to blame." Such views were even expressed in Hollywood. Joseph Breen, the industry's chief censor as head of the Production Code office (PCA), expressed his disgust at the very moguls with whom he worked on a daily basis. In confidential letters to fellow Catholics, Breen labeled Jews "the scum of the scum of the earth." His anti-Semitism was surpassed only by his anticommunism. And both topics preoccupied his mind as the centralizing authority on motion picture content.

Breen, Nye, Rankin, and others were in some ways responding to a demographic transformation taking place in Hollywood. Many refugees from Europe—actors, writers, directors, technicians—were fleeing to the safety and opportunity of the American motion picture community. Lionel Stander recalled that 1930s Hollywood became, in an ironic choice of words, "the Mecca" for Jewish artists and intellectuals.[13] Together, Hollywood Jews and their allies showed increasing political power during the European Jewish refugee crisis before the war. In 1938, as steamships wandered the Caribbean seeking a port of entry, several actors, some Jewish and some not, raised thousands of dollars to purchase visas for the passengers. Their representatives in Washington lobbied the State Department to cut diplomatic ties with Hitler's Germany. Some used personal contacts to negotiate with Mexican president Lázaro Cárdenas, urging him to accept more refugees as he had in the previous year, despite much local opposition. Such renegade diplomacy did not go unnoticed by the American press or Congress. Nor did these activities escape the notice of wary studio executives who wished to downplay their heritage and any opposition to American foreign policy.[14]

Amid congressional charges of a heavy Jewish hand, industry leaders moved away from old, ethnic film "factories" to modern American institutions. For example, Louis B. Mayer told a reporter that he "forgot" what part of Russia he emigrated from; he took July 4 for his birthday, one of the rare days of the year when his film studio shut down. Few executives practiced Judaism openly; several flirted with other religions. In some ways, Mayer's son-in-law, David O. Selznick, represented a new breed of independent producer who refused to be bound by studio tradition any more than by his ethnic heritage. He repeatedly rejected offers to join his father-in-law at MGM, preferring the life of an independent instead. Selznick's son later recalled that his father distanced himself from his Orthodox Jewish background, holding the sentiment, "You let a little Judaism in the house and where does it stop?"[15] Neal Gabler writes in *An Empire of Their Own* that studio heads were driven "to a ferocious, even pathological, embrace of America."[16] Studio executives—most of whom were Jews operating at a time when anti-Semitism was accepted with frustrating regularity—exhibited themselves and their studios as superpatriotic institutions during the impending war.

While anticommunism and anti-Semitism bedeviled Hollywood, so-called isolationists charged studios with encouraging American intervention in the European war. Members of the America First Committee worried that an "International Jewish conspiracy" was leading America into an unwanted war to aid the European refugees fleeing totalitarianism.[17] Noninterventionists had much to fret over in 1940 and 1941: the presidential contest between Franklin Roosevelt and Wendell Willkie offered little choice, since both preached preparedness; Britain's plight brought about worrisome programs such as Cash-and-Carry and Lend-Lease aid; Germany's dramatic invasion of the Soviet Union expanded the war and increased domestic political charges of "appeasement"; and *Time-Life* publisher Henry Luce's famous article "The American Century" made the firm case for internationalism. All combined to put nonintervention-ists even more on the defensive against what they perceived as the country's internationalist cabal.

In the fall of 1941, two leading noninterventionist congressmen, Burton K. Wheeler and Gerald Nye, announced their intention to hold hearings on Hollywood's propaganda machine, which they believed was warmongering in films such as Alfred Hitchcock's *Foreign Correspondent* (1940) and Charlie Chaplin's *The Great Dictator* (1940). They intended to bring the Interstate Commerce Commission into the investigation, thereby threatening Hollywood with the nightmare of antitrust accusations. In truth, Hollywood did produce several pro-intervention motion pictures. In *Sergeant York* (1941), Gary Cooper played the pacifist farmer who became a shy hero of the Great War; President Roosevelt even invited the aging York into the Oval Office after having viewed the film. In *Foreign Correspondent*, Joel McCrea played a wisecracking reporter who uncovers real danger in Europe and implores Americans to wake up to the realities he has discovered. (In an early treatment for the film, the PCA's Breen was dismissive, calling it "pro-Jewish propaganda.")[18] Similarly, Charlie Chaplin made an unmistakable interventionist plea in the guise of a Jewish barber in *The Great Dictator* (1940), his satire of Hitler. So powerful and memorable was his final soliloquy that Chaplin recited it over and over in several political settings, thereby extending the film into the real world. These and other movies provided enough evidence to motivate powerful noninterventionists into holding hearings.

On September 9, 1941, the Senate Interstate Commerce Committee hearings began. The Hollywood community was represented by the liberal Republican and interventionist Wendell Willkie. Noninterventionists charged that filmmakers were like any other munitions-makers leading the nation into an unwanted war. Motion picture content was seen as ammunition for a dubious cause, that of preparing the nation for intervention at a time when efforts at conciliation should surpass belligerence. Investigators subpoenaed Charlie Chaplin and called Henry Luce to testify about the *March of Time* documentary series. In a determined defense, Willkie charged Nye and others with overt government censorship. Worse yet, Willkie explained, Hollywood's opponents favored unrealistic portrayals of the European situation and sought to divide Americans along religious and racial lines.[19] Agreeing with Willkie, California's governor wrote to the committee: "To the extent that [movies] contribute to American unity in support of America's stand in its foreign relations during this grave world crisis, we believe the moving picture industry should be praised, not condemned."[20]

For the most part, Hollywood united against the unwelcome interference of Congress. Studio executives, industry talent, and their political allies joined forces against any inference linking them to the real "merchants of death." In November, shortly before Pearl Harbor, the hearings ended without resolution. Judging from the words and deeds of Dies, Rankin, Wheeler, and Nye, conservatives in Washington fussed over how insidious Jews and menacing communists had infiltrated the nation's motion picture industry and infected film content with their dreaded interventionism.[21] Such an image most certainly pained studio executives who were presiding over an empire under assault.

In fact, the empire was crumbling in some respects. Contributing to their other headaches, studio magnates and investors watched as their foreign markets vanished. This important development provided yet another reason for moguls to exhibit their Americanism when the war came, because executives would have appreciated government assistance in maintaining their hold on the world's lucrative motion picture trade. The European war significantly disrupted Hollywood's business abroad, especially in three prominent film-producing countries: Germany, Japan, and Italy. In 1937, citing the need to end contaminating outside influences, Germany cut Hollywood imports to the Fatherland, and the East European markets receded, virtually evaporating in proportion to the Nazi advance. In 1938, Japan cut its motion picture imports from 400 per year to 60. The following year, Italy threatened to suspend trade, thereby compounding difficulties.

By 1940 nearly all of Europe was lost as its markets to American exports dried up, except for a few neutral nations and Britain. Just as Britain became the free world's last great hope for European democracy in 1940, the British market became the studio moguls' final refuge. Yet even there, in the months before Pearl Harbor, over 650 theaters closed as a blitz-weary audience's attendance dropped by a quarter. Despite the domestic market's vitality, studio executives lamented the loss of overseas business, finding that they could do little other than make a few pro-British films. They hoped that the United States government could find a way to help them recoup some of their losses in the rapidly shrinking world by focusing on forming trade agreements with Latin America, Canada, and neutral Europe. But who would come to the aid of communists, Jews, and warmongers? The war seemed bad for business. Studios lost their world markets, and because of congressional oversight, content could no longer address the dominant issues of the day. A poor public image in Washington, anxious moguls assumed, prevented the studios from securing the full assistance they needed.[22]

Events propelled some desperate producers to seek deals with the Axis. David O. Selznick wrote to his associates in September 1940, "It should go without saying that no one in the organization could possibly have more violent feelings against the Axis countries than I have; and in view of these feelings I certainly would be the last one to want to engage in any business with them that I thought might remotely be beneficial to these countries." The cash-strapped Selznick expressed a view shared by others, however, that such trade *could* be right and good: "In my opinion the very worst thing that, in our limited way, we can do against these countries is to sell them our pictures!" Indeed, he believed that "the picture companies almost ought to be *forced* by Washington to sell their product in Italy, to get American films on the screens there as the one single medium of propaganda for glorifying Americans still open to this country."[23] Although the profit motive was certainly at the forefront of his thinking, Selznick understood that gaining the government's assistance in this endeavor required donning the garb of a nationalist. Apparently he believed that by portraying his product as propaganda he could win support to expand overseas. Producers held fast to the axiom that by serving national interests, they would be serving their personal interests. The war would provide them with an opportunity to display their patriotic credentials and to boost their financial well-being.

Given so many causes for concern, it may be easy to see why a diverse coalition—including conservatives and New Dealers, anticommunists, anti-Semites, noninterventionists, labor activists, small businessmen, Congressmen, and the Justice Department—all joined the attack on Hollywood. Antitrust legislation was a potent billy club at the government's disposal, for the mere mention of its application was threat enough to alter the outlook and action of even the most powerful movie mogul. Though the issue seemed to be a domestic one, the United States was not alone in its move toward dramatic government regulation.

During the 1930s, a decade noted for totalitarian regimes, virtually all the major motion picture–producing countries went beyond earlier practices of government involvement. In this way even American antitrust issues could be seen in international terms. In Germany, Hitler's ascent marked a significant change in that nation's thriving motion picture industry. The Nazi reliance on propaganda sparked an exodus of film-makers to Hollywood. In the Soviet Union, Stalin replaced Lenin's com-missar for information with his own bureaucrat, Boris Shumyatsky, who controlled the Soviet cinema and helped to construct Stalin's cult of per-sonality. Famed director Sergei Eisenstein's artistry did not appear on screen for a decade. Mussolini funneled substantial financial aid to the industry in Italy and founded both a studio (Cinecittà) and a film school (Centro Sperimentale); he then coddled the industry further by removing American competition. Japanese studios (particularly Nikkatsu, Shochiku, and Toho) turned their attention from facing their own violent labor dis-putes to buckling under the militarist government's increasing demands for cinematic support.[24]

Western republics too moved toward greater government involvement, which was also a central unifying mission of Roosevelt's diverse New Deal programs. But national boundaries solidified even among allies. Brit-ain imposed protectionist policies in the form of quotas on Hollywood exports, so that a frustrated London theater owner was compelled to show a certain number of British movies. A restrictive atmosphere for producers in Britain, combined with opportunities in Hollywood, convinced several great English directors and performers—such as Alfred Hitchcock, Lau-rence Olivier, and David Lean—that independence awaited them in Holly-wood during the 1930s.[25]

Foreign governments that involved themselves in their domestic motion picture industries emphasized the importance of nationhood in the lives of their citizens. Through film, such a country could rally its populace and disseminate its national values. The trend toward government involve-ment in these film industries provided for many needs of each nation: to control political content, to manage public opinion, to protect the finan-cial well-being of a home industry, and ultimately to project power and to prepare for war. In sum, many nations adopted a policy of cultural activ-ism, for doing so served national interests. In the late 1930s the United States was no different.[26]

In the United States, a determined government—consisting of indi-viduals with various motives—involved itself in the motion picture in-dustry and initiated antitrust legislation and litigation. A bill attacking block-booking passed the Senate Interstate Commerce Committee and the full Senate by 1939, only to fail in the House of Representatives. Undeterred, New Dealers in the Justice Department filed suit, and the federal court set a trial date for May Day in 1940. Already by then, over thirty private antitrust lawsuits had been filed against the major studios. Rightly fearing the worst and attempting to stanch the bleeding, studio executives signed a consent decree in 1940, essentially pleading nolo contendre to their crimes. Yet the antitrust campaign would continue intermittently during the war and relentlessly after it.[27] Even during the studios' greatest years of the 1930s and 1940s, antitrust suits signaled years of doom ahead.

International issues of communist conspiracy, anti-Semitism, the war, foreign trade, and state control affected the film industry by driving a wedge between studio executives, their talent, and individuals in government. At the very moment when Hollywood executives sought ways to overcome their differences with government, however, the war intervened and provided the means for reconciliation. Hollywood would support the American war effort for a complex set of reasons: personal, political, patriotic, and financial. Even so, Hollywood producers and talent entered into a debate over the national purpose in the international arena. That contest influenced events on the screen and behind the scenes.

Hollywood's "Reel" War

One evening in January 1943, the actor Walter Huston joined more than three hundred of Hollywood's elite for an organizational meeting of the new Hollywood Democratic Committee (HDC) at the stately Roosevelt Hotel in Los Angeles, an appropriately named place for the film community to discuss political matters. The HDC became one of Hollywood's key institutions for promoting Roosevelt's foreign policy and the war effort. At this early meeting, Huston explained Hollywood's purpose to those assembled with his resonant voice: "The eighty million Americans who unfailingly patronize pictures believe that we will not fail them. And we must not. We will not. We are proud to have a chance to offer our very best." Hollywood, he claimed, had a popular mandate for political activity. Although a staunch supporter of Franklin Roosevelt in the previous election, Huston invoked Roosevelt's opponent in order to raise awareness of, and increase membership in, the HDC: "Wendell Willkie said the other day, that 'experience has shown that you only get out of a war what you put into it.'. . . Well, let us put democracy into this war and we will get a democratic peace out of it. The Hollywood Democratic Committee is our weapon. Let us use it with a will to victory."[28] In just three months' time, the HDC wrote a constitution, held elections, and boasted a membership of 2,000. The artistic community agreed: cultural institutions had a critical role to play in this ideological war and beyond, a contest that could also ambitiously expand democracy at home.[29]

The diverse membership of the HDC cross-pollinated with the Independent Citizens Committee of the Arts, Sciences, and Professions (ICCASP), an affiliation that resulted in a veritable Who's Who of influential Americans. It included future anticommunist crusaders such as Ronald Reagan, future blacklistees such as Larry Adler, and radicals such as Paul Robeson. It included radio personalities such as Gertrude Berg, George Burns, and Eddie Cantor. It included studio executives such as Joseph Schenck and Jesse Lasky, directors such as George Cukor, and character actors such as Harry Carey. Generally, individuals with progressive perspectives joined the HDC, as did Lewis Milestone, director of the award-winning pacifist drama *All Quiet on the Western Front* (1930), and actress Gloria Stuart, a founder of the Screen Actors Guild. Composers Oscar Hammerstein and Ira Gershwin joined; so too did screenwriters Donald Ogden Stewart and Clifford Odets. In sum, the HDC contained a cross-section of the American artistic community: Tallulah Bankhead, Ethel Barrymore, Louis Calhern, Bennett Cerf, Norman Corwin, George Coulouris, Cheryl Crawford, Jane Darwell, Bette Davis, Olivia de Havilland, Jose Ferrer, John Garfield, Paulette Goddard, Ruth Gordon, Uta Hagen, Rita Hayworth, Walter Huston, George Jessel, Gene Kelly, Canada Lee, Fredric March, Groucho and Harpo Marx, Paul Muni, Edward G. Robinson, Richard Rodgers, Jerome Robbins, Franchot Tone, and Orson Welles. But the larger ICCASP organization extended far beyond Hollywood to include notable poets, composers, Broadway playwrights, novelists, graphic artists, scientists, and academicians such as W. E. B. Du Bois, Albert Einstein, Duke Ellington, Howard Fast, Lillian Hellman, Al Hirschfeld, James Montgomery Flagg, Langston Hughes, George S. Kaufman, Helen Keller, Sinclair Lewis, Helen Lynd, Dorothy Parker, Carl Sandburg, James Thurber, Mark Van Doren, and Max Weber. What happened to the HDC during and after the war shows in microcosm the transition of the nation from World War to Cold War. During the Second World War, the HDC enthusiastically supported the Allied effort.

Like other industries, the motion picture industry transformed itself for war. The government put the brakes on its antitrust litigation, signaling what John Morton Blum has called an across-the-board wartime "holiday for the trusts."[30] Ironically, the motion picture industry became even more heavily regulated by government with the intention of employing cinema for specific purposes: to boost morale, to convey information, to demonize the enemy, and to construct an easily recognizable national image. This transformation reinvigorated Hollywood creatively and financially as it forestalled further collapse.

Studios churned out war-related material on a large scale. Within a year after Pearl Harbor, no fewer than one-third of all features dealt directly with the war. In addition, newsreels, documentaries, and training films firmly established Hollywood as an important player, linking the war to audiences of all kinds. In the film cathedrals, congregations of Americans exposed themselves to cinematic sermons preaching certain truths. In general, Hollywood praised America's Soviet ally for courage and determination, employed racial stereotypes of the enemy "Other," and glorified American military heroism in defense of a united and diverse America. These common themes, confirmed merely by their repeated use, constructed a familiar belief system whereby Americans could understand the nation's involvement in the war and world affairs.[31] This image would undergo a spectacular change after the war as the same architects of its construction debated a new Cold War–era national identity. But for the time being, at least, most agreed on how these several wartime themes applied to the nation.

Two segments of the population recognizing Hollywood's importance were the government and the military. Franklin Roosevelt invested his faith in popular culture to drive public action. General George Marshall eventually came to view the motion picture on a par with military aircraft as "two new weapons" in the Allies' arsenal. As ad man Arthur Mayer wrote later in the war in an article for *Public Opinion Quarterly*, "The juxtaposition will seem startling to the average movie-goer," but, Mayer agreed with Marshall, nothing less than a "revolution" was taking place in their "own backyard."[32] Abroad, motion pictures proved significant in Roosevelt's efforts to build Pan-American goodwill in the Western Hemisphere, to introduce America to the Chinese, and to rehabilitate relations with the Soviets. For example, Frank Capra's famous *Why We Fight* series was dubbed in French, Spanish, Russian, and Chinese before being distributed abroad.[33] The heaviest output of motion pictures came only after an intense process of negotiation by some fifty military and civilian agencies, including Washington's Office of War Information (OWI) and Hollywood's Production Code, two institutions that repeatedly bickered over wartime film content.[34]

Government involvement in the cultural production process was certainly nothing new, but it rarely met with anything but grudging acceptance in Hollywood. During wartime, artists became increasingly sensitive to government interference in content decisions.[35] This was especially true as writers and directors learned about the propaganda machines in European totalitarian states. During the Great War, the United States, too, had experienced heavy-handed activity by an emerging regulatory state. At that time, George Creel's Committee on Public Information bludgeoned citizens with "100 percent Americanism" and unleashed hysteria. Haunted by that prospect, the old Wilsonian bureaucrat, President Roosevelt, cautioned his own propaganda man to show restraint and to avoid blatant jingoism. The soft sell, agreed OWI chief Elmer Davis, was the best form of propaganda even in a war where the choice seemed most obvious and the sacrifice most acceptable.[36] The subtle infusion of propagandist themes, passed subliminally into the American mind, was deemed right, good, and necessary by government officials; only after the war was this method questioned with frequency. But in mid-1942, Roosevelt approved the practice, and he appointed Lowell Mellett, a former editor of the *Washington Daily News*, to act as a liaison between the government and Hollywood as head of the Bureau of Motion Pictures (BMP) within the OWI. "The American motion picture is one of the most effective mediums in informing and entertaining our citizens," the president told Mellett. "The motion picture must remain free in so far as national security will permit. I want no censorship of the motion picture," he added with a only a bit of Rooseveltian hyperbole.[37]

Mellett explained to Hollywood producers that although not every motion picture had to be "*about* the war, or have a war background," studios should adapt their genres to the situation so that their output would "involve a consciousness of war."[38] Putting those ideas into practice, Mellett encouraged Hollywood to define the Allies, the enemies, the home front, industrial production, and the armed forces. Accordingly, the BMP's production code defined the "good society" as liberal, democratic, and internationalist. "We were always told by people in the OWI," Warner Bros. screenwriter Emmett Lavery recalled, "ask yourself if you can go into a projection room ten years from now and bear to look at it. If you think you can ten years in advance, it is probably reasonably close to the truth, and that is the line we want."[39] While the Hollywood Production Code continued to clamp down on the minutiae of morals and vice, the OWI primarily provided a general mission. That left the bulk of content decisions with the studios themselves.

When conservative enemies in Congress, fresh from electoral gains the previous fall, proposed slashing the OWI's funding in 1943, Elmer Davis warned them that they would be allowing an unregulated motion

Hollywood produces for the Overseas Picture Division of the Office of War Information, 1943. Courtesy Library of Congress, Prints & Photographs Division, LC-USW3-031481-C.

picture industry to control wartime content. That is precisely what happened. Although noted by historians for its influence, the OWI shaped Hollywood features through its domestic desk only for a single year and, even then, took Roosevelt's lead and primarily encouraged rather than dictated. With the OWI's budget gutted and its activities severely curtailed, Hollywood executives continued to define war themes just as Davis had foreseen. As Dorothy Jones, the OWI's head of film review and analysis explained later, "Final responsibility for the films made in Hollywood during the war has rested with the motion-picture industry."[40] The OWI hardly outlasted the war; President Harry Truman ended it in August 1945, transferring its foreign distribution component to the State Department. For the bulk of the war years, though, the motion picture industry enjoyed a high degree of autonomy to define the American national character.

Writers, producers, and government regulators collaborated to define the nation in liberal terms. Together, they emphasized themes of expansive democracy and the tangible benefits of internationalism. To buttress those themes, cultural producers designed readily identifiable participants in the drama: Americans, allies, and enemies. In practical terms, wartime Hollywood valorized the archetypal GI; praised his allies, particularly the Red Army soldier; relied on racial stereotypes to demonize the enemy; and displayed a united home front celebratory of its diversity. In each case, audiences accepted the theme as part of what can be considered their wartime collective memory, which lasted for the duration of the war. During the Cold War this network of themes underwent dramatic changes as battle lines were redrawn, enemies were made allies, and allies were made enemies. In some sense, these stock characters changed while the "script's formula" remained the same. Before looking at the changes in the "cast" during the Cold War, one should first look at the narrative written during the Second World War.

Racial identities underpinned many wartime depictions of foreign nationals. In some ways tagging other ethnicities with racial motifs amounted to a form of celluloid eugenics, whereby stereotypes were adapted and normalized in the name of the war effort. Filmmakers essentially classified Asian allies and enemies in relation to the Anglo-Saxon Western powers. By doing so, for example, Japanese militarists were no longer merely the temporary holders of political power within an island nation of distinct borders; rather, Hollywood transformed them into broader beings with fundamental and everlasting biological differences from those of Churchill's "English-speaking peoples of the world." Applying familiar and easily recognizable racial stereotypes to foreign peoples allowed Americans to make sense of the modern chaos around them and framed the way they viewed the *backward* allies they rescued and the sinister enemies they defeated. The significance of this activity would become apparent when these depictions of race continued after the war with respect to American radicals and Russian communists.

In contrast to the Japanese, the Chinese appeared as good friends of the West and sympathetic victims of Japanese aggression. In line with Roosevelt's desire to elevate Jiang Jieshi (Chiang Kai-Shek) and his nation to that of Asian "policeman," the OWI pleaded with Hollywood to depict the ancient culture as great and liberal. There was virtually no mention of Chiang's notoriously corrupt regime nor of the internal conflict between his nationalist Kuomintang and Mao Zedong's communists. Rather, the Chinese were portrayed as exotic peasants in the throes of unspeakable horror, devoted to a common purpose, and worthy of rescue by the West. Take, for example, the noble peasant family in the film adaptation of Pearl S. Buck's *The Dragon Seed* (1944). The sagacious father, Ling Tan (played by Walter Huston), struggles mightily to instill ancient customs into his modern-minded daughter, Jade (played by Katharine Hepburn). When their small Chinese village is invaded by the Japanese, the same rebelliousness she has exhibited against her father serves her well against the Japanese. Jade becomes heroic and rouses her father and community to action. The film poses two *threats* in this tale: the same Chinese traditionalists that confront the evil Axis also confront modernity in the form of Jade. But whereas the former threat is malevolent, the latter is benign, good, necessary, and Western.

This portrayal of the Chinese was put forth by a cast notable for the absence of Asian actors (for which later critics saw the patronizing film

as appalling). As in minstrel shows of old, whites donned a new face—
this one yellow rather than black—in this instance, to define the Chinese
as "diligent, honest, brave, and religious." These very terms are the ones
Americans applied to the Chinese people in public opinion surveys during the war.[41] Ultimately, the Chinese needed American help to repel the
Japanese aggressors, to make the transformation into a modern democracy and, apparently, to portray their own behavior.

The representation of the Chinese was thus sanitized for the war. Oddly,
old stereotypes, many of which had first been applied to the Chinese, were
reapplied to the Japanese. To Americans, Japanese soldiers were animalistic
subhumans: "yellow vermin," "mad dogs," "monkey men." The Japanese
"ape"—not unlike the cartoonish Irish simian and the beastly Hun depicted during the Great War—became an easily identifiable representation
of the Japanese. His thick glasses and his lean-and-hungry gaze combined
to form what John Dower calls the "dehumanization of the Other."[42] *Time*
magazine, published by China-born Henry Luce, employed racial "truths"
to help readers "Tell Your Friends from the Japs": eugenicists provided a
side-by-side comparison between tall, thin, lanky Chinese and short, fat,
stocky Japanese. The Chinese complexion was "parchment yellow" rather
than the deep, "earthy yellow" common to Japanese; the Japanese nose was
flatter, the face was bearded—all identifiers to make the Chinese more
"white" and the Japanese darker and stereotypically inferior. Moreover, the
Japanese were "dogmatic, arrogant."[43] Similar ideas were expressed by the
U.S. Army in a *Pocket Guide to China*.

Likewise, the Japanese were seen as the advance army of the Yellow
Peril, made up of menacing children and hard-working drones. They
spied here and planned secret attacks there; they led sadistic death
marches, pronounced boundless devotion to their emperor, beheaded civilians, and piloted kamikaze missions. Dower adds, "It was a common
observation among Western war correspondents that the fighting in the
Pacific was more savage than in the European theater. Kill or be killed.
No quarter, no surrender. Take no prisoners. Fight to the bitter end."[44]
Such terms repeated on a daily basis contributed to an image of an "orgy
of bloodletting" in the Pacific theater. To be sure, the image of the preda-
tory Japanese was based on actual atrocities, but it was often amplified by
exaggeration.[45] One OWI official labeled the characterizations "inappropriate. At a time when the public needed above all a sober evaluation of
the strength of the enemy," Hollywood fed them extremism.[46] In one
memorable scene of Capra's *Why We Fight* series, audiences witnessed
the "conquering Jap army" marching down Pennsylvania Avenue. The

free world had to win the war to prevent the rapists of Nanking from overrunning democracy, polluting white America, and defiling Western womanhood.

Yet once the war ended and Japan became the Asian front against communist expansion, the diabolical fiends portrayed in American war films were nowhere to be found. Instead, the Japanese became reformed democrats who could now look upon their emperor *and* cheer General Douglas MacArthur.

It has become commonplace for historians to describe the transition from the Second World War to the Cold War in terms of "Red fascism": that is, from Hitler's authoritarian Nazism to Stalin's authoritarian communism.[47] Yet the cultural producers, still years away from uncovering the extent of the Nazis' dirtiest secrets, portrayed Germans in film as cultured individuals momentarily gone mad. They made distinctions between good Germans and evil Nazis. In *Casablanca* (1942), evil Major Strasser is surrounded by Prussian soldiers (who happen to be robust *biergarten* singers). In *The Moon is Down* (1943), based on the John Steinbeck novel, the German is seen as a lonesome romantic who succumbs to a Norwegian widow. Most important, portrayals of Germany were almost completely devoid of anti-Semitism.

One reason for the lack of condemnation of Germans on a par with that of the Japanese was the moguls' sensitivities to the religious issue that had dogged them before the war. When several Hollywood Jews met in 1942 to discuss forming an organization to confront domestic anti-Semitism, Selznick acknowledged that "the combination of the words 'Hollywood' and 'Jewish' may be unfortunate and may give color to untruths that have been spread about the control of Hollywood. . . . It must be made crystal-clear that this is no Jewish cabal, meeting in cellars to devise ways and means of slaughtering Gentiles; and that it is not designed to preserve alleged Jewish control of the motion picture business. . . . [We must show that we] support the war effort, patriotic activities of every sort, and worthy charities of a nonsectarian nature."[48] Fearing that "one wrong step can do more harm than all the good we hope to accomplish," Selznick and others swept their heritage aside, preferring to have their countrymen "think of us as Americans only."[49] Publicly rejecting identification with what Selznick called "the Ellis Island group of producers" became paramount.[50] Such inhibitions frustrated many Jewish groups around the country who found it "tragic" that few Jewish themes entered wartime films despite the accusation that Jews controlled the industry.[51]

This reluctance to present anti-Semitism also had significance for film portrayals of Germany and limited America's blanket condemnation of racial and religious intolerance. As much as studio moguls bristled privately over anti-Semitism, they never emphasized it in their films, in part because it was not a theme upon which to build a united war effort. Rather, the more effective image of a relentless enemy of half-robots, half-animals marching on Main Streets in America would enter the Cold War–era propaganda wars when the Yellow Peril metamorphosed into the Red Menace.[52]

During the Second World War, though, standing in stark contrast to the Japanese soldier, the soldiers of the Soviet Red Army represented something entirely different to Americans. For Hollywood, no year defined the Red Army ally more than 1943, the year in which the Soviets triumphed after the siege of Stalingrad. In that year alone, different studios released several important "Russian" movies: Metro's *Song of Russia*, United Artists' *Three Russian Girls*, Columbia's *Boy from Stalingrad*, Goldwyn's *Mission to Moscow*, and Warner Bros.' *The North Star*. The same year he helped organize wartime Hollywood, Walter Huston appeared in these latter two films.

Before the war, *Ninotchka* (1939) probably sealed the profile of the Soviet woman in the minds of most Americans. Here, the capitalist West finally seduces the automated communist, played by the enigmatic Greta Garbo. Getting her to shed her frigidity for femininity became the central plot. During the war, though, Soviet citizens were reclaimed from androidism, backwardness, and barbarism. *The North Star* had top-notch talent behind it: producer Samuel Goldwyn, director Lewis Milestone, and screenwriter Lillian Hellman. *Dragon Seed* portrayed a Chinese village as noble bulwark against further Japanese aggression; *The North Star* simply substituted Russians for Chinese, and Germans for Japanese. The film is credited with humanizing the average Russians as Hellman praised their courage in the face of the Nazi onslaught.[53] Hellman further publicized herself, her film, and Russian bravery by accepting an extensive tour of the Russian front, from which she reported to Americans that Russians were "polite, Puritan, romantic, terrific."[54]

In *Mission to Moscow*, Americans see the "true nature" of communist Russia and the statesman's side of Joseph Stalin through the gentle eyes of ambassador Joseph Davies, played by Huston. In fact, Davies himself introduces the documentary-like picture, which was produced at the request of Roosevelt, who hoped to foster compassion for America's comrade. Huston's voice accompanied real Nazi propaganda newsreels interspersed throughout the picture. Interestingly, Huston provided the narration for

Capra's *Why We Fight* series as well, which also used Nazi footage to great advantage. In *Mission to Moscow*, scenes of Stalinist show trials were followed by scenes in which Ambassador Davies praises the Red Army and the "greatness" of Stalin himself; in short, Davies learned to respect the Russians, and so should you. As with the German case, Americans were urged to make distinctions between good Russians and bad Soviets—this time, for the sake of Allied bliss.

Regardless of these sympathetic portrayals, patriotic studio executives still held the Soviets at arm's length. For example, some executives decried Hellman's overripe romanticization of Russians. They ordered editors to cut twenty minutes from *The North Star* to deemphasize the positive portrayal of Russians and had the publicity department promote Hellman's visit with the anguished director Sergei Eisenstein as an example of Stalin's oppressive regime.[55] Still, they undoubtedly hoped audiences and the government would come away from *Mission to Moscow* seeing the value in collective security to halt Hitler's expansion. The Russo-American alliance, they could argue, also restrained Stalin's tendencies in that the Allies could keep the Soviets in check by keeping the Soviets close. Even as the wartime alliance flourished, the perceived ideological threat endured, albeit in a dormant state.[56] According to Hollywood, the Soviets proved themselves to be good fighters, if not good friends. But during the Cold War, even such lukewarm approval appeared, in hindsight, to be lavish praise. Within a few years, the writers of both films would be blacklisted in part for their authorship of scripts deemed to be pro-Soviet.

Nevertheless, the cinematic treatments of Soviet soldiers and citizens had much in common with the portrayal of their American counterparts: the citizens of both nations fought courageously, united by a noble cause. Both nations were also subjected to Hollywood manipulation. In the absence of more real, personal information to flesh out the human side of war, motion pictures and the media provided the story. Blum writes that this process "freed them from the sterile anonymity of official communiqués, but it also made them exemplars of national life, heroic symbols that satisfied the normal social preferences and the wartime psychological needs of American civilians."[57] In films such as *Wake Island* (1942), *Bataan* (1943), *The Fighting Sullivans* (1944), and *Back to Bataan* (1945), each "Willie" and "Joe" was a humble, hard-working hero and, with his buddies, a defender of the democratic-capitalistic ideal.

At the same time that Hollywood and the government relied on race to depict foreign nationals, they did the same when profiling wartime

America. The OWI, responsible for more than motion pictures, published a wartime pamphlet titled "Negroes and the War," which praised African Americans for their contributions to the war effort even as segregation separated the races at home and abroad.[58] This sentiment extended into films as well. Langston Hughes called *The Negro Soldier*, part of Capra's wartime output, "the most remarkable Negro film ever," and *Time* tagged it as "a brave, important and helpful event in the history of U.S. race relations."[59] In Luce's *Life* magazine offices in 1943, one editor complained that further racial progress remained stifled only because blacks "have been given not nearly enough opportunity to prove their worth."[60]

Features continued the theme. In *Bataan* (1943), for example, multiracial and multiethnic battle units fought together as one against the forces of evil and died as American martyrs for liberal democracy.[61] Gender, race, and class divisions gave way to a national community that embraced social and economic progress. Even the simple characterization of noble, independent blacks in *Cabin in the Sky* (1943) and *Lifeboat* (1944) raised African Americans above the worst of old stereotypes, those of dutiful mammies and dice-throwing rascals. To be sure, although obstacles to fairer treatment remained, African Americans were becoming known as righteous and loving citizens, and the character in *Lifeboat*, at least, as a valuable member of a community that subdues a devious Nazi.

The home front was hardly different; motion pictures showed how gender and class cleavages in society adapted to the wartime circumstances. The family endured while Dad was away; daughters sacrificed their boyfriends to the noble purpose. Together, mothers and children found solace amid the disruptions: they put up with rationing and purchased war bonds. In *Since You Went Away* (1944), Selznick wrote and produced an idealized version of America in hopes of doing for his country what the acclaimed *Mrs. Miniver* (1942) had done for British morale. In *Tender Comrade* (1943), writer Dalton Trumbo showed that a woman who worked was good, while a woman who hoarded was bad. Women who lost their men in battle accepted their loss as necessary because the international situation had forced them to put the needs of the community over their own. While similar ideas in the postwar period would become anathema, at the time, Trumbo's ideas were readily acceptable given the circumstances. As in other times, war served as an opportunity for social change. The wartime contributions of women and African Americans—publicized by film—laid the basis for claiming equal rights of citizenship after the war.[62]

Class differences so apparent prior to the war vanished on the screen. MGM's *Joe Smith, American* (1942) explained to average citizens not only why we fight but how we fight by exhibiting the importance of home-front production. Corporations benefited from the medium when film shorts publicized their products and contributions to the war. DuPont, enjoying its own "holiday" from antitrust proceedings, showcased its agricultural products in *Soldiers of the Soil*; Aetna downplayed the nettlesome problems of unemployment and industrial accidents in *Men Working*. Wartime America, as portrayed on celluloid, was the nation at its best, when its better angels prevailed.

While this national image was helping the government build unity for the war, Hollywood's efforts in this regard also benefited the studio executives who had experienced so many dire problems before the war. Wartime rationing limited Americans' free-spending habits *except* when it came to attending Hollywood motion pictures. Audiences continued to fill theaters for an easy escape from their daily concerns and confirmation that their sacrifices were necessary. They must have appreciated what they saw on screens, because they continued to patronize theaters in record numbers. If box office receipts offer any guide, movie attendance became "an essential wartime ritual for Americans"; indeed, attendance and studio profits increased year by year from $740 million in 1940 to $1 billion in 1942 to $1.45 billion by the end of the war.[63] Like ships, airplanes, and tanks, motion pictures were the product of round-the-clock factory work. As a result, the president commended Hollywood studios "for the enthusiasm with which your entire industry is tackling the remaining big job."[64] Hollywood's assembly line thus helped to cleanse the prewar image of the industry. But these activities also had unintended consequences, as innovative filmmakers experimented with new styles and techniques: the same battle-hardened and introspective writers and directors who helped the studios and the government with their handiwork soon became enamored of documentary realism and progressive themes that questioned basic assumptions of American unity and satisfaction.

Meanwhile, though, as important as training films, newsreels, and full-length features were in providing information and building community, arguably the most important Hollywood products were the floods of documentaries. Before the war, European documentaries of the 1920s and 1930s had been typically experimental, avant-garde productions. With the advent of war, though, "film for film's sake" gave way to "blood-and-thunder" propaganda. During the war, more American documentaries were turned out in a week than in an entire year before the war, many with progressive themes. But few Americans would pay the price of admission to see what they hoped to leave behind for a few hours. Rather, escapism and entertainment were critical ingredients in affecting the American mind. Arthur Mayer, owner of the Rialto Theatre in New York, explained, "No people in the world are more eager for education and information than the American public" as long as "it can be acquired with a minimum of effort and a maximum of comfort."[65] The documentary style, not the documentary itself, combined education with entertainment. By the last two years of the war, the documentary style allowed filmmakers to bring realistic treatments of the war to audiences. According to one OWI official, the repeated use of this stylistic innovation "led to confusion as to what was fact and what fantasy."[66] Ultimately, by blurring the lines between fact and fiction, filmmakers had acquired extraordinary power to define a potent national identity.

Some of the more progressive Hollywood producers looked to the postwar world as an opportunity to combine entertainment with both documentary realism and a social conscience for audiences at home and abroad. Young, tall, and capable Dore Schary was something of a film-producing anomaly. He had risen from the ranks of screenwriting to become production chief for major and independent studios. While other producers hid their Jewish backgrounds, Schary gave speeches in behalf of B'nai Brith. He also embraced liberal internationalism and actively promoted it in his professional life. Schary acknowledged Hollywood's great contributions to manpower, morale, and propaganda when he wrote in 1944, "Since Pearl Harbor the industry has presented a group of pictures that has been of value not only to the war effort but to the attitude of the people toward the post-war world and pictures that will also give occupied countries an accurate concept of the American way of life."[67] He referred specifically to *Wake Island* and *Guadalcanal Diary* as examples of innovative motion pictures that combined entertainment with documentary realism in 1943. As the war concluded, Schary hailed two new films produced in a similar style: *Pride of the Marines* (1945) and *The Best Years of Our Lives* (1946). Together, these important movies foreshadowed things to come for returning veterans and for the motion picture industry. As great critical and financial successes, these two films opened the floodgates for similar exposés of the American postwar landscape.

Written by Albert Maltz, *Pride of the Marines* employed documentary realism to tell the story of one man's war. The lead character, Al Schmid (played by John Garfield), is awakened to his duty by Pearl Harbor. His nationalistic enthusiasm gives way to the horrors of war when in one scene he uses his machine gun to annihilate wave after wave of advancing Japanese soldiers. Here, Maltz echoes director John Huston's wartime documentaries *The Battle of San Pietro* (1944) and *Let There Be Light* (1945) by showing the grisly nature of war, the "needless slaughter" and "how the shock of war drove men temporarily insane."[68] Unlike other overtly heroic portrayals of GIs, Maltz's marines were hardened by their experiences. Even so, his GI is serious without becoming fanatic; he fires off his gun but not his mouth. He refrains from spewing the racial epithets ("Japs" and "Yellow Dogs") so common in other films.[69] After the war, Schmid, exhausted, beaten, and literally blinded, is rehabilitated into the community for which he has sacrificed so much. Although blind, he can see his true reward.

Even so, the soldier's story did not end with the end of the war. Viewing *Pride of the Marines* in 1945, audiences were made aware that new challenges awaited. Maltz connected war aims with postwar concerns by showing that the American man, once a soldier of war, now found himself fundamentally and permanently changed into a soldier of peace. For Maltz, Americans, like butterflies, could not slip back into cocoons of isolation. Schmid, who befriends a Jewish GI named Lee Diamond, is forced to see his comrade's humanity. Here, Diamond is presented as a contributing member of the war effort who, in some ways, fights a personal crusade against Nazi intolerance that Schmid can hardly understand. The domestic and the foreign have intersected when Schmid is compelled to open his eyes to anti-Semitism back home. Critics applauded the meaningful transition of motion pictures from prowar pabulum to postwar nourishment of ideas.[70]

Despite its serious themes and sobering drama, the film met with popular and critical approval. The director of the army's Morale Films Division congratulated Maltz on persevering through red tape and censorship and for making it possible for the returning veteran "to continue to fight for the ultimate realization of the things that sent us to war" in the first place.[71] Motion pictures had provided the rationale for war and also instructed Americans about how the war had changed the nation.

Some movies late in the war explored how soldiers would be affected once they returned. Made wise by the conflict, veterans would seek to fight fascism when they found it at home. Scripts for the novel *Coming Home* (1944), for *They Dream of Home* (1944), and for *Decision* (1944) told of GIs who literally find fascists at home to hunt. Dore Schary expressed to Selznick the need to find and fight subtle forms of "native fascism" on the home front, and fascism became a useful ruler against which to measure domestic activities. For example, several writers and producers—Lillian Hellman, Dore Schary, Sam Goldwyn, Tennessee Williams, and others—prepared treatments for a Huey Long bio-epic. When they looked back on the American flirtation with Huey Long in the 1930s, they emphasized his rise to pseudo-dictatorship by manipulating common folks through his rhetoric. Like Hitler, Long's means were every bit as important as his ends. "He was a dangerous, vain, selfish man, whom somebody clipped just in time," as far as Schary was concerned.[72] Selznick, though, wondered about presenting a "pretty terrible picture of American political life . . . in foreign countries" and openly worried about the export censor's office nixing its distribution abroad. The film was still made.[73]

Native fascism aside, returning GIs faced many other problems more directly. With the war in Europe coming to an end, Dore Schary took a leading role in bringing progressive themes to Hollywood productions during this "more enlightened era." After the war, he assured advertisers, audiences will demand "pictures of more moment" and will reject "all tinsel and rose colored and creampuff!"[74] Schary and other producers believed that veterans and their families were looking for stories that addressed pressing domestic problems in a realistic manner. A series of "male melodramas" hit the screens in 1946 alone: *The Razor's Edge*, *The Yearling*, *It's a Wonderful Life*, and even, to an extent, Laurence Olivier's acclaimed *Hamlet*.[75]

Two films, though, look at the difficult adjustments returning soldiers would have to make. *Till the End of Time* (1946), produced by Dore Schary and directed by Edward Dmytryk (a year before he was blacklisted), shows that emotional scars were matched only by physical afflictions. In this picture Perry has lost the use of his legs, William has bad debts, and Cliff is undecided about his future. Audiences experienced another film with similar title, plot, and characters at the same time. Written by Roosevelt's speechwriter, Robert Sherwood, *The Best Years of Our Lives* (1946) takes a look at how three returning veterans adapt to fluctuations in their personal relationships and to their demons within. Indeed, change is the predominant theme of the movie, and it comes to a cross-section of middle America, where Al, Fred, and Homer—a banker, a working-class Joe, and a wounded veteran—lead lives devoid of unparalleled optimism and easy resolution. Even the things they took for granted before the war—respect, a steady paycheck, an understanding wife—have changed.

In one scene, Al comes home to his loving family and finds that much has changed while he was at war. He must reacquaint himself with the strangers in his own home, especially a grown-up daughter and a college-student son. In struggling to tell his wife what he has seen overseas, he distances himself from her. Fred, weighted-down by medals as a pilot, is now paraded about by his wife while he quietly endures nightmares of bombing runs over Germany. He discovers that the battle ribbons are worthless to a man who cannot find a job, and so he seeks solace in drink. In another instance, Homer attends a family reunion, an icon of postwar prosperity, and in reaching for a cold drink—still not fully accustomed to the hooks on the ends of his arms—clumsily knocks over the glass. Embarrassed, he runs to the safety of a local hangout. This picture shows postwar America populated by complex if not broken men; the nation housed inescapable challenges, not the quick release of responsibility signaled by victory parades.

As liberation continued late in the war, more and more individuals within government, the military, and Hollywood focused with intensity on the national image as conveyed in movies. The controversial themes and documentary realism that the two foregoing films represent ignited a conservative backlash. The overt political activism of the progressive writers, producers, directors, and performers involved in these films also contributed to a rift within the Hollywood community. The Motion Picture Alliance for Preservation of American Ideals, for example, was formed in February 1944 by Gary Cooper, Walt Disney, King Vidor, and Sam Wood in response to what they perceived as undue leftist influence in Hollywood. With a mission "to uphold the American way of life, on the screen and among screen workers," the Alliance promised to silence "the highly vocal, lunatic fringe" in both the industry and film content.[76] They distributed a *Screen Guide for Americans*, written by Ayn Rand, a Russian émigré who was then working as a $35-a-week reader for Paramount. The wartime film industry had found great opportunities to build morale, sell bonds, and form opinion. Ironically, these were the very things that left the industry open to charges of propagandizing for the wrong cause.

Just as soon as the Alliance was organized, it provoked a heated response by Hollywood progressives. Producer Walter Wanger cautioned against testing the loyalties of filmmakers and "preaching Americanism."[77] Dore Schary was even more pointed in his criticisms of the Alliance. In a scathing memo to the organization, Schary ridiculed any effort to root out "un-American" motion pictures. "There are a number of pictures that I would like to bring to your attention," he wrote with heavy sarcasm. One of these towed "the Communist line" as it seemed to

"build up class hatred," and another ridiculed democratic institutions—
yet Schary noted that all the scrutinized films had been produced by
founders of the Alliance. He then attached a list of Alliance members,
including Wood, Disney, and Vidor, and linked them to their "suspect"
films, thereby showing the subjective nature of interpreting un-American
themes. "I am heartily in favor of any organization founded to preserve
American ideals," Schary explained, "but I do not believe that the members of the Motion Picture Alliance are the sole defenders of these ideals." He quickly noted that the industry had been fully investigated and
vindicated back in 1941. He demanded "that the Motion Picture Alliance
name names, pictures, dates and influences concerning un-American
activities they claim exist in Hollywood."[78]

Members of the Alliance would do precisely that when they made up
the list of "friendly" witnesses testifying before Congress three years later.
The war had served as an opportunity to cleanse Hollywood's image, but it
had also created a fissure of seismic proportions within the industry.

Even as "war pictures" temporarily vanished from the screen, the influence of the war on the film industry, its content and style, remained.
Their wartime respite ended, studios again faced daunting problems related to their labor situation, their foreign markets, their public image,
and their antitrust woes. Meanwhile, the government would build on its
wartime censorship and propaganda experiences. And talent had learned
much about building influential political organizations and affecting social change through motion picture content and style. These issues would
have great relevance for the way Americans in government, in Hollywood, and in the nation at large would react to the coming of the Cold
War. But first they would have to define just what the national postwar
American purpose would be.

2

One World or Two?

The American Postwar Mission

THE SECOND world War represented a triumph for Ameri-
can internationalists yet also ushered in a period of uncertainty and debate over the American postwar mission in the world. American internationalists uniformly agreed that overseas events compelled the nation
to enter the war, but as the conflict subsided, they disagreed among themselves over the reasons *why* the nation had fought the war. With the help
of Hollywood, the war marked a watershed for public conceptions of
"the way things ought to be." The Allied leadership and influential
opinion-makers characterized the war in epochal terms of democracy
versus fascism, lovers of peace versus bloodthirsty militarists, life versus
death. Whether appropriate or exaggerated, these wartime characterizations prompted the Allied citizenry to imagine the postwar world in similar ways. In other words, whereas the Great War's denouement was seen
as a missed opportunity, the later global conflict provided another rare,
momentous chance to remake the world. Many Americans believed they
could reconstruct their world on the basis of liberal principles at home
and abroad.

The war's leaders contributed to this view of the war as an epic moment. Adolf Hitler promised a thousand-year Reich. Benito Mussolini
hailed a new Roman empire. Japanese propaganda linked contemporary
events with images of shoguns and samurai. In each case, Axis leaders
put the present day in terms of restoring national glory and recreating an
idealized past. Similarly, Winston Churchill and Franklin Roosevelt
framed the war in ideological terms as an unmistakable contest between
good and evil. Both leaders defended their alliance with Stalin by suggesting that they would sooner make a pact with the Devil himself than
allow Hitler to march uncontested into hell. Such rhetoric continued
after the war when the Allies set out to transform themselves from

military powers into "Four Policemen" vowing to keep the "order" in new world order.[1] It may be assumed that any war is epochal to its combatants, but the Second World War seemed more so. If the Great War was about militarism, open covenants, colonial possessions, and national self-determination, then the Second World War involved those things and more to Americans: an ideological contest between liberalism and the metastasizing cancer of fascism.

World leaders were not the only ones to view the conflict in such momentous terms. Opinion-makers—journalists, publishers, theologians, educators, and motion picture producers among them—shared that sense. The actions of these cultural formulators took on an even greater significance. While Roosevelt hemmed and hawed to a frustrating extent about his concrete postwar plans, cultural producers presented their visions of the postwar world to an anxious public. Roosevelt, ever mindful of the history of rash actions, shared few thoughts, undoubtedly because he recalled Woodrow Wilson's troubles keeping an alliance together in the wake of the Great War. Roosevelt hoped to avoid the pitfalls that befell Wilson when American internationalism itself was tied to the broken peace.[2] Silence helped FDR keep open his options for compromise. His ambiguity and his untimely death left his legacy and postwar plans open to much debate by his "heirs," just as Lincoln's death had left the country adrift during the era of Civil War Reconstruction. Amid much uncertainty and in the absence of an "official" presidential blueprint, popular culture helped fill the void.

American internationalists turned away from the fight against so-called isolationists, who had lost their struggle when Japan bombed Pearl Harbor, and increasingly focused on shades of internationalism. Two competing internationalist camps emerged in the mid-1940s: unilateralists and multilateralists. These were hardly monolithic groups, but some generalizations can be made. The former, an emerging group of Cold Warriors, came to view the postwar world as a bipolar contest between the United States and the former Soviet ally. To them, the United States was best suited to lead the free world against monolithic, totalitarian communism. The multilateralists, by contrast, advocated One World universalism. Including many cultural producers, these advocates believed the United States should lead a group of nations united for international harmony and mutual security. When official policy reflected the Cold War perspective, Hollywood's producers and executives soon found themselves identified as naive dissenters.

Two Worlds: Cold Warriors and Bipolarity

In the mid-1940s, opinion-makers such as Henry Luce, Reinhold Niebuhr, Walter Lippmann, and Wendell Willkie joined many others in debating what course the United States should take for the remainder of the war and in its aftermath. With equal measures of uncertainty and possibility swirling about them, Americans attended to this debate over America's postwar national purpose with eagerness. These writers considered issues as narrow as who should vote in the United Nations and as broad as the manifestations of evil. Virtually all of them tied their musings on human nature to the American people and prescribed changes in the nation's attitudes and activities. All believed that a great moment confronted the nation, one in which the people must choose their destiny. While most of the debaters agreed that Americans ought to embrace internationalism over isolationism, they disagreed vehemently on the scope and character of American internationalism. The differences between unilateralists and multilateralists involved an array of issues: relations with the Soviets, the United Nations, European recovery, collective security, control over the atom, colonialism, and the domestic social changes demanded by the war. What characteristics would compose the nation's postwar identity after the momentous victory over totalitarianism? The question would be debated intensely within the field of popular culture, and Hollywood would play a significant role in conveying the answer to the American public.

Henry Luce's popular *Life* magazine editorial titled "The American Century" was among the most notable of such tracts.[3] "We Americans are unhappy," he told his Depression-era readers in February 1941. This restlessness, however, was based not on domestic economic misery but on confusion over a world inflamed by war. "The future doesn't seem to hold anything for us except conflict, disruption, war" unless, Luce argued, Americans embraced internationalism. Rather than shrink from responsibility, the country should embrace its position in world affairs because, like it or not, "America is in the war. . . . But are we in it?" An exceptional nation—a sleeping giant—lay at an exceptional moment, Luce insisted. The choice was neither between war and peace nor between isolationism and internationalism. Rather, Luce's millennialism offered a choice between apocalypse and utopia. Wake up, America, Luce heralded. If the nation accepted its international commitments and faced its unavoidable challenges, there would be peace. If not, he warned, "we shall flounder

for ten or twenty or thirty bitter years in a chartless and meaningless series of disasters."[4] Of course, the war put noninterventionists on the defensive, from which they never recovered. Pearl Harbor, Senator Arthur Vandenberg explained, bombed us into internationalism.[5]

Just as noninterventionism encompassed a loose confederation of individuals, internationalism was likewise a banner raised by a diverse lot.[6]
Internationalism included members along the political spectrum: Democrats, Republicans, conservatives, Cold War liberals, socialists. But different people defined American internationalism in just as many ways. During and after the war, internationalist ideology underwent a dynamic
national debate among a wide variety of thinkers in many walks of life.
Although they agreed on the fundamental point that America had to wake
up to its responsibilities in world affairs, they differed on what the nation
was to do in international affairs.

Luce's close friend and fellow unilateralist Hollywood producer David
O. Selznick appreciated Luce's public advocacy of internationalism and
hoped their shared ideas would be promoted. "Dear Harry," he wrote his
friend soon after "The American Century" was published, "I think it is
one of the most important pieces that has appeared any place in recent
months," and he sincerely hoped "for the sake of the country" that internationalists would continue to preach the gospel of internationalism from
many pulpits.[7]

One preacher was Nicholas Doman, an international lawyer serving in
the army and attached to the Office of Strategic Services (OSS). After the
war, he was assigned to the legal staff of Robert H. Jackson, U.S. chief
prosecutor at the Nuremberg war crimes trials. Coming to believe that
American involvement in world affairs was not voluntary, he put his faith
in world government rather than in American preeminence: world government would advance "social control within the national community,"
and such regimentation "often checks the operation of antisocial factors
and becomes the source of greater freedom for the community."[8] Internationalists who promoted multilateralism and universalism held the belief
that the United States should enter world affairs to bring binding, peaceful coexistence among nations. As Akira Iriye has noted, universalists
valued the fundamental interests of people over those of nations.[9]

This was not the international world order that Luce had envisioned,
yet he had to contend with its appeal. He and theologian Reinhold
Niebuhr, columnist Walter Lippmann, and a host of more conservative
foreign-policy hawks such as James Byrnes and John Foster Dulles, believed that everything else flowed from one central truth: international

relationships had to be based on vital national security interests and not on more idealistic, universalistic considerations. In the years to come, as far as they were concerned, this pragmatic perspective would dictate America's relations with Western Europe and with the Soviets. Their chief targets, then, were not the noninterventionists, whom Pearl Harbor already had silenced, but those other internationalists who favored multilateralism and universalism.

Unilateralists were internationalists who envisioned a bipolar world order and expressed grave concerns about those universalists who held out hope for good relations with the Soviet Union. The grand wartime alliance was, at the very least, strained and awkward. Stalin's "Uncle Joe" persona belied a brutal regime. His 1939 pact with Hitler haunted some who wondered if the Soviet Union would sign a separate peace with Germany and shut down the Eastern Front. From another perspective, Stalin's pleas for a second front in the West were put off for three long years. As attention turned to the postwar map, many suspected that Stalin would make demands on Eastern Europe. American radicals tended to accept or at least explain Stalin's desire for a buffer of security. Whether Russia was, as one writer noted, "the most frightened, or the most ambitious, of all the nations" would help determine the future of American and Soviet relations—and the future of universalism.[10]

From his study in New York's Morningside Heights, theologian Reinhold Niebuhr wrote that the best way to preserve peace was for the United States to distance itself from the Soviet Union and from universalism. In *The Nature and Destiny of Man*, Niebuhr explained that America must face evil rationally and defeat it because the nation could not reform the unreformable. The shocking revelations at the Nuremberg trials offered satisfactory evidence that humanity must surrender any hope for utopianism. If Pearl Harbor bombed Americans into internationalism, then Nuremberg horrified them into a realistic appraisal of Stalin. After the war, Niebuhr drew parallels between Hitler and Stalin and admonished universalists for their "optimistic estimates of human nature." The country could not afford to be idealistic in a world populated by genocidal dictators.[11] Niebuhr's close associate, Arthur Schlesinger Jr., put it more pointedly: Universalism appeared "shallow and shaky."[12]

By 1944 America's foes looked less like retreating Germans and more like advancing Russians. Luce, Niebuhr, and their cohort became self-appointed educators, using the popular media to persuade the public that American foreign policy required a heavy dose of sober nationalism rather than universalism. Years later Niebuhr remarked that "one of the greatest educators preparing a young and powerful nation to assume responsibilities commensurate with its power" was columnist Walter Lippmann.[13] Although he criticized leftist idealism, Lippmann was anything but a conservative. Indeed, in a career spanning the twentieth century, Lippmann played an important part in Progressive reforms of domestic and foreign policy. He served as secretary to muckraker Lincoln Steffens, and he supported Theodore Roosevelt. In 1913 he founded the liberal journal *New Republic* and feverishly rejected the socialism he had flirted with while enrolled at Harvard. He helped draft Wilson's Fourteen Points and the Covenant of the League of Nations before becoming more skeptical of universalism. In later years he openly opposed wars in Korea and Vietnam, thereby becoming known as a Cold War critic.[14] Lippmann was an equal-opportunity voter, having supported six Republican nominees and seven Democratic nominees for the presidency. He was an early promoter of Wendell Willkie until he read Willkie's utopian plans for the postwar era; as the United States emerged from the war, Lippmann became, in the words of his biographer, "distressed by one-world euphoria," and so he embraced Realpolitik.[15]

Lippmann published *U.S. Foreign Policy: Shield of the Republic* in the same year, 1943, as Willkie published his treatise, *One World*.[16] Together, the old friends joined the debate on America's postwar purpose. Although Willkie's book sold more copies, Lippmann's book reached just as wide an audience when it was circulated in *Reader's Digest* and the *Ladies' Home Journal*. Ostensibly a columnist, Lippmann's influence reached into American homes and into dinner party conversations among the Washington elite. He "merited the title of unofficial—and often uninvited—public adviser to the makers of American foreign policy," one biographer wrote. "Even when they disagreed with him, they could not easily ignore his arguments."[17]

In his book, Lippmann emphasized the necessity of retaining a measure of nationalism in foreign policy considerations. The United States had to project its power overseas to protect its vital national interests. The demise of Hitler as a common foe doomed American-Soviet comity. But he did not mourn this inevitability; rather, Lippmann stated that this was simply the way things were. Americans had to prepare for other realities. Unsavory compromises, the hallmark of a realistic approach to foreign policy, proved a rational course of action in the volatile atomic age. The Soviets, who had endured two German assaults in a single generation, could not be denied an East European buffer. Lippmann argued the United States could no more force Soviet compliance in this regard than it could impose chastity upon a lover from afar. Such a recognition certainly contributed to Lippmann's legacy as a critic of the policy of containment, but in fact he was simply a realist. The danger of universalism, which he opposed, was that it threatened American sovereignty and flexibility.[18]

What Lippmann questioned was nothing less than the primary purpose of the United Nations. Would such an institution preserve security through universalism, or deal with raw power in the real world? Whereas universalists invested in the former, Lippmann knew that the latter would prove to be the case. Vital national interests would always prevail; the institution would succumb to voting blocs. Carving the globe into spheres of influence protected by militarized regional alliances made sense to Lippmann and other advocates of Realpolitik. Such alliances—like the one that Churchill proposed at Westminster College in 1946, or the formation of NATO in 1949, or those that John Foster Dulles formed in the 1950s—make Walter Lippmann's Cold War criticism look remarkably like the behavior of a Cold War hawk. When looking for true alternatives to American foreign policy in the Cold War, one may do well to look at the universalist ideas of One Worldism.

One World: The Universalists' Moment

Luce, Niebuhr, and Lippmann were three wise men who attached a nationalistic purpose to the American war aims. When Roosevelt and Churchill signed the historic Atlantic Charter that bound their two nations together as soldiers for freedom in a common purpose, others sought to use this moment of American internationalism as a stepping-stone toward ultimate universalism.[19] According to the advocates of universalism, the United States should use its immense postwar prestige to move the world away from petty nationalism and toward consensus, to emphasize individual human rights, and to bring about a lasting peace among nations. This One World movement marked a great step in world progress: from nationalism to humanity, from darkness to light. These ideas, first expressed during the Second World War, would influence cultural producers in the film and television industries and instruct them on how to carry the debate over American national identity into the Cold War.

In *Democracy's World*, writer Robert Clark Keough assured readers that American-led universalism would ensure the sanctity of the individual around the world. Even if democratic principles would "not eliminate all evil," a postnationalist age could prevent tragedies on the scale they were witnessing.[20] The nation-state system had lacked a universal moral code, had corrupted the world, and had led to "division and disintegration." After rejecting the notion of "my country right or wrong," a new international order based on loyalties other than those for the nation could prevent future holocausts.[21] The historic opportunity existed now, they declared; having entered the war, the United States could next become an architect of a new world order.

As idealistic as universalism sounded, only a vocal minority in the country considered it completely quixotic. The less-graceful among these critics tagged universalism "a craze," even "screwball."[22] But Luce, Niebuhr, Lippmann, and Cold War hawks took universalism seriously, primarily because its chief spokesman commanded a popular following from his perch in the middle class, the Midwest, and the mainstream.

Although universalism had existed earlier, perhaps no one lent greater credence to these ideas than Wendell Willkie. Where Niebuhr and Lippmann were both quiet, contemplative, and prim, Willkie was a tousle-haired populist. Whereas Niebuhr and Lippmann were reformed socialists, Willkie was a reformed Democrat; this "poor farm boy from Wall Street" left FDR's party to become the Republican standard-bearer in 1940 and Hollywood's defender in 1941. In 1943 Willkie published the most popular and influential exploration of universalism in *One World*. Like Luce, Willkie pressed for internationalism within his party and viewed the war in epochal, ideological terms. Ideas matter, he told anyone who would listen to his raspy voice. However "important the role of bayonets and guns may have been in the development of mankind, the role of ideas has been vastly more important," he wrote. Postwar America must possess an ideology well suited to lead the world in a peaceful, moral direction. He explained that "a war without a purpose is a war won without victory."[23]

In 1942 Willkie embarked on an exhausting wartime mission aboard the bomber *Gulliver*, traveling around the world in fifty days to over a dozen destinations: Edmonton, Chungking, Tashkent, Moscow, Teheran, Baghdad, Ankara, El Alamein and Cairo, Khartoum, Ghana, Brazil, Puerto Rico, and Washington, D.C. Joining him was Gardner Cowles, publisher of *Look* magazine, who had recently taken charge of the OWI's domestic desk. Together, Willkie and Cowles hoped to explain the purpose of the war to the American people.[24]

"The world has become small and completely interdependent," Willkie wrote. He learned that Americans are much closer to the people of the world than he had ever before realized, and therefore, "what concerns them *must* concern us." Like Luce, Willkie believed that the United States had to play the leading role in world affairs. The United States enjoyed a "reservoir of good will," Willkie explained, thanks to its military assistance, its shared technology, its consumer goods, and most of all its democratic principles. "Our motion pictures," Willkie explained, "are shown all over the world. People of every country can see with their own eyes what we look like, can hear our voices. From Natal to Chungking I was plied with questions about American motion picture stars— questions asked eagerly by shopgirls and those who served me coffee, and just as eagerly by the wives of prime ministers and kings."[25]

Similarly, when Lillian Hellman toured the Russian front, a Red Army soldier toasted "Stalin, Roosevelt, Churchill, Betty Grable and Dorothy Lamour." On the Western front, America represented all good things: virility, wealth, jazz, chocolate, and freedom.[26] The world knew, Willkie claimed, "We are not fighting for profit, or loot, or territory, or mandatory power over the lives or the governments of other people." He thought just the opposite: The United States sought to "cash in" on its reservoir of goodwill to promote universalism at home and abroad.[27]

Universalists sought to promote several general principles in foreign and domestic contexts: humane capitalism, anticolonialism, self-determination, civil liberties, and impartiality in dealing with all nations. These broad ideas underpinned the universalist agenda in Cold War politics, culture, and foreign relations. Because these ideas occasioned debates between Cold Warriors and dissenters over the next fifteen years, it is worthwhile to examine them further.

Willkie, the Wall Street lawyer, found little fault with American capitalism, but other advocates of universalism questioned expansive capitalism, and radicals spoke openly about the exploitation inherent in the system. Even many who embraced Willkie's general views believed him naive. One plainly proposed abandoning "the present extreme emphasis on making money, and then more money."[28] Like the camp of Cold Warriors, universalism comprised individuals who occupied an ideological site reserved for advocates who shared basic principles. Historians tend to emphasize the radical-liberal split in the late 1930s, a break that, they claim, irreparably tore the American left asunder. One can see however, that before postwar anticommunism took hold, these individuals were generally united in their conceptions of American foreign policy. This was certainly true even on so complex and controversial an issue as colonialism.

"This is a war of liberation," Willkie declared in his book. "All people deserved and required freedom to govern themselves." During his trip Willkie had adopted anticolonialism. At a time when Americans honored Winston Churchill as a beloved figure staring down Hitler, universalists scolded the prime minister for his efforts to perpetuate the British Empire. "The old imperialism must pass," Willkie wrote emphatically. Likewise, they wanted to hold Stalin to his words of November 6, 1942, when the Soviet leader had reassured "a worried world" that the Red Army would not prevent the restoration of sovereign rights in Eastern Europe. Imperialism left colonies bankrupt and dependent. The United States could lead the world toward liberation even after the defeat of the Axis. In practical terms, universalists used language such as "firm timetables," "ironclad guarantees," and a rejection of "colonial status" when promoting their cause.[29]

Decisions over decolonization created a tangle of problems for the United States. On one hand, Washington hoped to side with the noble anti-imperialist tradition that democracies were supposed to favor, remain consistent with its anti-Axis rhetoric, and also go on the record with early opposition to slow withdrawals by the Red Army in Eastern Europe. On the other hand, Washington faced the inevitable scenario of supporting its imperial allies, notably France and Britain, and propping up their colonial regimes in Africa, the Middle East, Southeast Asia, and elsewhere. Indeed, there were almost daily reminders in 1945 of this sticky situation as the Red Army replaced the Nazis in Warsaw in January, the Allies divided Korea in August, Ho Chi Minh declared an independent Vietnam in September, and Sukarno declared an independent Indonesia in November. Balancing national security and unilateralism was a delicate act.

Willkie and others refused to keep the light of scrutiny from shining on America. They frequently recognized Allied hypocrisy in fighting a war of liberation while subjugating minorities around the world. Therefore, universalists extended the ideas of decolonization and self-determination to America itself. This meant granting independence to the Philippines, continuing the Good Neighbor policy toward Latin America, and looking inward at the plight of African Americans, Jews, and the poor. "We cannot, with good conscience, expect the British to set up an orderly schedule for the liberation of India before we have decided for ourselves to make all who live in America free," Willkie explained.[30] Willkie's foreign policy views encompassed a civil rights dimension. There was no line of demarcation between the two; the domestic and the foreign intertwined.[31]

"[W]e have our domestic imperialisms," he reminded Americans. Rather than treading lightly on the controversial subject of race relations during wartime, Willkie faced the issue squarely and devoted an entire chapter to "Our Imperialisms at Home." Universalists invoked the Atlantic Charter and Stalin's wartime statements to the level of promises to keep. Even before the full extent of the Holocaust came to light, proponents of multilateralism observed signs of "insidious anti-Semitism in our own country" and in the halls of the State Department itself. American "race imperialism" at home was linked to the anticolonial project abroad. In this way, Progressives in Hollywood could find signs of domestic fascism to attack after the war.[32]

Having absorbed multilateralism, producer Dore Schary asked an audience in 1944, "Is there a "Jewish problem?" Yes, "but there is also a Mexican one, a colored one, a Catholic one, a Protestant one, and this problem is not unique to Los Angeles," Schary added, but "to every community" in America and the world beyond.[33] The prejudice abroad existed at home; the problems of race and ethnicity transcended national boundaries.

Many civil rights leaders appreciated Willkie's candor as they also linked the war with what occurred on the home front in the celebrated Double V campaign.[34] Both promised a double victory for democratic principles, one against Hitler and the other against racism. Indeed, Willkie enjoyed the support and warm friendship of the chairman of the National Association for the Advancement of Colored People (NAACP), Walter White. In a wartime article in the *Journal of Negro Education*, White applauded the "wise advice" emanating from "enlightened leaders" such as Willkie. He went so far as to express dismay over how Americans viewed the Japanese in crass, racialized terms, as a "colored people and not because they are our enemies."[35] Multilateralism helped the civil rights agenda because universalism linked the cause of African Americans with Africans seeking independence and, asserted Benjamin Mays, with "the exploited poor whites; the untouchables of India; the suffering Chinese; [and] the persecuted Jews."[36]

With similarity to their civil rights critique, proponents of universalism cast a critical eye toward abuses of civil liberties at home. They questioned how the United States could fight a war in the name of democracy against the fascists' ill regard for civil liberties as long as political opponents and innocents remained in jail in America. The Japanese American internment served as the most obvious abuse, but others existed as well. Communist Party leader Earl Browder sat in the Atlanta

Federal Penitentiary when the United States and the Soviet Union became wartime allies. Civil libertarians urged Browder's release for pragmatic as well as idealistic reasons. Not only was his imprisonment seen
as a blot on America as the world's leading democracy, but the jailing of
communists became a potential sore point with Stalin. On May 16, 1942,
Roosevelt released Browder in order "to promote national unity." One
World began at home with one America.[37]

Universalists hoped a public consensus would form around multilateralism. In the early postwar years, advocates would promote their agenda
constantly, directly, and vigilantly in an effort to steer the nation onto this
path. They would seek to shape public opinion and encourage public activism. To do otherwise was "utmost folly—it is just short of suicide."[38] The
public had a role to play in formulating its foreign policy. The Second
World War and the advent of global media invited the public into these debates and encouraged people's active participation. The period from the
1940s onward would see unprecedented public involvement in foreign relations on a daily basis. Whereas diplomacy once engaged a small number of
elites operating in secret, wrote Emil Lengyel, by 1945 "the people were to
become the craftsmen of the new diplomacy. . . . The dark niches of foreign
offices had to be flooded with the light of public curiosity. The masses
would have to become acquainted with the problems of other countries—
now their own problems."[39] A new democratic age of diplomacy was born.

One World ideas attracted attention. Even amid wartime rationing and
hardship, Willkie's book went through several printings. His trip, moreover, engaged the public and changed popular perceptions as Americans
stood on the precipice of peace. In part because "Willkie's *One World* was
widely discussed," one pollster concluded in 1944, "our distrust [of the
Soviets] fell to its nadir of 27%."[40] Conservative critics worried openly
about the "highly controversial" Willkie and the popular appeal of his
"One World theory."[41] At the moment of his greatest influence, Willkie
suddenly died of a massive coronary. Followers dedicated Freedom House,
a building in Manhattan, with the words "One World" chiseled on its facade. Others sought to establish a world university near his birthplace.[42]
Such monuments were physical manifestations of the movement he
helped launch. Willkie arguably left a greater footprint on society than in
politics, on the postwar world than on wartime America. Although he
wrote in part to establish his internationalist credentials to fellow Republicans, Willkie firmly believed in the ideas he set forth in his slender
volume. And those ideas framed some early debates over America's postwar direction, particularly in Hollywood.

Where American foreign relations meet popular culture: Wendell Willkie and Daryl Zanuck of Twentieth Century-Fox review the script for *One World*, 1942. Courtesy John Florea / Time-Life Pictures / Getty Images.

Members of Hollywood certainly took Willkie's call to heart. Top studio directors, such as John Ford, John Huston, and William Wyler, who also trudged along many battlefronts, drew great significance from the war when they returned. So too did mogul Darryl Zanuck, who, upon reentering civilian life in 1943, best illustrates this change. He added Louis de Rochemont of the newsy *March of Time* to his staff and secured the rights to produce two features: *Wilson* (1944) and *One World*.[43] Although the film version of Willkie's book was never completed, *Wilson* was released in 1944 with much hype. It combined elaborate sets with Wilsonian sermonizing over the saving grace of internationalism. Elsewhere in Hollywood, industry observers expected veterans to return to the studios ready to bring realism and topical themes to the screen.[44] Dore Schary repeatedly cited Willkie and saw "no reason why pictures cannot aid in molding public opinion" for progressive principles. After all, "Hollywood . . . is part of the world."[45] But Hollywood Progressives would also work away from the soundstage to promote universalism on the political stage.

In 1944, conferences at Dumbarton Oaks and Bretton Woods unmistakably signaled the start of the postwar era: that is, an effort to put the universalist ideology of *One World* into practice. Held on a manicured estate in Washington, D.C., a short walk from the home where Woodrow Wilson died, Dumbarton Oaks sketched out the blueprints of the United Nations. Here, a potential world government was born, promising in theory to respect national self-determination and to mediate disputes. The other meeting, held at Bretton Woods, New Hampshire, established an International Bank for Reconstruction and Development—a "World Bank" as it was called—and an International Monetary Fund, ostensibly to rebuild the world. The lion's share of the bank's $7.6 billion treasury would come from the United States. With $7.3 billion of its own, the IMF promised to stabilize foreign currencies, reduce crippling trade deficits, and promote free trade.

Not surprisingly, One World idealists hailed the United Nations as a fulfillment of Wilson's dream, but they exhibited more caution with respect to the two financial institutions because of their skepticism about unfettered capitalism. All three institutions proved that American internationalism had triumphed over the forces of noninterventionism by institutionalizing American engagement in world affairs. Furthermore, these institutions sought not only to reconstruct war-ravaged Europe but also to help emerging democracies to develop in Africa, Asia, and Latin America. Even before the Marshall Plan was born, Washington planned to use economic incentives for purposes both humanitarian and self-interested.

The World Bank and the IMF promised to remake a global economy along American lines. The United States would enjoy a substantial advantage in a postwar free-trade system, as America's wartime allies understood. Churchill resisted an international economic system that favored American exports. At Quebec in 1944, their actions and words showed that Roosevelt and his advisers continued to view the British as a crumbling empire. In response, Churchill looked at Roosevelt at one point and growled, "Do you want me to beg, like Fala?"[46] Stalin, for his part, rejected joining either financial institution. These important events, which offered both promise and caution to followers of multilateralism, foreshadowed Yalta, Potsdam, and Churchill's "Iron Curtain" speech. The economic institutions, launched as they were before the end of the war, signaled America's willingness to involve itself in rebuilding the world, but they also contributed to fracturing the alliance and initiating a geostrategic Cold War.

In the first week of 1945 the Hollywood Democratic Committee held its first membership meeting of the new year, two years after Walter Huston addressed the initial gathering at the Roosevelt Hotel. Boasting a membership of over 2,700, having been at the forefront of rallying the wartime home front and contributing to the war's victorious conclusion, collectively the HDC asked, "What now?" During the war it had combined politics, education, and culture for a national purpose. The postwar years would prove no different.

"What now?" was answered quickly when the HDC lobbied for the ratification of the United Nations and the passage of the Bretton Woods agreement. In March 1945 the HDC opened a lobbying office in Washington, to "use the prestige and weight of cultural America to fight for the issues we are committed to support." It issued a "Report from Washington" on a wide variety of legislative issues ranging far beyond those directly related to the entertainment industry. The HDC fastened on the Bretton Woods agreement and circulated petitions at several Hollywood studios, sent telegrams to members of Congress, and printed an eight-page brochure explaining for interested citizens the purpose and organization of the new international institution. "The Bretton Woods Plan is too complicated for you to understand," claimed a cartoon fat cat in the brochure. "Don't you believe it!" insisted the Hollywood writers. "It's easy to understand." Americans and the world faced a choice: Bretton Woods or World War III. For the amount of money it takes to wage three weeks of war, the HDC promised, Americans could secure world peace and prevent a renewed depression.[47]

Bretton Woods offered a choice for motion picture producers as well: profit or stagnation. Indeed, much of the studios' income derived from leasing films abroad. In some cases, the Treasury Department estimated, nearly one-third of their rental income emanated from overseas markets. Of that, half came from Britain. Foreign trade expansion, the likes of which Bretton Woods promised, would allow Britain to export enough to pay for its imports, including American films. Without the trade agreements, American businessmen worried, Britain and the rest of Europe would raise tariffs, lower quotas, or even close their domestic markets to American exports. The World Bank and International Monetary Fund, however, could artfully prop up the world's markets and allow the American government and business leaders to influence its course. Economics aside, Treasury Secretary Henry Morgenthau saw an innocent rationale for increasing American film exports: such trade would make it possible for "English-speaking people everywhere" to "enjoy the pictures they desire, irrespective of where they have been produced."[48]

Fully aware of these business concerns, HDC executive George Pepper worked tirelessly to fashion a united Hollywood front in support of Bretton Woods. He encouraged Democratic Party chairman Bob Hannegan to convince "certain producers that their true interests are represented in the establishment and acceptance of the Bretton Woods proposals." He also wrote Fox chief Joseph Schenck about what the international agreements would do for American business.[49] With Hollywood effectively shut out of European markets because of precarious trade relations, Morgenthau assured Pepper that if Britain joined the agreements, as she was sure to do, "she will have to relax her exchange controls as quickly as possible" and allow the influx of American motion pictures.[50] On the eve of V-E Day, over fifty actors, artists, writers, scientists, educators, and musicians, including Fredric March, Myrna Loy, Jo Davidson, Howard Fast, and Lillian Hellman, joined to endorse Bretton Woods, for without it they warned, the world would surely "suffer the fate of the League of Nations."[51] For diverse groups in Hollywood, international cooperation, American foreign aid, and studio business all demanded full support for Bretton Woods.

Since civilians had fought the war, endured the sacrifices, and perished in concentration camps, human rights and individual freedoms demanded an educated populace. The HDC satisfied that need by sponsoring a series of radio broadcasts, in March 1945 inviting Bette Davis, Walter Huston, Humphrey Bogart, and Olivia De Havilland to make a public service radio show for ABC to educate listeners about their role in the postwar world.[52] In April 1945, John Houseman produced a program written by Abraham Polonsky, just two years before he became a victim of the blacklist. "Our voice"—referring to a farmer, a housewife, and a "Negro clerk"—must be heard in San Francisco and Washington, the narrator demanded. The show included a scene in which a fictitious American calls the Treasury Department to speak with Secretary Morgenthau about Bretton Woods. A very real Henry Morgenthau "answered" the character's phone call and explained in direct terms the purpose of the dramatic portion of the broadcast. "Dumbarton Oaks is the police force and the court that bring quarreling nations into custody and try to make them settle their differences," the secretary explained. "Bretton Woods is the traffic system to prevent collisions in the first place." Repeating Willkie's sentiments, Morgenthau said, "Oceans can no longer keep us from being neighbors in the World Community."[53] Putting such political issues in cultural form proved popular and persuasive. One Kansas woman wrote the radio network that her husband was overseas with the navy, and she wanted a copy of the script for her two children, ages six and ten. "I never had a story affect me like this before," she explained, adding that it "made me feel proud to be an American."[54]

Hollywood leaders looked at other ways to drive the message home. In one star-studded organizing meeting at the Chasen's Restaurant, Bette Davis suggested that studio shorts might be produced to further explain international organizations to American audiences. With a wartime eye set firmly on the postwar world, these celebrities set out to inform Americans that Bretton Woods would be the engine driving the postwar economy.[55] At this critical moment, Franklin Roosevelt suddenly died, but the work continued in his name. "The long awaited victory apparently is ours, but its fruit is bitter," David O. Selznick mournfully told a radio audience on the day of FDR's death. Hollywood had united behind internationalism, publicized Bretton Woods, and looked to do its part to ensure the creation of the United Nations.[56]

The United Nations was, of course, an obvious manifestation of One World thinking with its stated respect for the self-determination of nations, promotion of negotiation, and reliance on collective security against aggressor nations. Dozens of representatives of nongovernmental organizations advised the U.S. delegation; many more attended the early sessions. The charter refers to "peoples" as often as to "nations" and the Universal Declaration of Human Rights, adopted in 1948, demonstrates the strength of universalism in these years.[57]

As tensions developed between the United States and the Soviet Union, however, universalists struggled to promote the tenets they so strongly believed. One example of One World idealism encountering an emerging Cold War pragmatism occurred during the United Nations conference in San Francisco in the spring of 1945. While deliberations over the UN covenant continued, Secretary of State Edward Stettinius employed a Hollywood screenwriter to ghostwrite a speech for him. The screenwriter, Dalton Trumbo, later gained notoriety as a member of the blacklisted Hollywood Ten who refused to divulge his affiliation with the Communist Party (CPUSA). But in May 1945, still two years from that predicament, Trumbo was enlisted quietly by his former fraternity brother, diplomat Llewellyn Thompson, as well as the Motion Picture Academy president, Walter Wanger, a member of the American delegation, to help draft a speech for the secretary of state.[58]

Admittedly, Trumbo's experience in San Francisco is insignificant on its own merit. His attendance appears as a trivial oddity, a footnote to history. Furthermore, Trumbo rarely mentioned the episode even months later when such a relationship could have embarrassed the government that investigated him. The interplay between a Hollywood radical who favored universalism and an upper-level State Department bureaucrat who had invested in bipolarity, however, can show the not-so-subtle ideological differences that would be exposed in the coming years. More important, this anecdote demonstrates that even the staunchest Cold Warriors could appropriate the language of universalism at the very time they corrupted its meaning for the sake of expediency.

Dalton Trumbo's inclusion at San Francisco was hardly surprising, especially given that the American delegation included the director Walter Wanger. Trumbo had served previously as the national chairman of Writers for Roosevelt, even composing Roosevelt's final national radio speech before his reelection in 1944. Later, Trumbo moonlighted as a speechwriter for the mayor of Los Angeles, who enthusiastically endorsed the conferences at Bretton Woods, Dumbarton Oaks, and San Francisco.

State Department bureaucrats initially gave Trumbo wide latitude to express his views, and Trumbo believed himself able to put his stamp on the United Nations, what he called "one of the most important projects that the peoples of the world have ever attempted to put over." Trumbo signaled his credentials to discuss these matters by equating what he had done in Hollywood with what he was about to do in San Francisco: whether writing a studio's screenplay or a State Department speech, he reminded the diplomats, "I am not entirely an idiot in terms of understanding what the public wants to hear about men and issues." To Trumbo, expressing political views in one venue was not so dissimilar to doing so in the other.[59]

Trumbo settled into the Hotel Fairmont in a room sandwiched between those of delegates John Foster Dulles and Harold Stassen. There the writer spent entire days typing out his ideas for the Stettinius speech, only to have revisions made by Assistant Secretary of State Thomas Finletter, who later held several top-level appointments in the 1950s and 1960s. The written give-and-take between the two men highlights the growing differences between One World idealism and the emerging State Department program, and demonstrates the growing discord among some Americans over the nation's purpose in the postwar world.

Both Finletter and Trumbo agreed that "the unaccustomed sound of open debate in a world assembly" was remarkable and refreshing. Internationalists recognized the value of open debate and its centrality to democracy. They also agreed that the United States was in a powerful position to shape the postwar world. But they differed on many of the specifics of the speech, principally on Soviet and American motives, bipolarity, and the role of negotiated settlements. Trumbo tried to persuade the State Department to downplay any hint of an Anglo-American alliance based on anticommunism. "I thought it was our intention, wherever possible," Trumbo wrote Finletter, "to allay the impression in some quarters that our policy is tied to the British, and that the two English-speaking powers always united in opposition to the Soviets." Trumbo believed the United States should use its unique position to encourage impartial mediation of disputes. "I think the objective of pointing out that we have an independent policy of our own an admirable one," and "then we might mention Roosevelt alone" in this speech, rather than including any reference to Winston Churchill.[60]

Consequently, Trumbo also attempted to emphasize American-Soviet comity, one key principle held by multilateralists. At Yalta, the Allies agreed to allow for the admission of two Soviet republics, as well as a pro–Soviet Polish representative, to the United Nations. Finletter characterized the agreement as Stalin's "request," one permitted by Roosevelt and Churchill. Stalin placed great importance upon the matter, Finletter wrote, because of the considerable wartime sacrifices of the Soviet Union. And why not, Trumbo responded to Finletter. The Soviets had borne the brunt of blitzkrieg. Trumbo believed that any commendation for valor was best expressed in the speech by the Americans without characterizing it as a Soviet "request," which sounded "unwarranted."[61]

These exchanges show Trumbo's frustration when the State Department appropriated universalistic sentiment to emphasize bipolarity. Finletter added in one passage, "I wish to make it absolutely clear that the primary objective of United States foreign policy is to continue and strengthen in the period of peace the war-time solidarity among the nations which have defeated Germany." Trumbo reminded Finletter of those words when he encouraged the State Department to stop attacking the Soviets over the Polish situation. "Why bring it up again?" Trumbo asked while pointing to another section of the speech. Problems with Britain, France, and China also existed over decolonization, occupation, and internal corruption, he reminded Finletter. Does the United States intend "to imply that disagreements in the past and future are between the four great powers and the Soviet Union? This seems dangerous. But if we mean to line up four against the fifth, we should state it clearly. And if we do *not* mean to do so, then these lines are very carelessly written."[62] Perhaps Finletter had gotten more political advice than he intended when he hired Trumbo to polish a speech.

Finletter adopted the language of One Worldism but, in Trumbo's mind, not the spirit. Where Finletter attempted to characterize American motives during the construction of the United Nations in wholly noble terms, Trumbo sought to maintain impartiality. The State Department hoped to show how the United States lived up to its Yalta agreements, implying Soviet noncompliance. Trumbo advised Finletter, "We should never say of our agreements that we 'loyally' fulfilled them." He added, "Only a man with a bad conscience praises his own loyalty and integrity. The position of the US on agreements, I think, should be simply this: 'We made an agreement and we fulfilled it.' . . . I never beat myself on my back because I pay off my note at the bank. The bank expects me to, and I expect to also."[63]

Once his contribution to the speech had been completed, Trumbo requested Secretary of State Edward Stettinius's assistant read over the speech—"before anyone else lays a hand on it"—and then have the secretary use it. Trumbo and Thomas Finletter hammered out final revisions before submitting it to the State Department, but Trumbo later discovered that the speech was given "the shaft" before being rewritten by another writer. After receiving a polite thanks for his government work, an exasperated Trumbo headed home to Hollywood with his large, signed photograph of Secretary of State Stettinius.[64] As he boarded his plane, he must have wondered to what extent his One World idealism could find harmony with the developing American foreign policy. Ironically, his ghostwriting in 1945 foreshadowed his later activities as a blacklisted writer.

Trumbo's reservations aside, HDC members now set out to dazzle Americans in "caravans" through several midwestern cities as a way of supporting the United Nations charter, a trip announced just hours after the charter was signed. In one radio broadcast, ventriloquist Edgar Bergen explained to his carved companion, Charlie McCarthy, that unlike the League of Nations, "all us Americans are going to have a voice in it. Our Senators and Congressmen want to know how we the common folks feel, and we're going to get word to them." Jimmy Durante echoed the sentiment by telling listeners that "we all can put in our two cents worth. . . . We all got to—because it's up to every one of us to help make the peace."[65] On their own, without government sanction, an organized and united Hollywood stepped onto the political field. In late July the Hollywood community joined those celebrating the Senate's ratification of the Bretton Woods agreements by a 61-16 vote, and the United Nations by an overwhelming 89-2 vote. As far as membership morale was concerned, the HDC was riding high with a clear purpose and proven success. By 1945 much of the film community had adopted some aspects of One World ideology. In turn, they had put those ideas into practice through their diplomatic activities.

Within a week after the Senate ratified the United Nations charter, the HDC's next crusade became blatantly apparent when the atomic bomb detonated over Hiroshima. Control of atomic energy became one of the most important early sites of sparring between universalists and burgeoning Cold Warriors. With the shocking advent of atomic weaponry, many believed multilateralism could forestall Doomsday. A progressive Secretary of Commerce Henry Wallace warned, "How we meet this issue will determine whether we live not in 'one world' or 'two worlds'—but whether we live at all." The HDC continued its foreign policy mission by moving from its support of international organizations to the issue of atomic energy control.[66]

A consensus of Hollywood activists favored international control abroad and civilian control at home. In early December 1945, under the banner "The Atom Has Bombed Us Into One World!" a "Crisis Meeting" convened at Madison Square Garden to publicize the problem of "international distrust and suspicion." At a program held at the Beverly-Wilshire Hotel, "Atomic Power and Foreign Policy," headliner actress-turned-politician Helen Gahagan Douglas shared the stage with actor-not-yet-turned-politician Ronald Reagan. The following night, people paid fifty-five cents for admission to Hollywood Legion Stadium to view an encore. Douglas told those assembled, "We can afford to split the atom, but we cannot afford to split the big three." Turning a Willkie-like critical eye homeward, the congresswoman asked, "Doesn't it ever occur to anyone, by the way, that the Russians might be a little fearful and suspicious of us—and with reason? . . . So Russia is cantankerous, is she? Well, what about us? And Russia interferes in the internal affairs of her neighbors, does she? Well, what are *we* doing in China? Why are *our* Lend-Lease materials being used in Java?" These themes of atomic energy control, international cooperation, and anticolonialism combined to form the Hollywood activists' agenda.[67]

Despite such programs, devout adherents of universalism soon became frustrated that Hollywood could do no more. Thinking the government could have produced public information films through the OWI, as they had in support of Bretton Woods and the United Nations, Progressives became disappointed when President Truman abolished the OWI two weeks after Hiroshima. It is doubtful that Truman and his advisers would have allowed such films to be distributed anyway. Bretton Woods and the United Nations had rallied the Hollywood community to the HDC, which then joined the government to build those institutions. The fight for international and civilian control over atomic energy, though, would illustrate the difficulties artists encountered in the political arena, especially when Hollywood's foreign policy diverged from that of Washington.

At the same time that Hollywood's activists weighed in on the atomic issue, they also tried to put One World ideas about self-determination into practice. On October 28, 1945, they called for antidiscrimination legislation to attack America's weakness on the race issue. The following March, they sponsored National Abolish the Poll Tax Week. A few weeks later, they presented an all-star variety show at the Elks Club in support of an anti–poll tax bill. The bill passed the House that June but stalled under a filibuster in the Senate. Given the wartime rhetoric, opponents of the poll tax framed the issue in terms of foreign policy. "The war has greatly clarified our democratic ideals," one pamphlet declared, and those who "helped bring democracy to countries overseas, want it at home, too." The actor Fredric March asked a radio audience, "Are we a nation that will allow Mexican Americans to die for us in France or Okinawa, and then condemn their sons and brothers to economic slavery? Are we a nation that will use Negroes as skilled draftsmen when our backs are to the wall, and drive them to shining shoes again when the heat is off?" Beyond lynching and exploitation, One-World activists put segregation and other racial issues in the context of war and foreign policy. Such incidents are a "disservice in world relations," a member of the HDC wrote, "Our representatives overseas are being constantly embarrassed" by allies and enemies alike.[68] As with the case of atomic control, as 1945 turned into 1946, a growing number of opponents criticized Hollywood activists for their outspoken criticism of the nation's "racial imperialisms."

For the remainder of the 1940s, Hollywood Progressives would seek to influence American foreign policy. They did so for voters in the political ways already illustrated, but also for audiences in their capacity as manufacturers of entertainment. Producer Dore Schary thought Hollywood had wasted its opportunity to promote internationalism and democratic principles after the First World War. This time, Schary argued, things would be different. Hollywood people had to recognize "our responsibility as citizens and picture makers" by promoting progressive themes for America. Better than radio broadcasts, public service announcements, and caravans, motion pictures could be employed in a new war against "sinister forces" abroad and at home, to "dramatize what the soldier must do to readjust himself to civilian life." The influential moviemaker urged his colleagues to act on both sides of the camera to this end. And audiences must realize they "are no longer the babies they were years ago, and if they're given more adult fare, they'll thrive on the diet . . . [and] so will the world." Speaking at the moment between ideological war and uncertain peace, Schary concluded at the end of 1945, "The motion picture makers must exercise the muscles they have put on."[69]

Hollywood became one site where a contest took place to identify the nation's postwar mission. To some extent, One World activists and their opponents, the adherents of the emerging Cold War consensus, stood on common ground with the belief that the United States was poised at a historic moment and had to choose internationalism and world leadership. But whereas Willkie's heirs sought to use this rare, historic opportunity to globalize liberal humanism, skeptics argued that the United States had no choice but to undertake the stewardship of the West against Soviet expansion. This ideological rivalry over the American postwar purpose was increasingly considered critical to all sides, especially in Hollywood. The half-decade after the war, wrote one historian, proved to be "the most turbulent and crisis-ridden period in industry history."[70]

Dissent emerged and matured in Hollywood in the late 1940s. Ideas about America's postwar purpose which were already being contested in 1945 would coalesce by 1950 into distinct ideological denominations because of threats both real and exaggerated. By looking to influential opinion-makers outside Washington—as far away as southern California—one can see that the emerging Cold War did not pit monolithic Americanism against the threat of communism. Therefore, the policy of containment—the military, economic, and cultural facets fashioned to meet the communist threat—would not go unchallenged or unchanged by Progressives in culture industries. Fueled by the ideas of Wendell Willkie and others, Hollywood activists promoted their vision in practical ways at the end the Second World War. Issues of particular interest to these advocates included the development of international organizations, the debate over controlling the atom, and the struggle for decolonization. Armed with early political successes and full of energy, Hollywood's internationalists looked at the postwar world with unbounded optimism. They hoped to use their positions of power in America's motion picture industry to advance their cause. But changes in the production process and the gradual onset of the Cold War would test the viability of multilateralism.

3

Casting the
Iron Curtain

IN SEPTEMBER 1946, while vacationing on the lovely island of Nantucket, literary agent Audrey Wood received a letter from a
friend and client, playwright Tennessee Williams. Accustomed as she was
to Williams's antics, she relished learning of his latest adventures and his
bursts of creative genius. At the conclusion of a letter updating his progress on the script for *A Streetcar Named Desire*, Williams swerved into
a non sequitur. Although nominally apolitical, he wrote, "The International outlook is becoming quite fearful. Don't you think there ought to
be an organized movement in the Theatre to insist upon a clarification of
U.S. foreign policy?" Instead of leaving it at that, Williams added specifics
regarding his reaction to a belligerent speech by Secretary of State James
Byrnes just days earlier.

> It appears to me that Byrnes and the administration have formulated a
> policy of their own in line with the most reactionary elements in the
> country and they are taking the shortest cut to world destruction through
> their inflammatory meddling in Europe. This is without the under-
> standing or sanction of the vast body of Americans who, like everybody
> else, will go down the drain if we're drawn into war with Russia. I think
> there ought to be popular demonstrations of all kinds in protest against
> it. The theatre could start such a program.[1]

The Cold War inflamed the passions of even the most politically disinterested individuals. Artists of all sorts, moreover, sought ways to use their
positions as purveyors of national culture to influence the American postwar character and foreign policy. For Progressives in Hollywood, this was
certainly the case.

From 1945 to 1947, just as the Cold War intensified, the entire motion
picture industry became associated in the minds of many Americans

63

with dangerous radicalism. Important events that linked Hollywood with radicalism included an industry-wide strike, affiliation with national radical organizations, and flirtation with the doomed candidacy of Henry Wallace. The One World idealism that infused many successful films (both critically and financially) during this period also contributed to the sense that Hollywood was promoting a radical agenda. Yet these same events revealed fissures within the motion picture community that would develop into a chasm amid the Red-baiting and witch-hunting that began in 1947. At first, Hollywood and the larger political left united against congressional interference, as they had done before the war. But that front soon crumbled as studio executives struggled to form bonds with the government and as liberals drew distinctions between themselves and the activities of purported "radicals." In sum, the early postwar era witnessed some members of a conflicted film community promoting universalism and others defining the communist menace.

Radicals in Hollywood

Freed from wartime restrictions and armed with renewed purpose, President Truman introduced a liberal, twenty-one-point program on September 6, 1945. He added other items haphazardly, Roosevelt-style, in the following months until he had compiled a sweeping legislative agenda encompassing full employment, a higher minimum wage, housing shortages, price supports, and health care. Principally, Truman sought to extend the New Deal beyond Roosevelt's grave, but his plans met with lethal resistance at the hands of a conservative Congress. In one area, though, Truman was successful: his administration set out to investigate and prosecute antitrust suits in a variety of industries after the war, including cement, sugar, steel, automobiles, and—to be sure—motion pictures.[2]

Whereas Truman looked to the future with optimism, studio moguls looked with dread. Hollywood labor strife and the renewal of the antitrust crusade provided headaches for studio executives. Pursuit of the antitrust case against the major studios was the most significant development for the industry in that era.[3] In October 1945, Attorney General Tom C. Clark renewed federal antitrust litigation against the Hollywood "Big Eight" in a New York federal district court. After a month, the government rested its case. In June 1946 a three-judge panel found the studios guilty of price-fixing and block-booking, and ordered fair and competitive bidding on a film-by-film, theater-by-theater basis. By 1947, even before the Supreme

Court settled the issue in dramatic form, Hollywood was already reeling. After the case made its way to the Supreme Court, on May 3, 1948, Justice William O. Douglas issued a unanimous opinion finding against the studios' monopolistic practices. Shockwaves hit Southern California as the Court ordered the studios to divorce themselves from their distribution and exhibition enterprises. On New Year's Day 1950 there were no revelers on the Paramount lot, for the studio was officially divorced from its theaters. A new day had dawned in Hollywood.

By 1947, at the same time that the government effectively handcuffed the moguls, the domestic and foreign markets had slowed dramatically. The huge profits of the war and the first two postwar years evaporated as uncertainty reigned over how to regain markets lost to the Axis and as foreign film industries regrouped in Allied countries. The war had been good to studios in the sense that their exports expanded as the Allied armies liberated occupied territory, but producers sought permanent security by coordinating their efforts to regain a foothold in foreign markets. After the war, studios policed content so as to avoid offending (if not appealing to) foreign audiences. In an article titled "Diplomatic Hollywood," the *New York Times* reported that studios were "bending backward to keep from stepping on international toes" in their postwar pictures. For example, in the interest of Pan-Americanism, editors deleted a wide range of scenes, from those exposing widespread poverty to those insinuating the harmful effects of coffee. Even "the Nazi and the Jap are no longer fair game," the paper explained.[4]

Content aside, studio executives needed to find a more comprehensive and systematic way to meet the new challenges of foreign trade, so the structure of overseas business changed as well. The Motion Picture Association of America (MPAA) and the overseas branch of the OWI merged to form a single trade association, the Motion Picture Export Association (MPEA). This institution, essentially a monopoly conspiring to restrain free trade, would bring government and the film industry in closer contact, particularly at the moment when producers were most fretful over the lucrative European market. Several obstacles stood in the way of the MPEA. Paris set up barriers to the import of hundreds of Hollywood films, including a law prohibiting the exhibition of any film over two years old in French theaters. Britain, Hollywood's chief client state, made up over 75 percent of American film revenue, and 1946 was a promising year. But things changed soon thereafter as Britain struggled amid great physical destruction, financial collapse, and rationing. With their domestic film industry in disarray, British producers looked to curb exports through protectionist policies. Given this situation, keeping "good relations with England remained the single most important item on Hollywood's overseas agenda." At the same time, however, the MPEA tussled with its British counterparts for control over the British cinema from production to exhibition.[5]

Sir Stafford Cripps, the president of the British Board of Trade, endeavored to de-Americanize British theaters. The means to that end included imposing a 75 percent tariff on all Hollywood films in August 1947. Obviously outraged and ready for a fight, American producers planned to test the diet Cripps had placed on the appetite of English theatergoers. The MPEA announced an embargo the very next day. With "friendly" markets closing down, "unfriendly" markets became a tantalizing option for studios. The MPEA "movie czar," Eric Johnston, acknowledged the temptation of the studios to sell pictures abroad, even if it meant exhibiting films that "show the seamy side of American life."[6] But most film executives undoubtedly realized that the government would not help with the distribution of such productions. The heads of the foreign departments of a number of studios met at Lucey's Restaurant on Melrose Boulevard, across the street from the Paramount and RKO lots. There they acknowledged the grave problems—rationing, quotas, tariffs, embargoes, and English pride—which prevented Hollywood from supplying its hungriest foreign consumers in Europe. By the fall of 1947, studio executives were bemoaning the situation and looking for ways to improve souring relations with Washington and with foreign governments.

Leaders of the motion picture industry had other worries in the years 1945 to 1947. In particular, studio executives suffered acute labor pains after the war, challenges that contributed to the mounting financial crisis and to an image problem. Several stars sought freelance status outside long-term studio contracts, and many performers investigated forming their own production companies.[7] Moreover, much of the film industry flirted with unions and progressive politics. One event in particular solidified in congressional minds, at least, Hollywood's liberal leanings: the industry-wide strike of 1945. That Hollywood had been thoroughly unionized before the war did not mean that harmony ruled the cinematic working class. To the contrary, unions engaged in pitched battles. The upstart Conference of Studio Unions, headed by former boxer Herbert Sorrell, challenged the studio-backed International Alliance of Theatrical and Stage Employees, now represented by former projectionist Roy Brewer (its former leaders, Bioff and Browne, had been convicted of racketeering).

Although industry labor woes were precipitated by this internal division among unionized talent, studio executives carefully watched (and participated in) the unfolding drama.[8]

Hollywood unions had signaled an end to wartime unity back in the fall of 1944 when set decorators, painters, and machinists walked off the Metro studio lot. MGM used the decision by the War Labor Board to withhold certification from the CSU as a pretense to refuse recognition of its collective bargaining efforts. In March 1945, Herb Sorrell of the CSU led an expansive (and ill-timed) strike of over 10,000 workers before the war concluded, calling out cartoonists and set decorators still in uniform to join the picket lines at studios and hundreds of theaters. The strike continued for seven months. Even though there was a nine-month supply of films already slated to appear that year, studios felt the pinch. A frustrated David O. Selznick felt compelled to suspend production of his latest epic, *Duel in the Sun*. By October 5, patience on both sides had worn thin. Herb Sorrell and some 700 striking workers assembled outside the gates of Warner Bros. just before dawn. Studio strikebreakers and police also appeared. The ensuing fight left cars overturned and people on both sides "knifed, clubbed and gassed." High-pressure fire hoses swept strikers "off their feet on the glass-littered pavement" before police apprehended Sorrell for "inciting" the riot.[9]

The strike had the residual effect of uniting other groups—the Screen Writers Guild, for one—in public sympathy with CSU over smoldering labor complaints. That October, promising "to keep my passions under control," one obviously irritated screenwriter, Dalton Trumbo, addressed a rally at Olympic Auditorium, a venue famous for its boxing matches. Although all workers in both IATSE and the CSU were "decent" folks "banded together to protect their living standards and their jobs," he said, the leaders in the more conservative, producer-supported, AFL-affiliated IATSE were "undemocratic." Producers locked out striking workers, contracted "scabs" to take their places, and recognized "independent" unions.[10] "Hollywood is a company town," a group of anonymous writers explained later, "and beneath the fancy publicity it is not so different from a coal town in Kentucky or a cotton town in Alabama."[11] Such rhetoric invited studio bosses to charge the CSU with communist infiltration. Amid wartime victory celebrations, Los Angeles newspapers showed Hollywood falling apart. Labor strife there appeared to outsiders as an internal struggle between working-class radicals and anticommunists. For moderates, the effort to purge radicals from organizations of the left became an obvious necessity.

Like the labor unions, the Screen Writers Guild (SWG) also appeared to have been taken over by radicals. When a slate of radical writers including Lester Cole and Ring Lardner Jr. swept the executive board elections in 1946, moderates in the SWG, including Emmett Lavery, looked for ways either to oust them or to form a rival organization, similar to the situation in organized labor. While the internal fight commenced, the House Committee on Un-American Activities (often referred to as HUAC) stepped in to purge the radicals. At first, Lavery sided with his fellow writers against congressional interference, but then he swiftly distanced himself and the SWG from the radicals by sacrificing them.

Like the unions, another organization that gradually became tainted by a radical image was the powerful Hollywood Democratic Committee. Since its founding during the war, and given its activism in support of the United Nations, the membership rolls of the HDC had swelled—from harmonica aficionado Larry Adler to studio mogul Darryl F. Zanuck, from radical John Howard Lawson to anticommunist Ronald Reagan. The organization prided itself on its diversity of membership and unity of purpose. The "fraternity of artists" cooperated for the same general cause: to promote multilateralism. Actor Edward G. Robinson explained that though he was a "citizen of America, I am part of the world." Gregory Peck added, "I joined [the HDC] because I believe in the liberal progressive view on politics and issues." Humphrey Bogart referred to Franklin Roosevelt while adhering to Willkie's principles. The director John Cromwell professed a belief in "independent liberalism," and actor John Garfield advocated "progress and world peace." The war politicized members of the HDC, and most agreed on the same fundamental values: a consciousness of world citizenship, activism for internationalism, and disdain for petty nationalism.[12] Yet despite this apparent harmony, fault lines soon appeared that would doom such a united effort for universalism. As the world situation grew tense, internal controversies swirled over the role radicals would play within the cultural left, over decolonization and self-determination, and over relations with the Soviet Union. In short, from 1945 to 1947, while studio chieftains dealt with a fragile foreign market and domestic labor disputes, Hollywood talent hotly contested not only the American postwar identity but who could define it.

On April 17, 1945, two hundred members of the HDC greeted the burly, white-bearded sculptor Jo Davidson as he stopped in Los Angeles before heading to San Francisco to sculpt some of the notables in attendance at the new United Nations. As the chairman of the Independent Citizens Committee of the Arts, Sciences, and Professions, Davidson hoped to convince members of the HDC to link their cause with his, to make a larger and more influential organization. In fact, Davidson's organization was quickly becoming a meeting place for a cross-section of notable Americans, including playwrights, atomic scientists, and educators, all seeking to influence the direction of the postwar nation. The ICCASP bylaws explained its purpose:

> Through a program of enlightenment, to promote and cultivate the continuance and extension of the democratic way of life in the United States; to combat all retrogressive and reactionary forces and tendencies calculated to circumscribe or limit in any way the continuance and extension of the democratic way of life in the United States; to promote and cultivate the continuance and extension of democracy among all peoples of the world and to combat every influence and tendency in world affairs calculated to circumscribe or limit the same; . . . to increase public interest in problems of national and international affairs; to enlighten its members and the public on matters relating to social, economic and political policies of the United States; . . . to disseminate among the people of the United States knowledge and information which shall inculcate in them an understanding of the necessity and desirability for attaining the foregoing objectives.[13]

Could Wendell Willkie have written it better? During his Los Angeles layover, Davidson urged the leadership of the HDC to bind its independent association in an even closer alliance with the 8,500 members of ICCASP. Such an association with a group including known radicals proved controversial, to say the least, and marked a final spasm of the Popular Front of the 1930s.

In June 1945 the HDC executive board met to discuss the proposal to associate with ICCASP. In a meeting aptly described by one member from Twentieth Century-Fox as "a lulu," members wrangled over the future of the HDC.[14] For some, the ICCASP represented a turn toward radical politics and a renewal of the Popular Front. Their heated debates raised a series of basic questions for the new organization to address in its statement of purpose: What was the meaning of the American "way of life?" Who was "retrogressive and reactionary?" Which "problems of national and international affairs" needed to be addressed? What was the difference between "to disseminate" and "to propagandize"? These questions represented the problem with promoting a singular national purpose. Among the outspoken advocates of association was screenwriter John Howard Lawson. "People in Hollywood can function better if HDC is affiliated with a national organization," he explained. "We must have a national organization."[15] After two hours of debate, as a compromise, the HDC rechristened itself the Hollywood Independent Citizens Committee of the Arts, Sciences, and Professions (HICCASP), which would become associated but remain independent. That was small consolation to members who opposed any association at all.

As a way to maintain organizational tranquillity and unity, members formed a special committee to discuss the direction and agenda of HICCASP. Made up of a cross-section of the membership—including moderates Ronald Reagan and James Roosevelt as well as radicals Dalton Trumbo and John Howard Lawson—the committee proposed a new statement of policy. With respect to foreign policy, however, the members could agree only on general notions of international cooperation, democracy, collective security, and bipartisanship.[16] They quoted Franklin Roosevelt, who favored "the ability of all peoples of all kinds, to live together in the same world, at peace."[17] Few would disagree with world peace, but grave disagreements would come over the practical manifestations of such peace. With its work discharged, the committee had provided HICCASP with only temporary organizational comity, a feeling that was fragile and fleeting.

On November 30, 1945, Lawson stood to address the HICCASP membership. With the atomic bomb, he began, "we now face the greatest and most terrifying crisis in the life of our country and the life of the world." Members rustled in their seats as the bombastic screenwriter indicted American capitalism, military policy, and the Truman administration. "It is not solely a question of the Soviet Union, which has demonstrated that it has a peaceful policy toward other nations." By preventing self-determination in Asia, by propping up "autocratic" regimes such as Chiang's in China, Lawson insisted, "we build up disruption and confusion and despair in the world." This "poison stew," he promised, "will come back to us."[18] Lawson's late-night tirade encapsulated the evolving situation.

Thus, at the very moment that studio executives were worrying about worsening relations with government, their lost markets, and violent labor disputes, the image of the industry became tainted by radicalism. Much of that stigma rested on disputes over American foreign policy. Whereas the United Nations and other international organizations united Hollywood in 1945, the international climate had changed substantially by 1947. Relations between Washington and Moscow soured significantly and contributed to a split within the influential motion picture community.

The Cold War afflicted Hollywood at a time when Americans were forming critical opinions about relations with the Soviet Union. Almost immediately after the V-J Day festivities became faded memories, Americans read in their newspapers throughout the remainder of 1945 of disagreements between Secretary of State Byrnes and the Soviet leaders at the Council of Foreign Ministers meetings in London and Moscow. A separate meeting was held in Washington with Britain and Canada to discuss atomic policy, while other nations remained noticeably uninvited. In November 1945, Josip Broz Tito's communist partisans took over Yugoslavia, while Mao's advancing forces prompted President Truman to dispatch George Marshall to mediate between Mao and Chiang for control over China. Good news was hard to find in the first half of 1946 as Stalin seemingly swept over much of Eastern Europe and also threatened Iranian oil fields.

In February 1946, Stalin delivered the famous "election" speech in which he intimated the incompatibility of communism and capitalism. His words set off alarms in the West. Two weeks later, George Kennan sent to the State Department his celebrated "long telegram" about dangerous Soviet intentions. Although many in Washington had already formulated reasons to doubt Stalin's motives, Kennan's famous cable from "the front" provided a nodding reassurance. In short order the document shocked several fence-sitters within the foreign policy establishment. Amid disagreements over borders, occupation, and UN membership, Kennan's survey of Russian behavior provided a synthesis for policymakers to seize hold of, allowing them to view themselves as actors "present at the creation" of a protracted conflict, to use Dean Acheson's phrase. Kennan's analysis armed Truman with the ammunition to "scare the hell out of the country" the following year, when Kennan's "Mr. X" article appeared in *Foreign Affairs*. As Lloyd Gardner has written, "If [Kennan] had not existed, Truman and Acheson would have had to have invented him."[19]

Despite the clear impact of the article, historians and Kennan himself have long noted the ambiguous language and, in some ways, muddled ideas in this early reference to containment. For example, while many agreed with Kennan on the need to shore up the West to resist communism, the means to achieve that end were open to competing (military, economic, political) translations. Beyond the simple recognition of a dire situation, the Truman administration was awash in a sea of policy options: Secretary of War Henry L. Stimson advocated internationalization of atomic technology; Secretary of Commerce Henry Wallace counseled conciliation; Byrnes urged belligerence; Marshall promoted moderation; and Kennan articulated containment. Nascent containment provided a starting point, a common language, and a strategy for confronting the challenge of physical Soviet expansion in Europe. Even after military and economic institutions were formed in the following years, containment remained a *moderate* device to protect geostrategic interests. The early ambiguity allowed for a modest brand of containment, relative to later, more stringent adaptations. What appeared so dramatic in the late 1940s was really quite limited in scope as compared to the early 1950s.

The moderate containment policies of the late 1940s hastened the alienation of the most radical elements of society, especially those who had direct connections to outlaw organizations and continued to work in the influential culture industries. (Once containment took on a more global and ideological reach after 1950, anticommunists targeted liberals regardless of those direct ties.) Throughout the late 1940s, ambiguity on the part of government and the temperate nature of containment allowed for heated negotiation in the public sphere over the national purpose, its foreign policy, and its international image. In the cultural arena, anticommunists effectively demonized the Soviets and further identified Hollywood leaders as "radical" supporters of Soviet communism. Three foreign policy issues in particular broke Hollywood unity apart: relations with the Soviet Union, control over atomic energy, and support for decolonization.

The winds blew away from conciliation with the Soviets when, in March 1946, Winston Churchill culminated his year-long crusade to tighten Anglo-American foreign policy with his famous "Iron Curtain" speech in Fulton, Missouri. Churchill presented the West with a choice between containment and appeasement. Accommodation with the Soviets amounted in his mind to the latter. Americans began taking sides that very week. "An octopus Communist–New Deal political alliance was in the making," the *Los Angeles Examiner* reported, "under the guise of a 'liberal' movement but following unswervingly the Moscow party line."[20]

Members of the Hollywood left worried about Churchill's red-meat remarks. "The stage is being set for future wars," Lillian Hellman said in response. "Let us not be asked to arrange crusades against Socialist Britain, Communist Russia, or Radical France." Rather, she exclaimed, "We must stand together."[21] Surprising to many moderates in HICCASP, the organization's leadership bitterly attacked the Iron Curtain speech as "a throwback to the power politics which have already plunged the world into two wars, and would now precipitate the final, atomic war."[22] Obviously not for Hellman and the HICCASP leadership, but for many others in the spring and summer of 1946, Churchill's words emboldened American anti-communists and sparked a campaign by influential internationalists to carry the message to the public. The wartime alliance with Stalin had faded quickly, and many Americans came to adopt Churchill's warnings about appeasement. The same week as his speech, invitations went out to attend a luncheon for Russian Relief and hear a speech by the ambassador to Moscow, Averell Harriman. "I doubt that I should be interested in the purpose for which your meeting is called," one prominent invitee wrote to Harriman. "So far as I can judge," he explained, "Russia is determined to follow closely the program of the despised Hitler, and frankly I can see little difference between the actions of the two dictators." The hardening of positions limited opportunities for fruitful dialogue.[23]

Such changes in the political climate took their toll on Hollywood, especially when members of the motion picture community addressed specific political issues such as control over atomic energy. Already by then, adherents to multilateralism had united behind an atomic policy that would grant international control abroad and civilian control at home. Under banners such as "The Atom Has Bombed Us Into One World!" activists raised awareness and collected funds and signatures. At one program a circulating petition garnered 1,000 names. Such events prompted excitement from George Pepper, who had moved from arthritic violinist to labor organizer of Hollywood musicians to HICCASP executive secretary. Pepper remarked giddily to producer Dore Schary, "We are going places."[24] While he undoubtedly meant HICCASP was going *up*, some members began to wonder about the validity of that sentiment.

When it came to control over atomic energy, many believed it prudent to take power out of the hands of the military and thus mitigate the destructive capabilities of the atom. Even Secretary of War Henry L. Stimson worried that wearing the bomb on "our hip" would lead to suspicion and proliferation.[25] The debate caused tension within the membership of HICCASP once the Senate opened debate on an amendment offered by internationalist Republican Arthur Vandenberg, who called for a military board to review all decisions made by the Atomic Energy Commission. Almost immediately, a diverse coalition of One World adherents formed public interest groups with the purpose of halting what they viewed as the further militarization of the atom.

Atomic scientists, undoubtedly feeling guilty over their role in releasing the atom from Pandora's box, also increased their political activity. Prominent scientists, including Albert Einstein, J. Robert Oppenheimer, Harold C. Urey, Hans A. Bethe, Linus Pauling, and Leo Szilard, believed that only by global unity could the unimaginable Apocalypse be avoided. Their organization, the Emergency Committee of Atomic Scientists, distributed a telegram over chairman Albert Einstein's name inviting prominent Americans (Hollywood producers among them) to meetings at Princeton in the fall. The scientists said of policymakers, "Our world faces a crisis as yet unperceived by those possessing power to make great decisions for good or evil." They continued, "We scientists who released this immense power have overwhelming responsibility in this world life and death struggle to harness atoms for benefit of mankind and not for humanity's destruction."[26] Another pamphlet intoned, "Putting atomic energy in the hands of the military is an announcement to the rest of the world that we have chosen to use this force primarily and almost exclusively as a weapon of war."[27] Control over the atom threatened the potential for world unity and possibly ensured another war.

These critics of the Vandenberg amendment had other motives that extended beyond merely preventing annihilation. Without civilian control over the atom, they argued, "peacetime development is impossible." Groups such as the atomic scientists believed that a world where national security dictated control over new technologies would prevent the full realization of what those new technologies promised. One statement of purpose explained, "Military control means delayed realization of the peacetime benefits of atomic energy—combatting cancer and other disease, a new cheap source of power and heat for undeveloped areas and ultimately for vehicle propulsion, new methods of analyzing industrial products," and other benefits.[28]

Like the atomic scientists, their associates in the Hollywood ICCASP branch worried not just about the destructive force of the bomb but also about how volatile men such as Secretary of State Byrnes threatened to use it. They viewed American foreign policy from the perspective of other nations: "We are brandishing it ferociously at the world," the actor Fredric March explained to a radio audience, "and the bomb might go off, and everybody knows it." Linking the Hollywood Progressives' fight to the scientists' political struggle, March continued, "We are here . . . because we have a profound conviction that the day is long past when the artist, the scientist, can sit musing in the studio or the laboratory, while the world batters itself to pieces outside his door. And that is what the world is doing."[29]

Just as relations with the Soviets and the atomic issue invited controversy and opponents, so too did the Progressives' focus on the issue of self-determination. Recall that advocates for multilateralism made direct connections between anticolonial struggles overseas and racial progress at home. They waged a universal fight for the democratic principle of self-determination and relied on taking an impartial view of all nations, including the United States. In the Cold War environment, critics mocked the Hollywood left's vocal outrage at lynchings while "the Soviets tore the Atlantic Charter to shreds" and lowered "a steel curtain of secrecy and tyranny" in Europe. "Why this abrupt bleating of your petty, perverted minds and Stalin-worshipping propaganda?" one individual asked of HICCASP.[30] Apparently in this case, both sides of the domestic civil rights issue viewed the controversy in terms of foreign policy. Just as Wendell Willkie had warned against "our domestic imperialisms," the executive board of HICCASP favored decolonization and racial self-determination wherever such struggles existed. "We support the growth of democracy, the growth of progressive self-government, throughout the world," HICCASP informed its critics. "The struggles of the colonial and semi-colonial people toward independence warrants our support." Members applauded Britain's Labour government for its anticipated withdrawal from India, Egypt, and Palestine. But HICCASP also promised to withhold support for states that were "inimical to progress and freedom," even if the United States was among them.[31]

Just as the Cold War heated up, HICCASP appeared to give voice to radicals who advocated an agenda in opposition to that of the government. The Truman administration warned of Stalin's warmongering; HICCASP appealed for understanding. Congress called for preserving atomic control; HICCASP counseled cooperation. Churchill sought an Anglo-American alliance; HICCASP raged against "undeclared wars" to prop up colonial regimes. For cautious moderates in HICCASP, suspicious of what they considered the radicalization of the executive board, the agenda had gone too far.

Of Soviets and Subversives: Stereotyping the Hollywood Left

In March 1946, the same month Churchill delivered his Iron Curtain speech and the Senate debated control over the atom, HICCASP had made known its outspoken opposition to official American foreign policy. The situation in Hollywood appeared critical to Cold Warriors who knew what a powerful role culture played in the new world order. Also in March 1946, Henry Luce met for a three-hour dinner and frank discussion with twelve "Hollywood men" about the future of film in a bipolar world. They all agreed "that the movies are a tremendously potent expression of America to the people of the world." But Luce expressed some concern that producers "delude themselves" and that the industry at times exported an image of "cheapness and shoddiness." Now more than ever, Luce said urgently, Hollywood must enlist in this new cause. His wife, the actress and playwright Clare Boothe Luce, then serving as a member of Congress, echoed similar convictions in writing to her friend David O. Selznick: "The 'Russian question' is *the* question of our day, even of our century."[32] For cultural anticommunists, defining the Russian in the "Russian question" became important.

Years later, George Kennan viewed the American mental transition from Hitler to Stalin as one of the great fundamental causes of the Cold War. "We like to have our enemies in the singular," Kennan explained, "our friends, if you will, multiple. But the enemy must always be at center, he must be totally evil, he must wish all the terrible things that could happen to us—whether [that] made sense from his standpoint or not."[33] American cinema contributed immeasurably to the process in the late 1940s. Hollywood propaganda—which included building support for heroic Russian allies in the Soviet Red Army—had been seen as instrumental during the Second World War. Even General George Marshall boldly claimed that Hollywood had won the war. But barely thirty-six months later, the old Soviet Ally pushing out Nazis became a ruthless anaconda strangling Eastern Europe. Containment demanded that the nation recast its collective memory of the Soviet Union from partner to thug in a remarkably short time. Motion pictures helped to cast the Iron Curtain when Stalin became the new Hitler.

The malleable image of the Soviet "Other" allowed it to be manipulated easily once the Cold War began. The fact that few Americans understood the Soviets with any sophistication or complexity meant that a new collective memory of the Russians could be constructed almost at will. One year after the war against fascism ended, it became easy to transfer public sentiments to the new situation. Tropes of totalitarianism, once applied to Russians from 1939 to 1941, were reapplied to the Soviet bogeyman in 1946.[34] That year, Herbert Matthews of the *New York Times* pondered, "Should we now place Stalinist Russia in the same category as Hitlerite Germany? Should we say that she is Fascist?" He concluded that, yes, "Fascism Is Not Dead." Likewise, the idea of appeasement resonated with the public. "Remember Munich," radio commentator H. V. Kaltenborn told listeners in his authoritative cadence after Churchill's Iron Curtain speech. A New Hampshire politician reminded voters that just as Hitler outlined his devilish plot in *Mein Kampf*, the Kremlin had never given up on their calls for world revolution. Clare Boothe Luce pointed out that the Soviet system, like the Nazi regime, "keeps eighteen million people out of 180 million in concentration and forced labor camps." As early as 1946, Soviet communists had become "Red Fascists" in the American popular imagination.[35]

For the remainder of the early Cold War period, cultural and political opponents worked in symbiosis to portray Soviets and communists in the inhuman terms employed against the Japanese during the Second World War. Whether in Hollywood scripts or politicians' speeches, Soviets and subversives were given particular characteristics: bestial, stubborn, abusive, deceptive, feminine, cultist, diseased, backward, barbaric. As Ellen Schrecker explains, popular conceptions of communists were powerful, consumable images.[36] Soviets and communists were often given contrary characteristics as both dupes and activists, Godless and fanatical, elitists and the downtrodden, monolithic yet desperate loners, bohemians and profligates, unemotional and seductive, deceived and trained, subhuman and superhuman. Whatever the tag, it was negative and, more important, extreme at a time when Americans were instructed to adhere to the mainstream.

Foreign films, including at least one Russian epic, contributed to the demonization of the Soviet image. In 1946 the great Russian director Sergei Eisenstein emerged from Stalin's artistic gulag to film his epic *Ivan the Terrible*. By this time Eisenstein had refined his formula for survival: relying on his status as an international icon to protect his life as a Soviet dissident. Stalinists had silenced him for over a decade, but he reappeared in the midst of a dangerous atmosphere to make a political statement. For those aware of Eisenstein's complex political situation, Ivan appears as a man obsessed by the joint venture of building state power and personal power. Americans could choose to see Eisenstein, alternatively hailed and silenced in Stalinist Russia, as the embodiment of stifled creativity and free expression. As critic James Agee wrote of *Ivan the Terrible* in *The Nation*, "It is a study of what such a fanatic becomes, given unprecedented power and opportunity, under the impingement of constant danger, treachery, and intrigue. Ivan, as Eisenstein presents him, is a fair parallel to Stalin; but he is still more suggestively a symbol of the whole history of Russian communism."[37]

"*Not* the Book of the Month." The Cold War heats up as Stalinism consumes One World ideas, 1947. Courtesy Library of Congress, Prints & Photographs Division, LC-USZ62-132578 / By permission of the Edwin Marcus Family.

While the image of Soviet communism was being manipulated, anti-communists turned up the heat on the political left in Hollywood by putting radicals under closer scrutiny. The nation took notice in September 1946 of ICCASP when Henry Luce's *Time* magazine devoted its cover story to the activist-artist Jo Davidson and the "stable of talent" in Hollywood under his direction.[38] The issue hit newsstands in the same week that Secretary of State Byrnes condemned the Soviet Union and promised that the United States would maintain a presence in Europe. With that backdrop, Luce's publication emphasized the dangerous turn Hollywood was taking. Previously, only studio moguls controlled "stables of talent," but the *Time* story implied that writers, directors, and performers now owed their loyalties to ICCASP: "There can be no denying that [ICCASP] is a political phenomenon unique in U.S. history." Whereas earlier screen stars blissfully enjoyed the perks of stardom, *Time* explained, "today, few stars, male or female, would be caught at a commissary lunch table without a Cause." Guilty over "being considered bloated capitalists," they "favor leftish causes." One such cause was accommodation with the Soviets, whose chief advocate appeared to be Truman's secretary of commerce, the former vice president Henry Wallace. By praising Wallace as a "fine fellow," Davidson's politics were clear to the emerging Cold War consensus.[39]

Time proceeded to give readers a primer on postwar ideological lines. "Liberalism is sort of like Bohemianism," the magazine writers quipped, "except that a liberal sits thinking in an ivory tower and has liquor and stuff while the Bohemian sits in an attic and starves." But together, *Time* warned, the Hollywood liberals and bohemians exercise "a unique leverage on thousands of U.S. voters" because "some men and women, whose every instinct rebels against the sound of a politician's voice, are so conditioned that they are unable to resist when their favorite movie star whoops up an issue." Suspect ideologies can have a far reach, Luce's writers seemed to be saying. The bearded Davidson, introduced on the cover under the heading "In Paris, the left bank; in Hollywood, the left wing," and inside the article as "Russian Jewish," probably looked to some like the iconic bomb-tossing Bundist in many an old political cartoon. He was portrayed as a struggling artist who lived in France—where a government composed of socialists and communists ruled—but who also dabbled in American politics. The cover story was accompanied by photographs of Davidson's sculpture studio, which looked remarkably like the attic of a bohemian. The face of Hollywood had become that of Jo Davidson and ICCASP. All the same, *Time* ignored the fact that Davidson led a quarrelsome group of liberals and bohemians.[40]

In the same week that fall, Commerce Secretary Henry Wallace delivered his famous Madison Square Garden speech in which he publicly questioned the Truman administration's embrace of bipolarity and containment. Just as the radical faction within the HDC was linked to a larger, national ICCASP organization, Hollywood Progressives flirted openly with the national movement supporting Wallace. After all, as Truman moved steadily into the Cold War camp, Wallace appeared to be following, in the words of screenwriter Ring Lardner Jr., "a sort of 'one world' approach."[41] After Wallace's speech and his subsequent dismissal

from the Cabinet, HICCASP adopted a new foreign policy program praising his "one strong, clear voice," embracing accommodation, and implor-
ing Truman to "return to the foreign policy" of what they imagined
would have belonged to Roosevelt: "We believe in mutual friendly and
permanent cooperation with the Soviet Union." They rejected aid to Chiang's Nationalist forces, favored international and civilian control over
atomic technology. World peace, they insisted, "rests on the cooperative
efforts of the whole world." They asked the membership to send telegrams to Wallace, "applauding his action, pledging support, and urging
him to continue his fight."[42]

Even when Wallace found few friends in Washington, he could always
rely on a cadre of devotees in the Hollywood community, especially
among Hollywood radicals. Long after Wallace's political descent, *Washington Post* columnist Marquis Childs reported that Wallace maintained
"substantial backing" in Southern California.[43] As it appeared likely that
Wallace would bolt the Democratic Party to lead a progressive movement, Cold War liberals increased their attacks. When Wallace claimed
to be the inheritor of Roosevelt's legacy, however, one notable critic
emerged. Eleanor Roosevelt, frustrated by Soviet intransigence at the
United Nations, devoted a handful of her *My Day* columns to chiding
Wallace, his burgeoning movement, and the radicals in his following.
Mrs. Roosevelt explained, "I am convinced that he has with him elements which are dangerous to this country and any use of my husband's
name in connection with that party is . . . entirely dishonest."[44] Although
these growing differences between radicals and liberals would prove crucial during the HUAC investigations the following year, for the moment
they remained largely unnoticed, especially on screen, as they worked
together to define the national character along the general lines of multilateralism: internationalism, humane capitalism, decolonization and
self-determination, collective security, respect for civil liberties, and impartiality in dealing with the behavior of all nations.

Having swelled its rolls with a diverse constituency, having broadened
its agenda, and having been targeted by congressional conservatives,
HICCASP found it increasingly difficult to keep its ranks in line, especially after Truman fired Wallace from the Cabinet. The standing committees within HICCASP became populated by leftists who would have
trouble in the years ahead: Robert Kenny, Sterling Hayden, Groucho Marx,
Lena Horne, Gene Kelly, Dalton Trumbo, Ring Lardner, Philip Dunne,
John Howard Lawson, and Howard Koch.[45] Furthermore, these individuals were associating Hollywood with the national ICCASP, an organiza-

tion already radicalized in the minds of Americans. "The Commies are boring in like weevils in a biscuit," one Chicago member claimed. Likewise, as *Time* plainly put it, there were a few too many "fleas on the dog."

Some liberals felt vulnerable on the issue, especially as the midterm elections approached. David O. Selznick chided his associate, Dore Schary, about the "Liberal problem and confusions now existing in the United States." Schary explained to his friend, "It's not that you're prejudiced, but you think all the Democrats spend their time hatching plots to wreck the Republic and that they are Communists or Party Travelers or rich Hollywood producers who are being used as dupes for the left wing, and that they have bad table manners, and that once they get into an organization they take over, and that they all hate the English and love the Russians."[46] Joking aside, Schary helped to outline the liberal position in a speech to a dinner sponsored by the liberal magazine *The Nation* a few days later. Addressing the "Challenge of the Post War World to the Liberal Movement," Schary spoke to an audience that included prominent Hollywood liberals—Democrats and Republicans, politicians and actors—at the Ambassador Hotel just after Wallace's very public break with Truman. Raising the importance of the postwar moment, Schary urged his influential audience to use motion pictures to advance liberal internationalism but also to defend against radicalism. Schary hoped to employ motion pictures to explain "definitions of imperialism," to fight old stereotypes, to reject "any motion picture trade paper editor as Hollywood's Supreme Court on un-American activities"—all points any good radical would raise. But Schary also explained, "We can make good pictures, about good things and make money for the stockholders at the same time," and he stated his strict "opposition to the American Communist Party."[47]

Several resignations took place within HICCASP; although the constituency still grew, 10 percent of the HICCASP executive council and several other members withdrew.[48] That same year, two prominent names left the organization, foreshadowing battles to come. James Roosevelt and Congressman Will Rogers Jr.—two HICCASP favorite sons—publicly departed the organization, claiming that it had gotten away from its roots. Even New Dealer Harold Ickes, executive chairman of ICCASP, grumbled about the group. When asked about Jo Davidson's political abilities, Ickes retorted, "He's a good sculptor."[49] James Roosevelt, the former West Coast executive director of ICCASP for $25,000 a year, broke with the committee and effectively drove a wedge between the left and the far left within the organization.[50] For an association that constantly invoked the memory of Franklin Roosevelt as savior and martyr, the loss of such New Deal connections must have been troubling. Most damning, at a time of labor unrest, the charge that the Hollywood outfit "behaves like a Communist front group" only prompted nods from Rankin and other members of Congress. Will Rogers Jr. and James Roosevelt looked to a rival organization: the Union for Democratic Action (UDA), later renamed the Americans for Democratic Action (ADA). In their new home they would wage a war with radicals over the Roosevelt legacy, the direction of the Cold War left, and the shape of the national image.

Liberals in and out of Hollywood expressed discomfort with the radicals among them and began a concerted effort to draw distinctions between themselves and the other faction. For two years liberals in the UDA had cited multilateralism in their organizational literature, and they had joined Progressives in a united effort favoring internationalism, the United Nations, the World Bank and International Monetary Fund, decolonization, and international control of the atom. After those early successes, drawing distinctions with Progressives became the rule. Liberals worried about several ominous events threatening to destabilize the world: communist expansion in Eastern Europe, a series of contentious foreign ministers' meetings, the revelation of Soviet spies in Canada, Truman's appointment of General Walter Bedell Smith to be ambassador to Moscow, Iran's appeal to the UN for assistance in ridding itself of the Soviet threat to its oil fields, and the renewed civil war in China. In the words of lawyer Joseph Rauh, Cold War liberals expressed the "need for a new liberal group, including as many New Dealers as possible, to pressure the Administration from the Left." But they were "even more eloquent on the need to untangle the existing 'popular front' by building a new organization wholly free of Stalinist influence." James Loeb, executive secretary of the UDA, was passionate especially about carving out the "vital center." Arthur Schlesinger Jr. wrote that Loeb's desire "to keep the liberal community pure was vital in a period when many liberals were still unduly tolerant of Stalinism." Loeb, Niebuhr, Rauh, Schlesinger, and others spent the year 1946 organizing the "vital center," in Schlesinger's famous phrase, and purging the far left, "brick by brick with quiet and persuasive efficiency." Eleanor Roosevelt, John Kenneth Galbraith, Walter Reuther, and Hubert Humphrey, became actively engaged in the effort as well.[51]

The UDA sought a clear break with perceived radicals when executive James Loeb wrote to the *New Republic* about the necessity to decide whether "[we] believe that the present critical tension in international affairs is due *exclusively* to the imperialistic, capitalistic, power-mad warmongering of the Western democracies aimed at the destruction of the peace-loving workers' democracy of the Soviet Union . . . or whether the problem is a more complicated one involving the achievement of mutual trust between differing forms of government, with both sides now seeking

"United Nations delegate, huh? Flighty, crackpot, radical One-Worlder, huh?" 1947. Library of Congress, Prints & Photographs Division, LC-UDZ62-130928 / Copyright by Bill Mauldin (1947). Courtesy of Bill Mauldin Estate LLC.

unilateral advantage and security and thereby deepening the distrust and tension." To promote One World ideas in the tense environment, Loeb and other Cold War liberals felt compelled to purge their organizations and unions of perceived radicals. Liberals must ask "whether or not they can or should work *within the same political organizations*" with those further left politically.[52] One UDA pamphlet asked, who is a liberal? The reader discovered, "He is your neighbor."[53] Of course, the same could be said for any member of the left. But simply asking the question and defining liberalism as something unique and separate from other members of the left was noteworthy. That the liberal is "your neighbor" implied that the radical was different, separate, unacceptable, and not particularly neighborly.

Reinhold Niebuhr and the board of directors of UDA outlined the liberal view in postwar foreign policy. While still seeking mutual agreements with the Soviet Union, the UDA chastised those further to the left for ignoring ominous signs from Stalin. "The progressive movement in America must find a solid position between those who regard Russia as the fixed point of international virtue and those who hate and fear Russia to the point of supporting every policy which widens the gulf between Russia and the west." The United States must defend Europe as a bastion of democratic capitalism against "communist dictatorship."[54]

Near the end of 1946, as more moderates fled the organization, HICCASP agreed to come under the auspices of ICCASP. The merger was consummated the next month. That merger was not the only union of radicals to take place. Before the year was out, ICCASP, now including its Hollywood chapter, associated with the National Citizens Political Action Committee to form the Progressive Citizens of America (PCA), also known as the ASP-PCA.[55] In December, at its first convention, the ASP-PCA announced its dissatisfaction with the two major political parties and threatened to form a third party.[56] Together, they heartily embraced Henry Wallace's call for peaceful coexistence with the Soviet Union and passionately objected to HUAC's threatened interference. "At this moment of profound crisis," Lena Horne told those assembled, "our government has fallen to men of shocking bigotry and ignorance, men dominated by the same stupid arrogance that brought the nation to its knees fifteen years ago." She labeled them "spokesmen of monopoly" and advocates for "international anarchy." Even the party of Roosevelt was "notoriously tainted" by John Rankin's Jim Crowism and the "machine greed" of Harry Truman, a sensitive man who had to work hard to distance himself from Kansas City's Pendergast political machine. Democrats now "abandoned" progressive causes in favor of "ignorance and bigotry." Looking to the near future, Horne declared, "The fight will be bitter."[57] Jo Davidson offered what he called "A Program for Peace, Prosperity and Freedom in One World" in the *California Daily News*: "They told us artists to stay in our ivory towers and practice our art and they'd run the world. Look what has happened. It seems to me that artists and scientists have an important contribution to make to the practical world."[58]

On its own, the ASP-PCA obviously had no intention of retiring from political activism, but any members of the alphabet soup that made up its history—the HDC, HICCASP, ICCASP, ASP-PCA—stood on shaky ground by 1947. By lining up against their studio bosses, by appearing "radical" to mainstream America, by increasing their attacks on American Cold War foreign policy, by cutting ties with the major political parties, and by alienating their moderate colleagues, the Hollywood members of the ASP-PCA opened themselves up to unchecked congressional scrutiny without the benefit of powerful defenders in an age of containment. Anticommunists had cast multilateral idealists in the motion picture industry as radicals— perhaps even agents of the Soviet bloc. The advocates of containment were soon searching the scripts bearing progressive names for evidence of subversion.

4

Projectors of Power
Containment Policy in Hollywood

ON NEW YEAR'S Day 1946, Bartley Crum, an urbane California attorney, received a telephone call informing him that President Truman had invited him to serve on the Anglo-American Committee of Inquiry into Palestine. Six American and Six British members investigated the Holocaust, the plight of 400,000 Jewish war refugees, the situation in Palestine, and worldwide anti-Semitism. Although many State Department officials favored controlling immigration to Palestine as a means to secure Arab oil, their efforts were balanced by Truman, who generally supported Zionism. A Roman Catholic, Crum held an awareness of domestic anti-Semitism and a sympathy for Jewish causes.

On his trips to Washington, Europe, and the Middle East, Crum carried with him a worn copy of Wendell Willkie's *One World*. Crum's daughter later found many copies of the text—hardback, paperback, illustrated, limited edition—amid the thousands of books in his library, one of which was inscribed by the author. But Crum considered the single frayed edition he carried with him "a good-luck charm, a talisman, like the crucifix he needed to have near him wherever he was, and which he never forgot."[1] Once when he forgot the book, Crum instructed his wife to mail it special delivery. *One World* was clearly his bible for universalism in the real world. Willkie, Crum noted, had supported Jewish refugees during the war. With Willkie dead, Crum would carry his torch.

At Blair House in Washington, Crum met with the president, Dean Acheson, James Forrestal, many reporters, Zionists, and the British representatives, who warned against "forcing any solution." In Stuttgart, Germany, Crum discovered there were only 200 Jews left. In Nuremberg he witnessed the war crimes proceedings and viewed uncensored films detailing the crimes committed in the concentration camps. He handed copies of *One World* to Arab intellectuals he met in Cairo and to his

Palestinian driver in Jerusalem. At hearings, Crum invoked Willkie as he pleaded that fundamental, universal justice trumped any shortsighted national concerns. He concluded that a Jewish homeland could help end anti-Semitism. For two years the committee searched in vain for a lasting solution. Crum and his allies failed to create a new sensibility and sympathy for Jews, and they paid a political price for their advocacy. In the fall of 1946, Crum told reporters that "because I support European Jews' fight for life against·British and American diplomatic strangling, I'm a Communist. Bah!" Crum later expressed to his daughter that the committee was "one of the most futile missions in history."[2]

While the cause for Israel stalled in a political sense, Crum and other universalists used popular culture as a tool to spark a renewed effort. As a California lawyer, Crum had long held ties to Hollywood elites such as Walter Wanger and Daryl Zanuck, two more supporters of Willkie. But Crum also supported progressives who made films that helped the causes he favored, such as *Crossfire* (1947), which brought the issue of domestic anti-Semitism to the forefront of American minds. Within the year, Crum took on a new cause: that of defending the producer and director of *Crossfire* before HUAC. When his two clients pleaded the Fifth Amendment, Congress voted contempt citations in the fall of 1947, and Bartley Crum's career was finished.

At the same time that anticommunists defined the Soviet threat, cultural negotiators manipulated the image of the United States and affected the direction of American foreign relations. Amid the institutionalization of containment policy and the *appearance* of Hollywood's ascending radicalism, the motion picture industry produced several features that have since become known as the "social problem films" of the late 1940s. Here, many members of the Hollywood left joined together on studio backlots to shed light on nagging national problems: poverty, alcoholism, anti-Semitism, conformity, political demagoguery, so-called isolationism, and our own "racial imperialisms," among others. In many ways Hollywood combined a progressive ethic with a documentary style adapted from wartime experience to underscore realism in "message pictures."

These prestige dramas resonated with audiences as the films flourished commercially and critically throughout the late 1940s. The primary reason for their success may be that they crystallized for Americans their new world order as so many people struggled to make sense of the last war. In sum, these films helped to define the new postwar nation for Americans and for the world. They were significant for another reason:

such a dark treatment of the national landscape led many anticommunists, growing exponentially at the same time, to view these portrayals as poor representations of the nation, and they found ways to contest that image. Ultimately, they encouraged a very different image from that of the Hollywood "Dream Factories."

The Left Hunts for Domestic Fascism

In April 1946, Dore Schary pitched a story to his boss, David O. Selznick, about two brothers, the older a "cynical, disillusioned, and wary" veteran of the Great War, and the younger brother an "aware, determined, and realistically idealistic" veteran of the Second World War. The conflicts within the country become the conflicts within a single American family, where the younger brother must tell his older brother "not in broad, wordy terms, but in highly picturable terms about the future of the family and, symbolically, the future of the world." The film was never made, probably because detailing "all the conflicts and all the happenings of these last thirty-two or thirty-three years" proved daunting (even for an ambitious epic-maker like Selznick).[3] Smaller films, though, were imminently "picturable." Amid antitrust woes, studios and cash-strapped independents such as Selznick turned to original screenplays and "small pictures" as cost-cutting devices. They used Samuel Goldwyn's independent production of *The Best Years of Our Lives* as their guide.

Ideas for "message pictures" came from a variety of sources, but especially the daily news headlines. For example, *The Lost Weekend* (1945) showed alcoholism as dangerous and destructive, contrary to Hollywood's traditional portrayals of drinkers as sophisticated lushes. In *The Snake Pit* (1948) and *Caged* (1950), Hollywood castigated the sick mistreatment of the mentally ill. Critics lauded these productions, many of which received awards. Commercially, audiences flooded theaters to watch instructive and, at times, titillating, pictures of themselves and their neighbors. By looking at these dramas, Americans came to see a country remarkably different from the one portrayed during the war or earlier. The superpower had super problems, and some problems related to the international sphere.

One area ripe for public investigation was the social construction of race. President Truman's formation of a civil rights commission in 1946, the antilynching campaign, HUAC's links to segregationists, and Strom Thurmond's Dixiecrat candidacy in 1948 all coincided with the production of several films exploring racial issues in the new world order. The year 1949 saw three in particular: *Home of the Brave, Lost Boundaries,* and *Pinky. Home of the Brave,* written by Carl Foreman, is the story of an African American soldier named Peter Moss. What centers the picture in international issues is that Moss's unit is on a special mission to a Japanese-held island in the Pacific, where Moss disintegrates under the pressure. The cause for his collapse is explained in a series of flashbacks and conversations which reveal that he had long endured the racism of his comrades. White soldiers all too easily lumped people of color together without regard for who was an ally and who was the enemy. His experience is a revelation: "I learned that if you're colored, you stink. You're not like other people. You're—you're alone. You're something strange, different. . . . Well, you make us different, you rats." Racial integration has brought about his personal disintegration. In the end, however, Moss reconciles with his white tormentors, letting bygones be bygones.[4]

Different audiences may have reached different conclusions, of course. White audiences and critics appreciated the resolution and praised the theme that courage on behalf of the nation entitles one to social acceptance in America, the "home of the brave." The film even played to crowded theaters throughout the South: Memphis, New Orleans, Chattanooga, and Dallas, where the *Dallas Morning News* called it "brilliant." For black audiences, although Moss was far removed from the Mammy and Uncle Tom stereotypes of the recent past, he remains a tragic hero. The racial rapprochement at the end of the picture "may strike many as 'rigged' and false," concludes film historian Donald Bogle.[5]

Despite its apparent compromises, though, Foreman's story may have contained a powerful message for audiences. Here, a motion picture presented African Americans with a diasporic notion of race. Blacks who considered themselves part of a persecuted minority could gain strength in knowing that people of color make up the majority of the world's population. After all, in this film racism united the bloody Japanese aggressor, the Polynesian victim, and the troubled black liberator, showing common bonds between men of color regardless of national boundaries. African Americans found community beyond America's borders at a time when those boundaries were enforced by the Cold War consensus. Though unintended, perhaps, this transnational perspective remained one of the film's liberating themes.

Filmmakers also looked at racial acceptance in white America in two other motion pictures in 1949: *Lost Boundaries* and *Pinky.* Both films show the senselessness of racial categorization by considering the (improbably widespread) infiltration of light-skinned blacks "passing" in white society. Directed by Louis de Rochemont, the well-regarded war-time documentarian, *Lost Boundaries* tells of a light-skinned doctor and his wife who hide their dark secret from their New England neighbors and even their children. After they achieve status and respectability, their true racial identity is revealed by chance, as the patriotic doctor enlists for military service. *Pinky,* directed by Elia Kazan, deals with the story of a fair-skinned black woman who denies her true race and finds acceptance in the white community with her white husband. At a critical moment, Pinky's grandmother forcefully shames her granddaughter for not embracing her blackness. "That's a sin before God, and you know it," she tells Pinky. "Get down. Ask the Lord to forgive you." In the end, Pinky chooses self-respect over society's racial conventions.[6] Although these three "race pictures" have been scrutinized since their release dates and noted for their acquiescence to conservative conventions—as well as the fact that the stars of the last two films passed for "black" to play their roles—in many ways they were revolutionary because filmmakers ex-plored the inconsistencies of racial prejudice in the "land of the free" at this most politicized time.

Even when filmmakers missed the mark, as in Walt Disney's *Song of the South* (1946) and David O. Selznick's *Duel in the Sun* (1947), radicals entered into a civil debate over portrayals of the American racial land-scape. Disney's production relies on traditional racial stereotypes to show a bucolic Old South populated by "happy darkies"; Selznick exchanged bug-eyed imps in *Gone with the Wind* (1939) for exotic victims in *Duel in the Sun*. In a speech, the well-respected screenwriter and radical Dalton Trumbo remarked, "I am quite certain" that Disney "had no intention of traducing the Negro people in *Song of the South*," and Selznick "undoubt-edly felt that he was telling the story of a sweet and simple girl of mixed Indian and Caucasian parentage who was ruined by her contact with the sordidness of white culture." Trumbo concluded, "It seems clear, then, we should exonerate them at the outset of any conscious advocacy of racial doctrines" for "they simply made a mistake." Their common mistake was that all motion pictures, "no matter how trivial," make a serious com-ment on society. "A motion picture is *about* something. Whether we wish it or not, it conveys an impression, it carries a message." Trumbo believed the postwar world "cannot afford" to build stereotypes because "a great deal has happened" in the last few years. "Six million Jews have been slaughtered by careful exploitation of the racial stereotype." Therefore, Trumbo reminded listeners, "racial jokes are not funny anymore. There is too much blood on them." Such stereotypes impugned the American image, "and from what I read of Mr. Eric Johnston's quest for world markets, it will also be greeted with something less than stony silence when it hits the screens of Europe."[7]

After the Holocaust, anti-Semitism was at the forefront of Hollywood's collective mind. As suggested, myriad social problems that faced the nation in the postwar world, were explored by socially conscious filmmakers. Perhaps a good way to understand this phenomenon is to take a look at a single issue—anti-Semitism—and explore how Progressives attached it to representations of the nation on the screen. This process shows the intersection between the foreign and domestic spheres as reformers employed both political activism and cultural power to define the national character. Almost immediately, their efforts met controversy and prompted a backlash from opponents who favored an idealized national image in opposition to intolerant communism.

In 1945–1946, Americans were just coming to understand the extent of the horrors in Europe. Selznick and Schary, who were among those being educated, shared a series of articles on European anti-Semitism in the *New York Times*. The exposé looked at the plight of Jews seeking to reunite with lost families, to recoup lost property, to rebuild synagogues and cemeteries. Balkan Jews experienced "some of the worst tortures ever devised." Neutral Spain forced refugees from occupied France to register weekly to obtain jobs as menial day laborers; freedom to worship or produce kosher foods under Franco's regime was limited to the home. Although most Italians believed anti-Semitism was "imposed" on them by their alliance with Hitler, Mussolini and Pope Pius went beyond reluctant compliance. Jews avoided Polish displaced-persons camps, places notorious for anti-Semitism, preferring instead to scavenge for resources from the cellars of bombed-out buildings. Russian soldiers lobbed epithets at Jewish refugees on the road to Vienna. One foreign correspondent reported that "a lot of anti-Semitic propaganda remains implanted in German minds." No matter where one looked, Jews' troubles ranged in shades of bad and worse: persistent anti-Semitism was at the core of mistreatment, and the international nature of the issue extended to America.[8]

Progressive producers understood firsthand that persistent intolerance and anti-Semitism existed in America as well. They connected the international problem, which the war had made so apparent, to America. By 1945, Dore Schary and others knew that not only had the State Department neglected to find ways to aid the victims of the Holocaust, but the diplomatic corps had been slow to condemn atrocities or even to confirm reports that such a tragedy had occurred at all.[9] While most Americans could claim, "We didn't know," the government could not. In the absence of government outrage or sympathy, Hollywood Progressives believed they could confront the issue in politics and in film content. In a memo attached to the *New York Times* articles, Selznick inquired of Schary, "Don't you think it would be a good idea if you have some group in which you were interested . . . advise the Polish Ambassador that the continuing anti-Semitism among the Poles is receiving most unfavorable American attention?"[10] No evidence exists that Schary did apply personal pressure on the Polish ambassador, but there is sufficient proof that his organizations were deeply concerned about the well-being of Jews both in America and overseas.

The Palestine issue became the nexus for Progressives expressing concern over domestic fascism, anti-Semitism, and anticolonialism. One meeting in Beverly Hills on a summer evening in 1946 is representative of many such gatherings. Attendees discussed supporting a congressional bill barring religious or racial discrimination; they voted to wire American, British, and UN officials to protest the shooting of refugees in Haifa; they debated linking their efforts with the American Committee to Free Palestine and other like-minded groups; and they planned a mass meeting at American Legion Stadium for the following month.[11] Already, others were busy fund-raising for the Irgun, the militant Zionists seeking to overthrow British colonialism.[12]

The next month, 6,000 rallied at Legion Stadium, condemning British partition, encouraging Jewish settlement, and tying the cause to larger issues of colonialism. Actor Edward G. Robinson told the crowd:

> Our fight for a free Palestine will be futile—beyond that, it will be hypocritical—if we do not realize that it is only a portion of the larger fight. When we demand freedom for Palestine, we must also demand the freedom of the Arab peoples from their feudal tyrants, the freedom of Europe from the vestiges of fascist domination, the freedom of Indonesia and India and China from imperial overlords, the freedom of American labor from any threat to its legitimate rights and demands, the freedom of the Negro along with the Mexican, the Japanese, the Filipino, the Jew, the Protestant, the Catholic to live where he wishes, to vote as he pleases, to educate his children and to safeguard their future under a government which counts us all as equals before the law.[13]

Two weeks later, the group supported a UN mandate for Palestine and the immediate admission of 100,000 displaced persons.[14]

But political activity was only one way to address the problem of enduring anti-Semitism. Writer Albert Maltz broached anti-Semitism on the screen in *Pride of the Marines* (1945) but only by introducing a Jewish soldier who contributed to the war effort. Anti-Semitism was only an implied problem before 1945; after the war and the Holocaust, that view gradually began to change. Screenwriter Ring Lardner Jr. adapted the novel *Earth and High Heaven* for Samuel Goldwyn. Whereas Goldwyn had wanted to engage the subject of anti-Semitism lightly, he discovered that Lardner had written scenes that confronted the issue explicitly. "Lardner," Goldwyn told the writer, "one of the reasons I hired you . . . was the fact that you're a gentile. You have betrayed me by writing like a Jew."[15] Goldwyn abandoned the project.

At the same time, segments of the Hollywood community found ways to blend their political views of "domestic fascism" and anti-Semitism with their professions. Members of the Hollywood Branch of the American Arts Committee for Palestine sipped hot coffee at Lucey's while listening to progressive Senator Claude Pepper discuss the issue in October 1947. On that same night audiences by the thousands went to their local theaters to see *Gentleman's Agreement* and *Crossfire*, and many undoubtedly came away understanding why their nation should support a Jewish homeland.

Directed by Elia Kazan and starring Gregory Peck, *Gentleman's Agreement* tells the story of a gentile journalist trying to understand, by passing as Jewish, what it means to be an American Jew. In the course of events, he is mistreated and prevented from entering restaurants and other public facilities. Such anti-Semitic mistreatment knew no bounds in *Crossfire*. Taken from a book titled *The Brick Foxhole* by Richard Brooks and represented by the same agent who handled Tennessee Williams's provocative plays, the story landed at RKO, where Dore Schary was head of production. The story department reader described the treatment as "realistic, cynical, frequently unpleasant, but never lacking in suspense." In short, it had "excellent picture possibilities" when it was sent to Schary's desk just three days after V-E day.[16] Producer Adrian Scott, director Edward Dmytryk, and screenwriter John Paxton rounded out the production team that decided to focus on the issue of anti-Semitism. After thinking about how to approach his adaptation, Paxton "finally decided that a cops-and-robbers format might work best." The original victim, a gay man named Edwards, was replaced with a Jewish man named Samuels. By equating anti-Semitism with robbery and murder, the producers of *Crossfire* criminalized America's personal prejudices. They ardently hoped that sacrificing the nation's democratic rhetoric would become difficult in a postwar atmosphere that encompassed One World ideas. For the moment, courageous studio executives at RKO agreed. Production Code chief Joseph Breen put up several obstacles and demanded that a speech be added to the script explaining that the murderer was atypical among military personnel. After one month of shooting, one of the most controversial films of the postwar period headed to screens across America.[17]

The main character in *Crossfire* is Jeff, a soldier who has been stationed during the war in the "brick foxhole" of the American home front. Frustrated by his inactivity during the meaningful fight against fascism, and further devastated by a rumor that his wife has left him, Jeff goes on a drinking binge with other uniformed barflies—including Monty and Samuels—and ends up in the arms of a prostitute. When Samuels is found beaten to death, Jeff is mistakenly accused of the crime. The only way to win his freedom is to admit his dalliance the night before. Ultimately, the investigating detective and Jeff's buddy Keeley discover the truth: Monty murdered Samuels for the sole reason that he was Jewish. "This is the same war people are fighting all over the world," Keeley yells to Monty as they scuffle, "and you're the same enemy!"

Far from the stereotypical wartime GI, the characters in *Crossfire* are as different from each other in their temperaments as they are in their visions of a "good" America. Jeff is frustrated by the war; he is a drinker and carouser who is ensnared in a hate crime. In some respects, the producers inverted protagonist and antagonist by casting actors against type; Jeff and Keeley are far from likable, whereas the murderous Monty (played by Robert Ryan) is the dashing man in uniform. In fact, Monty is an everyman, a policeman who before the war "hates Jews, Negroes, foreigners and civilians." Producer Adrian Scott was eager to challenge notions of American exceptionalism by articulating the universality of evil apparent in domestic fascism. Samuels, the victim, is simply a "misfit."[18]

Crossfire clearly carried the political aims of progressives: to expose domestic fascism and to challenge American exceptionalism. Mindful of the wartime documentary style, Adrian Scott was "extremely anxious" to use these excerpts from a 1940 Roosevelt speech: "We are a nation of many nationalities, many races, many religions—bound together by a single unity, the unity of freedom and equality."[19] The sensitive and controversial nature of the film made some prominent Jewish leaders apprehensive. When the American Jewish Committee representative Dick Rothschild learned of RKO's project in February 1947, he understood that

Schary and Scott were "animated by the best of motives," but he worried that the anti-Semitic theme "was an extremely dangerous idea to project on the screen before 50 million or more people of all shades of emotional maturity or immaturity." Rothschild encouraged Schary to change the victim to an African American, an ironic suggestion, since Brooks's original homosexual victim had been changed by Schary to a Jewish victim. When Schary balked, Rothschild met with RKO president Peter Rathvon but failed to scuttle the film.[20]

Not just thematically but stylistically, *Crossfire* challenged notions of American exceptionalism when producers refused to add luster to grimy city streets. More than most of the other films mentioned here, *Crossfire* represents *film noir*, a 1940s cinema style noted for its exploration of realistic themes and psychoses in the dark, smoky shadows of the urban night. In some respects *noir* applied the wartime documentary style and its emphasis on realism to the home front. Here, disoriented antiheroes are trapped in psychological tension; cynicism and ambivalence are hallmarks for the genre.[21] This popular film style stood in contrast to an America standing as the beacon of democracy and military might in the world, and anticommunist critics took notice of this fact.

In 1947 John Foster Dulles spoke to reporters in Chicago and addressed the issue of American exceptionalism. He admitted, "No doubt our nation has at times been hypocritical. Some of our external exploits were ignoble. Some of our trade policies lacked enlightenment. We have not fully realized at home the human freedom and political equality of which we talk abroad. We have no call to be vainglorious. But we can humbly recognize that our foreign policies in their broad lines have reflected a great faith and a great tradition."[22] For Dulles, one could not judge the situation in America without comparing the nation to the imagined Soviet Union, an alternative defined by anticommunists as "Red Fascism."

Dulles had reason to care about how the nation was portrayed to audiences. "Message pictures" such as *Crossfire* were exhibited in a political climate that encompassed many critics.[23] In some cases, audiences were given an opportunity to discuss what meanings they drew from the film. Their responses offer a window through which later generations can gauge audience reception and constructions of the postwar national identity. Almost unanimously, at one such screening of *Crossfire*, those present believed that it would be "a worthy objective" if movies, though "designed presumably for entertainment," were made a "vehicle for educating the public in order to reduce intolerance." They believed that motion pictures could have the effect of moving public opinion in the same way that "particular speeches of Roosevelt and Churchill . . . created marked swings in public opinion."[24]

At the crux of *Crossfire* is the murder. Audiences understood the Jewish victim to be "a sweet, sympathetic, inoffensive fellow—the last person on earth to evoke murderous rage." But the portrayal of the anti-Semitic murderer provoked greater debate. Some viewers, fresh from war, easily identified with Montgomery, especially because the murderer was a soldier himself. As controversial as this device was, one viewer noted to Schary that "if the murderer were too abnormal a character, it was thought the murder would be regarded merely as an episode in the life of a criminal, with no further implications. The value of the propaganda would then be lost."[25] Elliot Cohen elaborated on this idea in his lengthy review for *Commentary*. Given the Holocaust,

> we know that the germs of this disease lie latent everywhere in this country, stimulating masses to relatively discreet discriminations and exclusions, stimulating others to more or less open hatred and scarce-hidden violences and aggressions. (Pre-war Germany seemed less infected.) But suddenly—and this is the great fear—the disease can flare epidemically—and tens of thousands cry "Kill the Jew"—while the other millions stand passively by. Six million Jews—not to speak of most of Europe itself—died of such an epidemic not so long ago.[26]

How did audiences receive this message picture? An examination of audience preview cards reveals that several viewers employed universalist rhetoric in their responses to the film, whether they liked *Crossfire* or not. When GIs banded together to hide the vicious crime, one female viewer said they were "loyal to their buddies but not to their society." One man explained, "You find it in every race. Somebody's always hating somebody else." Another man connected the international situation with the content of the film: "The motive behind the story interests me, because there's so much talk around lately about hating the Jews and Palestine." At one theater, the scene audiences liked most was the detective's concluding speech revealing the lesson linking subtle intolerance to hate crimes. To the question, "What will you primarily remember in terms of this picture?" one viewer mentioned "the timeliness of its theme."[27]

Famed philosopher Max Horkheimer, a Stuttgart Jew, offered his evaluation two months before the release of the film. He noted that the criminal motive had been so obvious that the detective just took it for granted. The detective, like the murderer he trails, shows "there are different categories of Jew-haters." Intolerance is universal, Horkheimer explained as he quoted the film: "In our days it is the Jews, tomorrow it may be the Quakers, or the people from Tennessee, and one day even those who wear different neckties." In August, Albert Einstein joined the One World Award Committee for a special screening of *Crossfire*, the first motion picture the scientist had seen in five years. "*Crossfire* is a picture I would like people to see," Einstein said to the gathering, even urging RKO to use his name in its publicity. The next year, Dore Schary received the One World Award for his work on the film. *Pride of the Marines* writer Albert Maltz added, "So long as there are people who have, not only the opportunity and the skill, but the personal principle to make films like *Crossfire*, the United States will never become meat for Fascism."[28] Willkie was right; the war continued at home.

Virtually all respondents remarked about the controversial nature of the film, and RKO played up the controversy in its trailer.[29] "I expect that," Dore Schary wrote Horkheimer. "I think it is normal and natural that anything which sets men's minds thinking creates an antagonism. The atom bomb won a war and created attention," Schary added with more than a bit of understatement.[30] According to response surveys, audiences understood the political nature of social problem films, evaluated One World messages contained in their content, and in some cases altered their conceptions of the postwar nation accordingly. The United States appeared sick with some of the symptoms that plagued totalitarian states.

One viewer from whom Schary did not hear was R. B. Hood. Hood had paid admission to many of the "message pictures" in the late 1940s: *The Best Years of Our Lives*, *Gentleman's Agreement*, and *Crossfire*, among them. Like any film fan, he sat in the darkened theater, absorbed the themes, and noted the names of the talent involved with each picture.[31] But Hood actually took copious notes to provide the basis for the memoranda he wrote to his superiors in Washington, for R. B. Hood was an FBI agent. In October 1947, he learned that the military had banned *Crossfire* from its bases and that the State Department applied pressure on the MPEA to restrict its export abroad. Information such as that gathered by Agent Hood proved harmful to filmmakers with a progressive bent as the government geared up for more hearings.

By uniting One World ideology and culture, creators of "social problem" films had intended for their movies to be political; they were unabashedly so. In such a charged environment, however, with the Truman administration fashioning a containment policy to meet the changing world situation, these motion pictures took on added meanings. By openly portraying America in such dark terms at a time when a growing number believed in sanitizing that same image, the entire Hollywood left risked becoming identified with the radicalism that seemingly infested the entire industry. By 1947, studio executives seeking government assistance to recoup overseas losses and congressional conservatives seeking political advantage found common cause through Red-baiting the perceived radicals in Hollywood. Containment policy and images of the Soviets made the process possible. Hollywood liberals, who distanced themselves from radicals in unions and other associations, quickly turned from vocal defenders of civil liberties to silence.

Criticism mounted against "social problem" films. The Legion of Decency, a powerful Roman Catholic institution brazenly intent on censorship, established a classification system for rating movies and issued the following pledge for all Catholic congregations in the country to take once a year:

> In the name of the Father and the Son and the Holy Ghost. Amen. I condemn indecent and immoral motion pictures, and those which glorify crime or criminals. I promise to do all that I can to strengthen public opinion against the production of indecent and immoral films, and to unite with all those who protest against them. I acknowledge my obligation to form a right conscience about pictures that are dangerous to my moral life. As a member of the Legion of Decency, I pledge myself to remain away from them. I promise, further, to stay away altogether from places of amusement which show them as a matter of policy.[32]

With its definition of "indecent and immoral" in mind, the Legion passed judgment on more than 400 films a year, *Gentleman's Agreement* and *Crossfire* among them, and they were downgraded for content. With the promise of organized boycotts, Hollywood had to pay attention.

To the Motion Picture Alliance for the Preservation of American Ideals (MPA) controversial representations of the nation were anathema, and so they proceeded to distribute the *Screen Guide for Americans*, written by Ayn Rand in 1947. Rand had worked at RKO before gaining fame and conservative appeal for her wartime novel *The Fountainhead*. Her MPA guide served as a primer on Americanism and stood in remarkable contrast to Willkie's *One World* ideas. Although intended only for an audience of motion picture producers, the MPA cleverly titled this a guide for producers who wanted to become more *American*. "If men believe that the American system is unjust," Rand wrote in the guide, "they will support those who wish to destroy it." Portrayals such as the ones in the social problem "message pictures" had to be contested. She acknowledged that the purpose of those filmmakers "is not the production of political movies openly advocating Communism"; rather, "their purpose is to corrupt our moral premises by corrupting non-political movies—by introducing small, casual bits of propaganda into innocent stories—thus making people absorb the basic premises of Collectivism by indirection and implication."[33]

Rand and the MPA acknowledged the politically charged environment in which they operated. The Cold War had invited them into the negotiation over the national image. The MPA warned producers, "Don't take politics lightly" in the face of critical choice: Churchill or Wallace, the West or the Soviet Union, Americanism or totalitarianism. They reminded studio executives that "Hitler, too, had stated openly that his aim was world conquest, but nobody believed him or took it seriously until it was too late." Moguls needed to avoid appeasement because communists valued, just as Hitler had, the utility of cinematic propaganda, so presenting an American image was crucial.[34]

On economic matters, Rand, who had recently sold the picture rights to *The Fountainhead* for $50,000, tied democracy and capitalism tightly together: "Don't pretend that Americanism and the Free Enterprise System are two different things. They are inseparable, like body and soul." In motion pictures, "don't preach or imply that all publicly owned projects are noble, humanitarian undertakings," she added. Furthermore, she told studio moguls, "don't smear industrialists" and "don't spit into your own face or, worse, pay miserable little rats to do it." Captains of capitalism should be seen by audiences for their "productive genius, energy, initiative, independence, courage." Too many films—such as *The Best Years of Our Lives*—show bankers and businessmen "as villains, crooks, chiselers or exploiters." Alliance members understood that a "constant stream of such pictures becomes pernicious" little truths in the minds of American audiences and the eyes of the world.[35]

The MPA, understanding the need to promote American exceptionalism without hesitation, urged producers to downplay class divisions, show consumption as virtuous, and portray "victims of circumstances" as sinful. "Don't deify 'the Common Man'" (rejecting years of Rooseveltian rhetoric); "America is the land of the uncommon man." In the new world order, motion pictures must show the nation as unique. "The American system," the *Screen Guide* added, "is the best ever devised in history." By contrast, the Soviet Union is a bastion of "depravity," so "don't suggest to the audience that the Russian people are free, secure and happy." Whereas

One World ideology emphasized the universality of the human, Rand and the MPA condemned efforts to show "that life in Russia is just about the same as in any other country." The MPA rejected accommodation, telling producers to forbid references to the old wartime alliance. Rather than merely offer an alternative to the ideas presented by One World advocates, the most militant members of the MPA endorsed the imposition of a blacklist. The MPA understood the need to preserve the American ideal of free speech but interpreted it narrowly. Free speech, Rand argued, "does not require that we furnish the Communists with the means to preach their ideas, and does not imply that we owe them jobs and support to advocate our own destruction at our own expense." In other words, "it does not require employers to be suckers. . . . Let them create their own motion picture studios, if they can. . . . Freedom of speech does not imply that it is our duty to provide a knife for the murderer who wants to cut our throat."[36] Rand soon came to the attention of HUAC as an expert on radical infiltration in Hollywood.

Given formidable concerns over labor, antitrust, and radicalism, studios searched for ways to cleanse the image of the industry and to rebuild foreign markets by forming new partnerships with government. Like the Second World War, the Cold War would provide an opportunity. In 1945 the old OWI had moved to the State Department with the intent of coordinating the American image abroad. At that time an official with the OWI explained, Hollywood producers and New York distributors had initiated "considerable discussion . . . about controlling, regulating, selecting, the type of films which will go overseas, with a view toward taking only those which show the American scene in a favorable light." Emmett Lavery held the screenwriters' view: "I think a great good can be accomplished, but in a changing world the moving pictures are a medium of free speech. It is one way to come together, and a wide exchange of pictures is desirable."[37] That contest between visions of the American nation would be played out in a world changing dramatically toward bipolarity and Cold War. At the very time a significant number among the Hollywood community appeared to be moving toward radicalism, independence, and universalism, others—notably the Democratic Party, the Truman administration, and Congress—were moving toward anticommunism and containment.

Although American containment policy was introduced in 1946, it was not institutionalized until 1947, with the advent of the Truman Doctrine and the Marshall Plan. In March, Arthur Vandenberg told President Truman to "scare the hell out of the country" in order to stiffen the nation's

backbone against the Soviet threat. The Truman Doctrine, ostensibly providing military aid to Greece and Turkey for their defense, went so far as
to draw the blueprint for military containment. That summer, Truman
signed the National Security Act, a wholesale reorganization of the military and intelligence services. Between these two significant events, the
president inaugurated a form of domestic containment with Executive
Order #9835, the Federal Loyalty Oath. As momentous as the Truman
Doctrine was, however, it was primarily the administration's attempt to
unite the executive and the Congress, Democrats and Republicans, and
the government and the public behind a single foreign policy. In keeping
with Kennan's limited vision of containment, the doctrine was not global,
not total, and not nearly as far-reaching as it would become after 1950.

Cultural producers understood that institutionalized containment
upped the ante on their work as negotiators of the national identity. "We
are this day, as a nation, proposed to set ourselves up as the supporters of
democracy" in Greece and Turkey, Dalton Trumbo told a group of writers.
"However we consider it, every story we write shall have meaning whether
we wish it or not," he added. "It is our absolute obligation to see that not
one of these films contains even the hint of fascist ideology." The extreme
rhetoric of those days framed the contest in Hollywood between "Communists" in the HICCASP and "Fascists" in the MPA. Trumbo concluded
that policing the purveyors of the national image was "a grave responsibility."[38] His anticommunist opponents could not have agreed more. On May
7, 1947, six days after listening to Truman "scare the hell out of the country" and voting to support the Truman Doctrine, members of an emboldened HUAC stepped off the plane in Los Angeles for preliminary meetings
about the upcoming investigative hearings.

As policymakers institutionalized the Cold War and prepared to dis-
sect Hollywood again, the studios found that the Marshall Plan offered
a timely opportunity. That June in Cambridge, Massachusetts, Secretary
of State George Marshall strode through the old Harvard Yard on his way
to deliver the famous commencement address in which he outlined the
economic arm of containment, the Marshall Plan. By offering funds to
reconstruct devastated, desperate Europe, Marshall explained, the United
States could help itself while helping others. Indeed, the rationale behind
the Marshall Plan was both political and altruistic. Churchill called it
"the most unsordid act in human history," and certainly Washington
could have appropriated the vast sums toward domestic reconversion instead. This was especially true, given the widespread fear of a renewed
depression after the war. But in other ways, given the volatility of postwar

Europe, the Marshall Plan served as a form of noble colonialism. As one State Department economist who joined the Marshall Plan team explained years later, "The United States had enormous self-interest in the success of the Marshall Plan. . . . If the United States had allowed Europe to collapse, it would have cost us much more than what we spent on the Marshall Plan—a great deal more. So it was in the self-interest of the United States to finance this program." He concluded, "We were doing well by doing good."[39] The Marshall Plan would have a remarkable impact on the motion picture industry and the contest over the Cold War national image. In the first two years after the war ended, Hollywood had struggled to regain its lost foreign markets. In 1947 the government offered Hollywood a panacea to help the industry recover, even as it took the form of European recovery.

Hollywood's problems were formidable primarily because cash-strapped Europeans hoped to revive their own once-vibrant film industries. Hollywood's coordinator of exports, the MPEA, struggled on its own to break open foreign markets. Only with intense pressure from Washington would Europe ease quota restrictions on imports of American motion pictures. The Marshall Plan, created in the name of anticommunism, now offered an opportunity spelled out in a handy booklet titled *How to Do Business under the Marshall Plan*. Published by Henry Luce's *Time-Life* corporation, the manual explained the Marshall Plan as a *"business plan* to be carried out by *businessmen*," with the government acting as facilitator in the short term but with the expectation that "at the end of the Plan private business will be in a position to operate the program entirely."[40]

To reclaim their foreign markets, Hollywood executives essentially promised the government that they would help "reprogram" Europe.[41] In October 1947, David O. Selznick warned that any aid to prop up European industries must not harm American industries in the process. "Fellow democracies must be helped regardless of the cost," he told a convention of bankers at the Hotel Del Coronado in San Diego, "but this help must not be given in a form that will hurt American industries. The foreign industries must not be built up so that we will throw people out of work here." Furthermore, he added, Washington could rely only on American motion picture producers to fashion a coordinated national image fit for the Cold War. "When the English public sees the American way of life," they will become "greatly dissatisfied with the type of socialistic government that is now in force in England," Selznick promised.[42] In the fall of 1947, just as HUAC put a spotlight on perceived radicalism in the motion picture industry, the State Department and studio executives would strike an informal deal convenient to both sides.

In the meantime, critics questioned Marshall Plan aid, given its connection to containment policy. For example, Marianne Debouzy, a French student in Paris in the late 1940s, and her friends had "mixed feelings" about American assistance. Even if the United States hoped to defend Europe and to help starving people, she and others also believed that Washington "thought of Europe as an outlet for their goods, as a market to export stuff."[43] The market for Hollywood movies, of course, served Washington's foreign policy interests. American educator Emil Lengyel worried that in order to reeducate the Nazis, Washington would allow only pro-American and anti-Soviet scripts to be exported. "Reading some of them," Lengyel wrote, "one would gain the impression that the Russians are our foes and not the Nazi Germans." This was poor policy for several reasons, he concluded: "One cannot teach a nation peace by talking war."[44] Whether true or not, the Cold War made even the most altruistic institutions appear to have been engineered solely for expediency.

From 1945 to 1947 the Cold War intensified, and Washington engaged in world affairs with the purpose of containing European communism militarily and economically. At the same time, Hollywood progressives put forth an abundant number of "message pictures" based on One World principles. Just how the advancement of these ideas on film meshed with Washington's preparations in foreign relations is a complex question to answer. But it is certain that "as the government became more sensitive to America's image abroad, it became more concerned about Hollywood's role in projecting that image."[45] By dissenting from official foreign policy and by offering alternative visions of the nation on the screen, Hollywood progressives had presented HUAC with a casus belli.

The Curtain Falls on the Hollywood Radicals

As the Cold War deepened in the years 1945 to 1947, Hollywood conservatives joined the government in making the case for democratic capitalism, bipolarity, containment, and American exceptionalism. Although other motives, such as political opportunism, explained congressional investigations into Hollywood's activities that fall, there is little doubt that negotiations over the American national identity in the Cold War played a crucial role in the developing cultural crisis. Recently opened congressional archives, including investigation records and executive session transcripts of HUAC, show that investigators and inquisitors paid as much attention to the message in "message pictures" as to the organizational activities of the Hollywood left.

During this same period, though, most of the film community presented a united front against the dangerous precedent of congressional interference. One knowledgeable insider, Robert Riskin, who wrote screenplays for Frank Capra and had worked in the wartime OWI, explained to a radio audience in 1945 that plenty of "good" Americans worked in Hollywood to counteract anyone "communistic": "The Chase National Bank is not communistic; the conservative industrialists who run this industry are not communistic; and the writer, if one can be found, who has tendencies in that direction is going to have a tough time getting any elements into a film past those gentlemen."[46]

As early as the summer of 1945, the question of HUAC's investigation of Hollywood turned from "if" to "when." Representatives of HICCASP, ICCASP, the Democratic Party, and Southern California's congressional delegation negotiated the terms of the hearings with the chairman, John Wood. When derailing the investigation proved impossible, Hollywood armed itself for a political confrontation. The Hollywood community built a coalition to keep the heat on Wood, and HICCASP attacked the committee's most prominent member, the anti-Semitic John Rankin. On July 12, 1945, HICCASP formally addressed letters to the Truman White House and to members of Congress protesting Rankin's vitriolic rebukes of a communist (Jewish)–dominated Hollywood. They further questioned the role HUAC would play in the film industry, now that it had become a permanent standing committee of the House.

In October the Hollywood community opened what it called a "fight-to-the-finish campaign" to abolish HUAC, which it claimed was aiming "to establish fascism in America."[47] Emboldened by its recent legislative prowess, HICCASP took on Rankin by publishing *Introducing Representative John Eliot Rankin*, a pamphlet full of his racist tirades and anti-Semitic rants, as well as his voting record. With little narration, they let the Mississippi Democrat speak for himself as they hoped Washington would come to its senses regarding any potential interference in Hollywood's affairs. HICCASP believed that only by such a strong reaction to HUAC could it prevent Congress from chipping away at Hollywood's edifice. At first the effort appeared to be working, prompting one Democratic Party official to report to HICCASP executive George Pepper, "House committee definitely not coming to California. Received assurances today that [Democratic Party] leadership will not permit witch-hunt." Of course, time would not confirm such an optimistic outlook. In fact, Pepper was suspicious and wrote back, "Hollywood people are sick and tired of working like the devil to elect decent candidates every two years and find their reward is an annual witch hunt."[48]

Hollywood's "sick and tired" included studio executives and representatives. Several exasperated moguls railed against the government for invading their kingdoms. "Nobody can tell me how to run my studio," Louis B. Mayer reportedly yelled from his desk at MGM. In fact, for years Mayer had known there were radicals within his studio walls but had chosen to joke with his talented "pinkos" rather than sacrifice them.[49] "Every studio in town is trying to figure out a way to whitewash itself," Jack Moffitt of the *Hollywood Reporter* informed HUAC.[50] In April 1947, Eric Johnston, given his position as a centralizing force for the industry as MPEA chief, inserted himself into the developing crisis and traveled to Washington to diffuse the situation. Believing he had to offer HUAC something, Johnston acknowledged that communists undoubtedly worked in the industry but asserted that they had no influence on the final film. Indeed, he could argue that Hollywood's reliance on traditional genres and on collaboration, so essential to the factory form of production, prevented any single individual from becoming dominant. Unfortunately for Johnston and the motion picture industry, HUAC was not satisfied.

In the spring of 1947, HUAC chairman J. Parnell Thomas, a moon-faced New Jersey Republican, held court at the Hotel Biltmore in Los Angeles. He arrived in Hollywood just as the industry bestowed its Academy Award for best picture on *The Best Years of Our Lives*. Although most critics and audiences had received the film warmly, the view was hardly unanimous. Anticommunists condemned the cinematic national image in a burst of vitriol and immediately fastened on the film as a prime example of un-Americanism. "This vicious picture," the *Tulsa Tribune* editorialized, "is a dangerous, anti-American film" and "a masterpiece of subversive half-truths." Amid the difficult reconversion process and with the Soviet menace looming, "America is exhibited as a social order that is not only unkind but cruel to youth. And that is a vicious and treasonous lie." Just as Hitler "knew how to use [Germany's] propaganda machine," anticommunists explained, "now we are getting the Russian propaganda," and "Hollywood is lending itself to the subtle infiltration of communistic propaganda." Progressive themes became easy proof of sinister behavior.[51]

In mid-May 1947, Thomas and his investigative staff began calling witnesses into closed-door executive sessions where their questions centered on two key issues: apparent radicalism in the guilds and unions,

House Committee on Un-American Activities chairman J. Parnell Thomas and investigator Robert Stripling search for signs of communist infiltration in the motion picture industry, 1947. Courtesy Library of Congress, Prints & Photographs Division, LC-USZ62-119702 /
Associated Press.

and subversive content in motion pictures. Virtually all the witnesses
were "friendly." Some eagerly embraced their new-found friends and tagged
their old ones as subversive. Trade paper reporter Jack Moffitt, whose
screenplay had been halted during the 1945 production strike, supplied
the names of twenty-nine individuals (including seven of the Hollywood
Ten) and twenty-one motion pictures he deemed suspect. Adolphe Menjou, the mustachioed and cosmopolitan character actor, savored his lead
role in front of the committee. Others, such as actor Robert Taylor and
producer Jack Warner, expressed anguish at performing their patriotic
duty. Regardless of their motives, the committee relied on the witnesses' testimony as a starting point from which to further their investigations into who defined the national character and what messages
they conveyed.[52]

Writers earned most of the attention for subversive themes, but witnesses explained how producers and actors as well could subvert a film.

"An actor can change it by an expression of his face," Menjou explained. "You can give me a scene that is just as nice and patriotic to America as you want, and I will change it by a sneer or anything I want." As for Dore Schary, he was "a brilliant man," Menjou told the committee, "belonging to the Independent Citizens Committee . . . and likes Wallace. Why? Well, watch his pictures awfully closely. They have to be watched." Witnesses criticized the activities of organizations that favored universalism. This became even easier once an organization appeared to be controlled by radicals.

Committee members and "friendly" witnesses lumped radicals and moderates together in their general attack on multilateralism. Actor Richard Arlen knew the problems within the industry were not caused just by communists when he charged, "I don't think they are out-and-out Communists running around with a sickle and hammer, but they are in sympathy with that phase of things." Moffitt noted that Roosevelt's speechwriter Robert Sherwood, who had penned *The Best Years of Our Lives*, advocated "a film policy that seemed to be related to the foreign policy." The script "indulges in one of the stock tricks of the Communist propaganda, and that is the identification of any criticism of the Reds . . . with such things as Jim Crowism, anti-Semitism, reactionary capitalism" and other signs of domestic fascism. Moffitt aligned himself with thoughts that "have also occurred to Secretary Marshall and to Mr. Byrnes." While written, directed, and produced by professed liberals, *The Best Years of Our Lives* nevertheless "serves the purpose of the Communists admirably," Moffitt told Chairman Thomas, because it "subconsciously creates a state of mind much better than open propaganda does." According to Hollywood conservatives, the critics of containment within the industry—who had been labeled recklessly as communist, un-American, and subversive—sought "a monopoly of ideas" in the cultural arena.[53]

In such a confining and fearful climate, when extreme patriotism was an insignia to be worn on the individual's sleeve, anticommunists looked for telltale signs of "softness." There were two methods of Red-baiting: guilt by linking the accused to suspect associations, and guilt by defaming their ideas (in petitions and pamphlets, on college campuses, and in Hollywood scripts). Zealous anticommunists cared greatly about both. HUAC compiled files containing content information on suspect motion pictures, even those made *before* the onset of the Cold War when the United States was allied with the Soviet Union: *Crossfire*, *Counter-Attack*, *The Grapes of Wrath*, *Juarez*, *The Little Foxes*, *Modern Times*,

Mission to Moscow, Mr. Smith Goes to Washington, My Man Godfrey, The North Star, Of Mice and Men, Pride of the Marines, Song of Russia, Watch on the Rhine, and many more. Many themes played better during a period of depression and world war than during the Cold War. Analysis of these films consumed HUAC's investigators for months. No one can doubt the centrality of content in negotiations over America's Cold War national identity.

Investigators gathered newspaper clippings and critical reviews of "subversive" films. They looked at both old and new motion pictures. "Some promising films" in production at Universal, one HUAC memo stated, included Lillian Hellman's *Another Part of the Forest*, Arthur Miller's *All My Sons*, and Albert Maltz's *The Naked City*.[54] Committee staff dutifully typed up the most damning excerpts in a digestible form for committee members. Even the most carefully trimmed extract included all personnel associated with the production, from producers, writers, and directors to cameramen, editors, and composers of scores. By looking at what they gleaned from the pages of mainstream New York newspapers, trade papers (*Variety*), and leftist publications (*New Masses, PM, People's World,* and the *Daily Worker*), one gains a more accurate picture of what Cold War conservatives feared and loathed about multilateralism.

The committee explicitly questioned witnesses about motion pictures that expressed progressive themes on the screen. Congressmen found subversion in the favorable portrayals of Soviets in films such as *Mission to Moscow* (1943). They grimaced at the exploration of American class tensions in *The Best Years of Our Lives* (1946). They noted films that challenged American exceptionalism in Elia Kazan's *Boomerang* (1947), which exposed the corrupt political forces that threatened the American justice system and in which, rather than sober and capable, the American man appeared troubled, unstable, intolerant, and unheroic. The HUAC investigator remarked that *Boomerang* showed "that all is not 100 percent pure in American life." The committee also focused on how filmmakers dealt with the issue of colonialism. John Howard Lawson's *Sahara* (1943), for example, favored the high ideal of decolonization over the nation's strategic self-interest. HUAC members expressed displeasure at portrayals of domestic fascism and anti-Semitism in two 1947 releases, *Gentleman's Agreement* and *Crossfire*. All together, the national image that appeared on the big screen at this time emerged just when the advocates of containment wished to reassure their allies and to intimidate their foes. In sum, the committee used its powerful position to directly challenge, piece by piece, progressive perspectives as they appeared in the cultural arena. They did so because multilateralism countered their view of what the national identity should be in the Cold War context.[55]

Fascist anti-Semitism had prompted Progressives to explore domestic fascism, as in *Crossfire*. In turn, Progressives noted that anticommunist criticism of such portrayals led to the real domestic fascism embodied by HUAC, and they responded with the requisite number of committees, rallies, and petitions. Activists hastily organized a protest meeting for almost 30,000 at Gilmore Stadium. Katharine Hepburn told those assembled that writers and actors had become the "primary target," because "silence the artist and you silence the most articulate voice the people have."[56] They followed up that event with a conference titled "Thought Control in the United States." The Voice of Freedom Committee, essentially a group of prominent individuals associated with the New York stage, joined the broad defense by protesting efforts that they believed would "cripple" liberal voices on the radio.[57]

Despite these attacks, HUAC issued over forty subpoenas to "friendly" and "unfriendly" witnesses, and they set public hearings on their October calendar. The appropriately colored pink subpoenas were served on writers primarily, including Stettinius's ghostwriter, Dalton Trumbo; the writer of *Pride of the Marines*, Albert Maltz; and the boisterous radical John Howard Lawson. But process servers also located two of the most prominent men associated with the controversial *Crossfire*: producer Adrian Scott and director Edward Dmytryk.

Combatants on both sides framed the hearings as a contest to define American national identity. As an ad in *Variety* asked plainly, "Who's Un-American?"[58] At Lucey's Restaurant, directors John Huston and William Wyler organized the Committee for the First Amendment, a group of moderates—not radicals—that counted Katharine Hepburn, Billy Wilder, Humphrey Bogart, Fredric March, Danny Kaye, and Walter Wanger among its ranks. At the first meeting, held at songwriter Ira Gershwin's house, the group discussed their air assault. HUAC "has called on the carpet some of the people who have been making your favorite movies," actor Gene Kelly told a radio audience. "Did you happen to see *The Best Years of Our Lives*, the picture that won seven Academy Awards? Did *you* enjoy it?" he continued. "Did you like it? Were you subverted by it? Did it make you Un-American? Did you come out of the movie with the desire to overthrow the government?" Actress Lauren Bacall asked in her sultry voice, "Have you seen *Crossfire* yet? Good picture?" she purred with conviction. "The American *people* have awarded it four stars, but the Un-American *Committee* gave the men who made it three subpoenas." William Wyler informed Americans, "I wouldn't be allowed to make *The Best Years of Our Lives* in Hollywood today."[59] Together, the members of the Committee for the First Amendment chartered a plane to carry their mission to Washington.

For liberals, censorship amounted to domestic fascism. But studio executives, producers, and Eric Johnston of the MPEA joined the fight because they especially bristled over government interference in hiring practices. David O. Selznick circulated petitions out of industrial loyalty, and on October 19, Eric Johnston declared flatly, "As long as I live I will never be a party to anything as un-American as a blacklist, and any statement purporting to quote me as agreeing to a blacklist is a libel upon me as a good American." He added words that would haunt him years later, "There'll never be a blacklist. We're not going totalitarian to please this committee." Two days later, Paul V. McNutt, the attorney for MPEA reiterated, "There has been a suggestion that the MPEA adopt a policy of blacklisting. That would be a conspiracy without warrant of law." For the time being, Hollywood produced a united front.

Washington was cool and breezy as Halloween approached. During the first week Thomas's committee allowed the well-coached "friendly" witnesses to set out the case. They discussed the role radicals played in the film colony, identified "subversive" pictures, and named names. They also offered their damning assessments of the expanding role of motion pictures in the Cold War. The week had damaged the "unfriendlies" before they arrived.

On the following Monday, as Thomas gaveled the hearings to order, flashbulbs popped and gasps greeted the members of the Committee for the First Amendment as they filed into the hearing room. They symbolized an industry united in support of Eric Johnston and nineteen "unfriendly" witnesses. Rather than give voice to Johnston and his measured, corporate-backed attack on HUAC, Thomas scheduled the nineteen "unfriendlies" first, starting with the vociferous radical John Howard Lawson. In his prepared statement, Lawson called Thomas a "petty politician" and charged the first witnesses as "stool-pigeons, neurotics, publicity-seeking clowns, Gestapo agents." What he could not read in public he expressed anyway. For half an hour, Lawson and Thomas sparred, interrupted each other, and bellowed before guards pulled Lawson out by force. Committee for the First Amendment members looked fidgety in their seats in light of the display. In turn, Dalton Trumbo, Albert Maltz, Alvah Bessie, Samuel Ornitz, Herbert Biberman, Edward Dmytryk, Adrian Scott, Ring Lardner Jr., and

Lester Cole followed the legal strategy they and their lawyers, including Bartley Crum, had already drawn up: to refuse to answer whether they were now or had ever been members of the Communist Party.[60] Although Edward Dmytryk explained later that the "defiant witnesses" had been encouraged "by the speeches of the late Wendell Willkie," there was little effort to engage the committee on such sound ideological grounds, or to pacify the committee by admitting party affiliation, or to cull sympathy with the audience watching the unfolding drama.[61]

After the histrionics, Hollywood unity evaporated. Rather than defend the writers, Eric Johnston clearly represented the studios and put his concerns in terms of competing for foreign markets. "A damaging impression of Hollywood has spread all over the country as a result of last week's hearings," Johnston began, a blemish affecting the export of films at the moment when "every other country in the world is trying to build up its motion picture industry, through government subsidies and devices of all kinds." A frustrated Johnston intended "to use every influence at my command to keep the screen free." Finally, he addressed the committee's complaint that Hollywood had not fully enlisted in the Cold War effort to promote Americanism:

> One of the most amazing paradoxes has grown out of this hearing. At one point we were accused of making Communist propaganda by not making pictures which show the advantages of our system. In other words, we were accused of putting propaganda on the screen by keeping it out. That sort of reasoning is a little staggering, especially when you know the story of American pictures in some foreign countries. We are accused of Communist propaganda at home, but in Communist-dominated countries in Europe our motion picture films are banned because they contain propaganda for capitalism. We can't be communistic and capitalistic at one and the same time. I've said it before, but I'd like to repeat it. There is nothing more feared or hated in Communist countries than the American motion picture.[62]

Johnston hoped he had shown the committee that Hollywood had an important contribution to make by fashioning a favorable national image to counter communist propaganda. He expressed the need to open foreign markets to those productions on nationalistic and economic grounds. Unintentionally, Johnston had laid the foundation for the studios' rehabilitated relationship with Washington by suggesting that the export of American films would benefit both the government and the studios.

The Hollywood hearings helped to institutionalize anticommunism, providing the government with a list of named organizations to distribute to blacklisting employers. In November 1947 the attorney general issued the first of many lists of radical and communist "front" organizations. Hollywood was heavily represented on the government's inventory of "subversives": Film Audiences for Democracy, Films for Democracy, Frontier Films, Hollywood Anti-Nazi League, Hollywood Community Radio Group, Hollywood League for Democratic Action, Motion Picture Democratic Committee, Hollywood Writers Mobilization, and even the Screen Writers Guild. Because moderates abandoned them and then smeared them, the Hollywood Democratic Committee and ICCASP both made the list. The Progressive Citizens of America and the National Council of American-Soviet Friendship were also marked.

HUAC encouraged the studios to adopt a blacklist as a means of ridding themselves of charges of fostering subversion. "It occurs to [us]," one committee investigator said, "that the quickest way Communism can be eliminated from Hollywood would be through the payroll route. In other words, if these Communist writers were cut off of the payroll by the studios, it would not be a very healthful place for them to live. In other words, they would be taken out."[63] One day after Congress declared the Hollywood Ten in contempt, Johnston and studio executives met at New York's Waldorf-Astoria for some frank discussion. On November 24 they issued what became known as the Waldorf Statement, formally consummating the relationship between studio executives and the officials in Cold War Washington. Johnston, the man who had promised months earlier that there would be no blacklist, now explained, "We will forthwith discharge or suspend without compensation . . . and we will not re-employ, any of the Ten until such time as he is acquitted or has purged himself of contempt, and declared under oath that he is not a Communist." The Screen Actors Guild endorsed the statement two weeks later, around the time that Bosley Crowther of the *New York Times* wrote, "It should be fully realized that this action was engineered by the major New York executives, the industry's overlords, and not by the 'Hollywood producers' who form a different and subordinate group."[64] To critics, an arm of the government had goaded the studios into illegal collusion in the name of Americanism.

Reaction outside Washington varied, of course. Some Americans castigated the Ten. "Trumbo, you *traitor—get out* of this country—go to Russia!" one man wrote from Houston. "You red Rats," another scrawled on a postcard from St. Petersburg, Florida. An "awakened American" in Buffalo concurred.[65] Other artists expressed their desire to help their persecuted colleagues. For example, the playwright Arthur Miller informed one of the Hollywood Ten, Herbert Biberman, that prominent New Yorkers had raised funds for an ad to run in the *New York Times*. Miller also issued an amicus curiae brief with the Supreme Court as the Ten awaited a decision on their appeal.[66]

The Hollywood Ten fought their contempt citations and sued the studios over their firings. But though they maintained confidence that the courts would rule in their favor, they found that the Cold War atmosphere

No caption in original. Congress shackles the motion picture industry while other nervous media look on. The television industry is noticeably absent, 1947. Library of Congress, Prints & Photographs Division, LC-USZ62-86589 / Copyright by Bill Mauldin (1947). Courtesy of Bill Mauldin Estate LLC.

had worsened by 1949–1950. Critical international events—including the fall of China to communists, the Soviet detonation of an atomic bomb, the revelation of an American spy ring, and the outbreak of the Korean War—poisoned their hopes for successful appeals, and the Hollywood Ten prepared for prison.[67] Their story, though, often hides the fact that unknown hundreds of Hollywood personnel lost their jobs because of the blacklist. It also leads to the popular perception that dissent died with them.[68]

Liberals and radicals waged a war of words. Arthur Miller noted that liberals avoided being seen with tainted friends much as gentiles in Hitler's Germany, seeing "their Jewish neighbors being trucked off, . . . turn[ed] away in fear of being identified with the condemned."[69] In the *Saturday Review of Literature*, Arthur Schlesinger Jr. labeled the Hollywood Ten "fellow-traveling ex-proletarian . . . hacks." In a heated letter to the editor, Trumbo chastised Schlesinger and "his breed" for their weak defense of civil liberties. Trumbo sneered at liberals for sitting in front of investigators and proclaiming, " 'I do not wish to imply approval of your questions, but I am not now nor have I ever been a dissenter. I am not now nor have I ever been a Communist. I am not now nor have I ever been a trade unionist. I am not now nor have I ever been a Jew. Prosecute those who answer differently, O masters, silence them, send them to jail, make soap of them if you wish.' "[70]

Anticommunists viewed the Hollywood Ten as enemies of the state for their opposition to the nation's foreign policy. While awaiting transfer to prison, Dalton Trumbo read newspaper headlines characterizing his crimes. Under photographs of former secretary of state Edward Stettinius, Alger Hiss, and Dalton Trumbo, the *Washington Times-Herald* reported, "A ghost goes to jail." In his work as a speechwriter, Trumbo had "advised" Stettinius at San Francisco to stack the voting in favor of the Soviet Union. Never mind, Trumbo wrote his wife, that these terms were agreed at Yalta and Dumbarton Oaks. The focus had shifted from issues of first amendment rights, fifth amendment rights, and contempt citations to the proximity of radicals to the machinery of foreign policy. "Thus do liars distort history," he concluded.[71]

Worlds away from Trumbo, Hollywood's divorcement from dissent promised tangible benefits from the hands of government. In the year after the HUAC hearings, when studio executives had agreed to contain progressive views in Hollywood, the government stepped up its efforts to help its new allies in the cultural Cold War. Even as the studios underwent court-ordered divorcement from their theater chains in 1948, the government approved of the MPEA monopoly as a clearinghouse for exported films. Eric Johnston won senate confirmation as a member of the bipartisan Public Advisory Board of the Marshall Plan, a group that met each month and reported directly to the chief administrator. With the Marshall Plan as a carrot in hand, the State Department helped negotiate a settlement to the British boycott of American motion pictures in March 1948. The following year Hollywood could boast that there were more than twice as many American films exhibiting in Britain as British-made productions.[72]

In some respects these events produced a hollow victory for the film capital. Audience demographics changed during the 1950s, and that did not bode well for motion picture producers. Consequently, studios produced fewer "A" pictures and cut budgets for their "B" pictures, serials, shorts, cartoons, and newsreels.[73] In 1950 *Fortune* prophesied, "With box office down, foreign revenues cut, critics pained, older fans dwindling, reorganization at hand and television looming, the motion-picture industry may be turning a historic corner."[74] Around that corner Hollywood constructed grand revivals and frothy confections, allowing foreign films, Broadway, the publishing industry, and television to "test the waters" of controversy. Studios operated new technologies to make bigger spectacles, including Cinerama (1952), 3-D (1952), and CinemaScope (1953). They invested in the drive-in boom, which accounted for one-third of all American movie theaters by 1958.[75] Studios also adapted by flirting with the very technology they had once scorned: television.

The HUAC investigations had opened the floodgates that had held back more flattering images of the nation. Hollywood in the 1950s generally portrayed the United States with heavy doses of nostalgia. Here, there was little mutiny in the land of bounty. In *Call Me Madam* (1953) the boisterous Ethel Merman played a wealthy socialite whom the president has appointed ambassador to a small, unimportant country. From her post there, Merman divides her time between advising the president on daughter Margaret's singing career and pursuing a love relationship with urbane George Sanders. Only ten years separated this film from the heavier diplomatic exploits in *Mission to Moscow*. *Pride of the Marines* was barely a memory when song-and-dance man Gene Kelly pranced abroad in the splashy spectacle *An American in Paris* (1951). *Crossfire's* anti-Semitism gave way to themes of assimilation in a remake of *The Jazz Singer* (1952), starring comedian Danny Thomas. Hollywood even took to remembering its own past in *Singin' in the Rain* (1952) and *A Star is Born!* (1954), showing actors who washed out for personal deficiencies rather than for their unpopular political positions.

When studio executives searched for other new content, they looked no further than their Bibles. The 1950s movie palace showcased several religious spectaculars: *Quo Vadis?* (1951), *David and Bathsheba* (1951), and *The Robe* (1953). In *The Ten Commandments* (1956) conservative director Cecil B. DeMille remade the silent screen classic for audiences of the 1950s. In a two-minute introduction to the epic, DeMille directly related biblical and modern wars fought against "the whims of a dictator." DeMille intended for audiences to draw clear connections between his cinematic spectacle and contemporary events, for as he said, "This same battle continues throughout the world today." In this way, he brought the box office and the soap box together. For this religious revival, De Mille rejected innovative acting techniques that were then in vogue in favor of lavish costumes, Technicolor set designs, and special effects. Here, pure entertainment and America's professed devotion to religion combined as Hollywood preferred to retell the stories of ancient Hebrews (including those who converted to Christianity in the case of *Ben-Hur*) rather than confront modern-day anti-Semitism, as in *Crossfire* and *Gentleman's Agreement*. William Wyler's *Ben-Hur* (1959) became an icon of the epic spectacles that DeMille championed. In it, Wyler, who had directed the controversial and progressive 1946 film *The Best Years of Our Lives*, adapted to the political climate of the 1950s. While undoubtedly entertaining, these and many other motion pictures showed a clear change in the way America would be portrayed on the big screen: pious, powerful, and devoid of systemic problems.

Anticommunist content became obvious as well. After 1947 and continuing into the 1950s, Hollywood contributed to demonizing the Soviets and defining subversives for audiences in approximately forty films, including *I Married a Communist* (1949), *The Red Menace* (1949), *I Was a Communist for the FBI* (1951), and *Walk East on Beacon* (1952). In *Big Jim McLain* (1952), two hard-edged HUAC investigators (played by Cold War cowboys John Wayne and James Arness) return to Pearl Harbor to foil communist infiltration in Hawaii.

Hollywood took themes of subversion one step further with themes of invasion. The Soviets attacked in *Invasion USA* (1952). Russian communists could be equated with aliens from outer space, as in the classic examples *Red Planet Mars* (1952) and *Invasion of the Body Snatchers* (1956), with soulless aliens infiltrating a California community to spread their poisonous philosophy across America. Invasion could work in reverse, too, to create American heroes penetrating the Iron Curtain. In *Prisoner of War*

(1954) Ronald Reagan enters a North Korean prisoner-of-war camp to document reports of torture and brainwashing.

Hollywood had been transformed in a short period of time, from 1940 to the mid-1950s, from a site where the national identity had been actively contested to a place where conformity and light entertainment ruled. In Hollywood, anticommunists had positioned the United States as an exceptional leader of the Free World, welcoming of diversity, united in purpose, and free from internal disabilities. The world was firmly divided between forces for good and forces for evil. Voices of dissent were banished, left alone to seek other outlets. In stark contrast to his speech to the students at Rochester in 1940, David O. Selznick now expressed relief that a politically neutered industry reigned. As he told an interviewer in 1958,

> I think that the concept that the commercial motion picture is an art form is ridiculous. It is entertainment and it is business, and it is backed by individual stockholders, tens of thousands of them, who expect to get returns on their investment, and I think this is no art form. This is a business. It is a mass entertainment, and I think that to pretentiously criticize or review commercial films as though they were an art form is precisely the same as reviewing the operations of Proctor and Gamble as though they were an art form.

Selznick's Hollywood had been cleansed of its contentious past: "I don't think there are any social lines" dividing the film community. At long last, he could say, the "very small percentage of extreme Leftists has evaporated."[76]

Despite the 1950s puffery, Hollywood is noted for having produced some fine, small pictures with progressive themes during the decade. Yet Hollywood "cleared" talent to work in movies. Suspect individuals cleansed themselves before a board of reconciliation, the members of which included Ronald Reagan, Emmet Lavery, and Dore Schary, a liberal who felt compelled to collaborate with anticommunists despite years of chiding their Red-baiting. Progressive director Elia Kazan flourished under these circumstances. He named names, prostrated himself, found work, and stepped lightly around political minefields.

Hollywood purified themes as well as personnel. In 1951 Harry Cohn, the head of Columbia Pictures, looked over a screenplay by Arthur Miller titled *The Hook*, a story about union corruption on the Brooklyn waterfront. Cohn took it to the FBI for some sort of "clearance" and returned with the suggestion of substituting communists for Miller's gangsters. "When I declined to commit this idiocy," Miller later recalled, "I got a wire from Cohn saying, 'The minute we try to make the script pro-American you pull out.'" Interference with progressive themes—"terribly serious insanity," as Miller put it—became routine.[77] Anticommunism robbed motion pictures of progressive talent and themes during the 1950s.

Even probing films such as *Rebel without a Cause* (1955) reinforced the family as a central organizing unit. Ultimately, there was more angst than rebellion. Off the stage, for all its salaciousness, Hollywood's adaptation of Tennessee Williams's *A Streetcar Named Desire* (1951) proved something less than cutting edge. *The Nation*'s film critic, Manny Farber, noted that "the story proceeds as Tennessee Williams first wrote it, except that all the frankest—and most crucial—dialogue has been excised and the last scene has been churned disastrously to satisfy the [censors] but confound the spectator." It appeared, Farber concluded, that "the author surrendered without firing a shot." Tennessee Williams, who was embarrassed but had been content to prostitute himself years earlier as an MGM hack while writing "something of value" on the sly, understood the difference between the restrictions placed on writers in Hollywood and the freedoms allowed in other arenas.[78] One World ideology had been sufficiently contained in the motion picture industry, but other outlets existed to carry the Cold War critique to audiences at home and abroad.

5

Test Patterns

Making Room for Dissent in Television

As THOUSANDS of readers picked up their copies of the August 20, 1945, issue of *Newsweek* magazine—the first postwar issue—they probably flipped the pages a little more slowly around the article titled "A New Era: The Secrets of Science." Within the previous week, Japan had succumbed to a "conquest by atom." Amid the articles detailing how American bombers flew over Japanese cities to unleash this new power, readers found a map showing planes cruising at 30,000 feet to "blanket" the United States with airborne antennas for television sending stations. In this, the same week that the Japanese surrendered, Westinghouse engineers joined with aircraft manufacturers to build B-29-sized planes for this new mission, called Stratovision. The map, duplicated in Henry Luce's *Time* magazine as well, showed aircraft hovering over New York, Chicago, Los Angeles, Atlanta, Memphis, Dallas, Salt Lake City, Portland, and other cities. *Time* reported that only fourteen planes were needed to cover 78 percent of the American population.

The "new era" in *Newsweek*'s title certainly referred to the atomic age, but readers quickly realized that modern science also ushered in a "new era" that promised to transform the nation in other fundamental ways. Americans who were fascinated with scientific achievement could marvel at two brilliant flashes of light: the atomic bomb and the television screen. The former ended horrific war; the latter symbolically inaugurated postwar prosperity. The two devices emerged in the national consciousness at the same time; both were seen as pathbreaking, and both developed in a Cold War environment.[1]

"If it works," NBC's president Niles Trammell said of Stratovision, "it will be revolutionary."[2] With the war over, Trammell informed the Federal

119

Communications Commission (FCC) a few weeks later, a new technological age was dawning in television transmission. He explained, "We no
longer are required to predicate plans for television on the winning of the
war. Victory has been won. Peace is here. Television is ready to go."[3] And
the public was ready for television.

Government officials, network executives, advertising agencies, the
artistic community, and citizen groups believed that television held great
promise as a democratizing medium. In particular, NBC archives show
that network executives viewed themselves as stewards of the public interest and guarantors of quality television. Their rivals at CBS were
little different in this regard. The networks institutionalized censorship
as a means to *promote* liberal themes rather than to excise them hastily.
In the late 1940s and early 1950s, these individuals believed television
should cultivate an educated populace, avoid racial stereotypes (especially of America's friends in the nonaligned world), and reject exaggerated
advertising claims by overzealous corporations. Though the Hollywood
left buckled at this same moment, universalism proved to be a portable
ideology, able to move from motion pictures to television.

The Democratic Promise of Early Television

Looking away from Washington and more deeply into the cultural arena,
shifting attention from one industry to another, broadens the scope of
foreign relations in general and of the Cold War in particular. Dissenters
carried the fight forward for One World values; they found open outlets
through which to shape public opinion about American foreign policy. By
1950, the year that the Hollywood Ten lost their final appeals, advocates
of global anticommunism had successfully discounted, demonized, and
demoralized their varied opponents inside and outside the Hollywood
community. Many histories end here, but what happens if we turn the
page of the story? What we find is that at the same time, the budding television industry provided a hospitable environment for cultural producers
to work, directly engaging the public "under the radar" of even the most
vigilant Cold Warriors.

Viewing a movie was (and remains) a far different experience from
viewing a television program. A film usually offers a singular experience
paid for at the door, a venue where viewers sit in public with strangers. In
the late 1940s and throughout the 1950s, children could watch "kid flicks,"
while for parents there were motion pictures with more mature themes.
Early television programs, though, could be seen in a weekly format, for

free, with viewers sitting in the privacy of the home, alone or only with family and friends. One historian wryly noted that television was "where families stayed together by staring together."[4] Given this practice, television became a popular medium of shared experience in which new programs had a remarkable impact. Despite their differences, cinema and television both served as sites of community-building, where universalism flourished. And even as ideology faded from the big screen, progressive worldviews found their way onto the small screen.

Not unlike cinema, television became a powerful, national, cultural institution. Like the motion picture industry, television is a contested site where various groups, recognizing the importance of mass communications in the construction of a national identity, fashion programs to complement their own social, political, and economic perspectives. Lyndon Johnson's press secretary, Bill Moyers, who moved on to a long career in television, likened TV viewing to citizens congregating around the national "campfire" to hear stories, thereby defining the national identity. In the sanctuary of the home, national audiences drew together by participating in the daily viewing ritual. In the early years of the Cold War, the paternal John Cameron Swayze, with carnation in his lapel, concluded his *Camel News Caravan* tenderly each night with "That's the story, folks. Glad we could get together."

In this warm environment, audiences saw the continuation of an ideological debate over the national character, between committed Cold Warriors and their progressive critics, on television in the 1940s and 1950s. Understanding the collaborative process in early television is the best way to understand how this contest developed. And perhaps no programming genre exemplifies this collaborative process and the contest over Cold War national identity better than the weekly anthology drama. The anthology drama—such as *Playhouse 90*, *Studio One*, and *Kraft Television Theater*—was a popular television series format in which a program's weekly episode consisted of a distinct story rather than continuity in plot, character, setting, and performers. In this art form, many people—writers, directors, producers, and ordinary citizens among them—strove to abandon what they perceived as the American national illusion of "harmony, homogeneity, and happiness" as portrayed on the big screen. Rather, they presented an alternative worldview in these teleplays, productions that generally advanced the values of multilateralism.

A few blacklisted writers from Hollywood, such as Walter Bernstein, Abraham Polonsky, and Arnold Manoff, found work in early television writing for the CBS show *You Are There*. Despite the powerful forces arrayed against them in Hollywood, they were able to use television to control their own destinies.[5] Ring Lardner Jr., a member of the Hollywood Ten, was another who, with his promising film career in shambles, found new outlets in early television. "The people for whom I was directly working knew who I was," Lardner explained later, "but the men who signed the checks in some instances did not." Success brought notice and threatened exposure, so he repeatedly created new pseudonyms for on-air credits and for all financial matters. For four years Lardner avoided meetings and lunches with network executives, sponsors, and others. Only after the blacklist silently ended did Cold War congressmen learn of Lardner's exploits.[6] But many television writers who were never blacklisted, having avoided dangerous ties to "subversive" organizations, still shared a similar belief system with those who had been.

The community of writers living in New York City which included Paddy Chayefsky, Rod Serling, Gore Vidal, Horton Foote, and Reginald Rose explored the issues of homosexuality, teenage pregnancy, alcoholism, juvenile delinquency, mental illness, and other behavior defined as "abnormal" at the time. They also confronted the Cold War when they promoted pacifism, indicted Red hysteria, and questioned the nuclear arms race. Together, on anthology drama programs they articulated dissent and an alternative worldview for Americans. These weekly teleplays emphasized gritty realism and universalism. In short, these writers shared their utopian dreams and apocalyptic nightmares with TV audiences throughout the 1950s at a time when contemporary politics constricted the possibilities for exploring these issues in more conventional arenas.

Anthology writers drew inspiration from many different sources, including Wendell Willkie's *One World*, the atomic scientists' qualms about the future, and the Hollywood Democratic Committee. For all, the war had been an epochal moment, providing an unprecedented opportunity to shape the world community that followed. Anthology writers particularly appreciated universalism as a transnational viewpoint emphasizing the world's common humanity. Like Hollywood progressives, anthology writers believed such an ideal could fill the vacuum once populated by fascism and militarism. With the war concluded, Willkie believed, "we may feel certain that when [soldiers] have battled over the world, they will not return home as provincial Americans."[7] Just as the horror of war aged young men, exposure to internationalism educated them. Unknowingly, Willkie was speaking about a veteran like Rod Serling. At one point during the war, Serling, then a young soldier from Ohio stationed in the Pacific theater, faced a near-fatal experience when a Japanese soldier aimed his gun at the American from only a few yards away. As Serling froze with fright at his impending death, a fellow GI shot the enemy soldier over his shoulder. Serling later recalled how he survived "through no dint of my own courage." Mixed with his relief were feelings of shame, anger, and a belief in pacifism. In December 1945, Serling wrote to his mother from Honshu, Japan, that he was coming home "scratched up a bit, a little older and more worldly."[8]

Thousands of other hardened veterans joined him on the trek home, not just to make a living but to make sense of the war they had just won. Like Serling, Paddy Chayefsky, Robert Alan Aurthur, Gore Vidal, Reginald Rose, Tad Mosel, and others had served in uniform before seeking careers as television writers. As they entered the profession, in many cases the writers' progressive worldviews later found their way into television programming.[9]

Looking back, several of these anthology writers felt compelled to put their complex thoughts down on paper. Gore Vidal examined his wartime tour on a freight supply ship in the Aleutians in his novel *Williwaw* (1946). Vidal wrote furiously in the years after the war, prompting one *New York Times* literary critic to ask, "By the way, could it be possible that you are writing too quickly? It seems to me that your rate of output is amazing."[10] Vidal's pace served him well as a writer of weekly television scripts. As Serling explained later, a script is "an extension of [the writer's] own mind." And there was much on Serling's mind while he attended college in 1947. For one classroom assignment, he wrote a courtroom drama—"In the Case of the Universe Versus War"—a pacifistic play with, appropriately enough, God presiding as judge. War was little more than "legalized murder" to a man embittered by his experience in the Pacific theater. In the play, Serling as the victorious GI asks an anonymous casualty on the witness stand what glory there is for the dead soldier.

> SOLDIER. I am told that my grave is littered with flowers. But I can't see or smell them. My lungs were rotted away by mustard gas and my eyes were blown out by a mortar shell. I am told that I am lauded by the world's greatest men, but I can't hear their praises. My ears were torn off by a shell concussion. But far worse I would want to speak to all these people and tell them that their emotions are misdirected—I deserve nothing but pity, but my mouth is stilled by the eternal silence of death.[11]

Serling's early writing revealed the impact of the war on his developing worldview, which would turn toward dissent in later years. It also reflected the feelings shared by many Americans during the period between

1945 and 1948, when the nation attempted to make sense of the past war while preparing for the new Cold War. The "worldly" veteran envisioned his fictional trial just weeks after publication of George Kennan's "Mr. X" article and after President Truman signed the National Security Act. In this play Serling expressed skepticism for any nation presuming to be "destined to rule," a designation that many Cold Warriors avowed. Writing during the same week as the HUAC hearings in Hollywood, Serling decried rampant domestic fascism at the hands of petty authoritarians. To him, extreme nationalism was an enemy to its citizens; he questioned "a colorful flag waved in front of my eyes" and "the empty platitudes of politicians exhorting us to fight for right, and honor, and homeland." From his perspective, Serling believed the United States was waging the Cold War for "false virtues." In the conclusion of his play, Serling's God delivers a damning verdict for all humanity living in the late 1940s.[12]

Other familiar ideas percolated in the writers' minds. In another college paper, Serling took the "yellowish" print media to task for promoting "distrust" and "a belligerent attitude of open hostility" to the Soviet Union. He later labeled the loyalty oath "ludicrous" and "demeaning."[13] Other Serling scripts and papers addressed the housing crisis and birth control. "A conducted tour through Utopia" demonstrated American hypocrisy on the civil rights issue. For example, Serling excoriated the fictional southern senator Theodore "Billboard" (a send-up of Mississippi's charismatic Senator Bilbo) for wishing to persecute Jews, Catholics, and African Americans. Senator Billboard even threatens a filibuster to keep the "red Communist ideas of equality" from subverting his white Utopia.[14] Similarly, Paddy Chayefsky wrote humorous poems about the postwar housing crisis, the GI Bill of Rights, and Senator Robert Taft.[15] Serling's and Chayefsky's early texts proved coarse and obvious compared with the more subtle arguments they honed for television in the following years. But these idealists expressed their worldviews in their scripts and plays, thereby offering an alternative to the developing Cold War consensus.[16] There was great synchronicity between One World ideology, the Hollywood left, and these future television writers.

The writers were, of course, only part of the collaborative process that produced anthology dramas. More returning veterans—Marc Daniels, Martin Ritt, Franklin Schaffner, Fielder Cook, Paul Bogart, George Roy Hill, and John Frankenheimer—became important television directors. Several of them viewed television as an opportunity that combined creative freedom, progressive activism, and good pay. Martin Ritt explained that television "was very interesting, it was exciting, and it was live."

This appealed to him especially because he had worked with the *March of Time* war documentaries that emphasized realism (and earned congressional scrutiny). Whereas Hollywood and Broadway appeared restrictive for various reasons, the blacklisted Ritt believed that in television "I could do virtually anything I wanted." In 1946, tired of school and loath to become a lawyer, the impatient Franklin Schaffner was in New York City working for an organization called Americans United for World Government when he wrangled a job as a radio producer, before entering television. At the young age of twenty-four, John Frankenheimer found "an ideal existence" as the assistant director on several shows. In subsequent years this partnership of progressive talents in television would only grow more influential as they would challenge the views of doctrinaire Cold Warriors.[17]

That anthology dramas "fascinated millions is abundantly clear from statistics," according to media historian Erik Barnouw. From 1950 to 1957 there was always at least one anthology drama in the top twenty most popular shows. In 1950, the same year that Senator Joseph McCarthy launched his first anticommunist salvo against the State Department, approximately one-third of the top twenty rated shows were anthology dramas. Furthermore, at a time when a top-ten show routinely garnered between 25 to 45 percent of the entire national television audience, the top twenty rankings included a variety of successful anthology dramas, nearly a dozen. Although NBC fortified its early programming schedule with the most anthology dramas, all networks relied on them to some extent. One program, NBC's *Kraft Television Theatre*, alone commissioned 18,845 scripts and presented 650 teleplays in its eleven-year run. Commercial America understood the draw of television very early on, and the most popular programs in this genre were sponsored by corporate giants: Ford, General Electric, Goodyear, Kraft, and U.S. Steel.[18] In short, the anthology dramas were generally popular and plentiful, and, notwithstanding the occasional schlock, they were thematically far-reaching.[19]

In these early years, the nature of the medium itself encouraged experimentation. The "proper" roles for sponsors, producers, programmers, affiliates, writers, directors, performers, and technicians fluctuated from network to network, from program to program, and literally from individual to individual. Many who worked in television looked to their experiences in radio, stage, print media, and advertising to guide them in the new industry.[20] Rod Serling later recalled, "There was a sense of bewilderment on the part of everyone"; pioneers of live television were "feeling their way around" trying to find "some reason for being, and some

WHAT IS THE FUTURE OF *television* ?

EM 27 GI ROUNDTABLE

War Department pamphlet, 1945. When the motion picture industry turned to the blacklist, progressive voices found opportunities in the new, democratizing medium of television. Courtesy American Historical Association / By permission of Robert B. Townsend.

set of techniques."[21] The ensuing disorder facilitated an environment where writers and directors could audition experimental themes as well. This atmosphere allowed for an intense debate over industry development and television content. Changing Cold War mentalities would play an important part in how those debates were resolved and what content would be produced over time.

Another important component of the collaborative process, and one that scholars have neglected, was the audience. The audience—especially the viewers as perceived by sponsors, networks, and writers—must be considered in order to explain the popularity of television, the acceptance of these controversial programs, and the reasons for changes in programming over time. Common citizens contributed to the rise of television during the postwar era for many reasons, but especially because of growing prosperity, suburbanization, and their willingness to accept innovative programming. All these factors not only helped to make television popular and accessible but also served to create a hospitable environment for progressive themes to thrive. However, some of the very same institutional forces that initially welcomed controversial themes later restrained them and promoted the Cold War consensus ideology of anticommunism, unfettered capitalism, and a national image of exceptionalism.

Owning a television set became an important gauge of a family's postwar success, something Vance Packard recognized as he prepared to publish *The Status Seekers* in the 1950s. "Even today," he wrote, "the TV aerial has symbolic significance in some areas of the nation. . . . Many two-room shacks have thirty-foot towers above them."[22] Television became a technological ruler by which to measure the American Dream. Its explosive popularity is confirmed by statistics: in the first winter after the Second World War, *Public Opinion Quarterly* reported that a quarter of Americans were willing to pay high prices for a television set. Despite the fact that in 1946 the cost of a receiver reached approximately $500, another poll showed that most Americans anticipated owning a set within three years.[23] Already in the next year, sets were down to $170, sales rose dramatically, and status came at bargain-basement prices.[24] Even those who did not own a set aspired to acquire one. Americans understood the blossoming importance of television, found ways to view it, and read about its programs in popular print media. Although many citizens did not own a set in the earliest years, very few ignored it altogether. Virtually all Americans were curious, expectant owners, seduced by the small screen's glow. Not surprisingly, viewership grew substantially in a short period of time.

Several scholars and critics have suggested that most Americans missed the "Golden Age" of television for the simple reason that they did not yet own a television set. Therefore, these observers argue, programs appealed only to this imagined audience: a relatively few, highly educated, upper-income urbanites who could afford television sets. (Were these the same highbrow snobs who also enjoyed wrestling, roller derby, and Milton Berle's borscht-belt variety show?) Actually, studies confirm that television homes rose from 10,000 in 1946 to a million in 1949, and from 4 million in 1950 to 12 million in 1951. And one NBC survey shows that as early as 1948, on average, each set entertained four viewers during prime time.[25] Almost half of the entire population had seen a television program by 1949, even if they did so in a neighbor's house, from a bar stool, or through a store window.[26] Television ownership grew rapidly from 12 percent of the population in 1950 to 71 percent in 1955.[27] Television had reached smaller metropolises in every region of the country by 1951: Providence, Lansing, Birmingham, Omaha, Albuquerque, Norfolk, Seattle, Fort Worth, Ames, Dayton, Salt Lake City, and Kalamazoo among them.[28] Most surprisingly, perhaps, by 1955 more Americans owned television sets than owned household telephones, a statistic that has held true ever since. Ownership reached 86 percent in 1958, still before the sun had set on the "Golden Age," and just shy of 90 percent by the end of the early Cold War period in 1960.

Furthermore, almost anyone who saw television understood immediately that mass communications had changed forever. The rising popularity of the new medium threatened and injured newspapers, motion pictures, and radio. Over 81 percent of Americans who recently had seen it predicted that television would affect radio if not outright kill it.[29] This view was expressed by a generation of loyal listeners who had been weaned on the indispensable radio, had marveled at its instant transmission, and had been comforted by its fireside chats during depression and war. Despite anxiety over reconversion to a domestic economy, insecurity over housing and job shortages, and dread over media reports of a renewed depression, many Americans soon looked to television as virtually a necessity.

Television remained popular for another reason that went beyond mere novelty or status: the public welcomed programming content that they could not receive elsewhere, certainly not from Hollywood. While HUAC members and other Cold Warriors may have spurned controversial One World themes, the American public had not joined that consensus blindly or completely. Anticommunist films probably appeased more members of HUAC than entertained members of the public at large.[30] Weekly anthology dramas, with their trim psychological focus, picked up where social problem films and Hollywood activism left off. Writer Paddy Chayefsky insisted that live television plays were "far and away superior to anything on the current Broadway stage or anything issued by the movie industry," and writer Rod Serling agreed that the anthology drama "consistently aimed high"; it was "adult, never hackneyed, and almost always honest," and "rarely dull."[31] In turn, anthology writers became known for their scripts. "We became a household word," Horton Foote recollected, especially as the networks marketed their stable of writing stars.[32] Television was popular for a variety of reasons, not least because people put their democratic hopes in audiovisual transmission.

Growing postwar suburbanization indirectly helped to create an atmosphere in which provocative programming could flourish. A baby boom and a housing shortage stimulated the migration to the suburbs. Americans turned away from urban centers but never fully let go of their invisible ties to other citizens. As they gained economic mobility to the middle class and physical mobility to the growing suburbs, television granted them the opportunity to stay connected to old neighbors they had left behind and even to Americans they had never met. Media scholar Tom Engelhardt writes in *The End of Victory Culture* that television "offered an even more expansive kind of mobility" than the automobile had to an earlier generation because "one could miraculously go anywhere without leaving one's couch or bed."[33] More important, Rod Serling believed, the physical location of the television set inside the home made it possible to address "intimate" themes to viewers. What some critics derided as "kitchen dramas," director Delbert Mann argued later, "seemed to make the strongest emotional connection with the audience."[34] Generally speaking, the small screen bound Americans together in an important way at a time when they were being physically separated from old bonds.

Just as churches, taverns, and political parties united individualistic and mobile pioneers in earlier generations, the television united Americans living on what urban historian Kenneth Jackson has labeled the "crabgrass frontier."[35] Television dramas appealed to American viewers in part because they had the sense that their concerns were represented on live television. Even if a broadcast focused on a subject unrelated to them, audiences could appreciate that they might be watching the story of their neighbors and fellow citizens. Programs became virtual "social news" broadcasts to audiences trying to cope with national and international upheaval.

Throughout much of this period, even as important events occurred on an international scale, newspapers and radios concentrated on domestic politics, not on social trends. Television news followed suit. When Senator Joseph McCarthy railed against perceived communists in the government, there were fewer than three hours of news and public affairs programming each week. Aside from the well-known broadcasts presented on CBS by Edward R. Murrow and Fred Friendly, the human side of anticommunist hysteria would have been more hidden if not for the televised drama. And when Alfred Kinsey released his report on American sexuality, nightly newscasts lasted a mere fifteen minutes, leaving little time for in-depth coverage.[36] Here again, dramas entered the public square. When the civil rights movement overtook Montgomery, Little Rock, and Selma, the networks had no more than two correspondents outside of Washington and New York City; and NBC "field reporter" John Chancellor's beat included the entire South and Midwest.[37] Screenwriters made sense of racial issues by adapting colonialism, lynching, and integration to dramatic form. For the "social news" of their world, postwar audiences found "truth" in an unlikely place: the television drama.

The public favored television over the Hollywood motion picture in the early 1950s. In 1951 almost all television cities showed massive drops in theater attendance, ranging from 20 to 40 percent, prompting many theaters to halt business altogether; that year, 3,000 movie houses closed their doors.[38] More than 50 theaters closed in New York City; more than 60 in the Boston and Chicago areas; more than 70 in metropolitan Philadelphia; and in Los Angeles, the film capital of the world, at least 130 movie houses shut their doors. In nontelevision areas, movie attendance remained steady, but in television cities, sporting events, restaurants, taxicabs, radio broadcasters, and even jukebox owners felt the sting of television. Throughout the 1950s, inflated ticket prices often hid the fact that attendance at movie theaters declined over 70 percent.[39] The hazy television picture that conveyed such remarkable content appeared to win the competition for the American eye. Indeed, viewers spent more and more time in front of their sets as the years went by.[40]

From 1948 to 1952, Hollywood executives responded to a dual challenge posed by the threat of television and by the decision in *United States v. Paramount Pictures, Inc.*, which had ordered the studios' divorcement from their theater chains. Better to back a few Technicolor epics, the thinking went, than a plethora of contentious dramas. Studios instituted austere budgets, slashed payrolls, limited the number of features, opened their back lots to television production, and after 1955 unlocked their film vaults to broadcasting opportunities.[41] Some studio employees released during cutbacks at Universal in the late 1940s moved on to television.[42] As time passed, studio moguls also came to embrace television, especially when they viewed its revenue as a potential life saver. Americans may have flocked to their television sets at first out of curiosity, but fresh programming content sustained the medium as television transformed from novelty into institution.

How could controversial themes appear on TV with such regularity during the apparent height of the global, anticommunist consensus? Television became a site of debate over Cold War politics and culture because of the collaborative process inherent in the industry, the epochal impact of war on veterans who turned to writing and directing, the novelty of technology and the excitement of live television, and the changing experiences of the audiences as nesting suburbanites. Two other critical forces that allowed for the articulation of progressive themes on television were government officials and network executives. During the late 1940s government officials and network executives undertook a conscious effort to democratize the medium in the name of the "public interest."

High atop the fifty-third floor in his Manhattan office, however, David Sarnoff and other network brass were not nearly as open to progressive ideology as were writers and directors on the lower floors. Indeed, many executives considered themselves patriotic Cold Warriors. But if men such as Richard Nixon, J. Parnell Thomas, and Joseph McCarthy were high priests of anticommunism, men such as David Sarnoff of NBC and William Paley of CBS were only members of the laity.

General Sarnoff, for example, joined in the chorus for peaceful coexistence with the Soviets. Sarnoff, on the very day in 1948 that the government indicted Alger Hiss, and while newspapers reported the ongoing Berlin Airlift, reiterated to an audience in New York City that although he was cognizant of the potential menace, "we should be willing to carry on discussions and negotiations, however fruitless or frustrating they may appear at the time."[43] He still believed in a deliberative process of revealing Soviet intentions, not unlike one proclaimed by George Kennan. In this way, Sarnoff supported the government's moderate policy of containment before 1950. Both Sarnoff and NBC president Niles Trammell served on the Committee for the Marshall Plan with notable Cold War liberals who expressed disdain for Red-baiters, including politician Hubert Humphrey and theologian Reinhold Niebuhr. The committee included Hollywood producer Walter Wanger, the man who introduced Dalton Trumbo to his friends in the American delegation at the United Nations. Producer Daryl Zanuck, who had brought his wartime documentary experience to such films as *Wilson* (1944) and *One World*, also joined in support of the Marshall Plan.[44] Like these individuals, network executives believed that the Marshall Plan and television remained two noble enterprises well suited for helping those in need, two vehicles that transported democracy to the public.

Because of the obvious public fascination and excitement surrounding television, the FCC started with an ambitious plan to license 400 stations in 140 American cities. The commissioners and the networks also felt the need to define the purpose of the new medium during the years 1945 to 1948. This period was crucial to the development of the medium that would help define the nation for Americans. As Eric Barnouw has written, these were "the formative years for television. Its program patterns, business practices, and institutions were being shaped." The intrepid national broadcasting plan and the need for a statement of purpose contributed to a macro view of early television rather than one dominated by regional or local considerations. Networks would dominate, affiliates would not. Given the democratic promise of early television, and given the national outlook of commissioners, the FCC came to place an imagined national audience at the forefront of its thinking.[45]

Early on, the FCC promoted universalism by promoting its particular definition of the "public interest." In March 1946, as the television industry began to build after the wartime hiatus, the FCC issued what scholars have called the "single most important programming policy document" in its history. The "Blue Book" of standards and practices urged broadcasters to consider the "public interest" when programming. It defined programming necessary to the "public interest" with great specificity: to provide a balance to advertising-supported material; to showcase the "unsponsorable"; to "serve minority tastes and interests"; and to "allow experimentation with new types of programs."[46] The commissioners concluded with an implied threat, "The FCC would favor renewal applications from stations that had met their public service responsibilities," which included a "discussion of public issues, and no excessive advertising."[47]

The commission extended its views to include even the most daring political content. In the summer of 1948, FCC chairman Wayne Coy announced the commissioners' interpretation of Section 315 of the Communications Act of 1934 and held that stations "may not censor political broadcasts because of allegedly libelous or slanderous material contained in them." This meant that the FCC would demand that licensees accept political broadcasts even by radicals and alleged "subversives."[48] The message was clear to broadcasters and the networks: television would be preserved as a democratic medium open to many perspectives, even the most provocative.

Beginning in September 1948 and lasting until April 1952, the FCC further maintained control of the new industry by declaring a "freeze" on station licensing (because of signal interference and other technological difficulties) and thus on television expansion. During this freeze, industry insiders fashioned important standards and precedents under the watchful eye of a progressive FCC. Freda Hennock, the first woman appointed to the commission, complained to the National Association of Broadcasters that weeks had gone by with virtually no "quality" programming. The FCC commissioners insisted that stations meet the "public service responsibility" if they hoped to have their broadcast licenses renewed.[49] During the formative years of television, the FCC freeze created a progressive laboratory in which multilateralist themes could grow.

At the same time, the FCC rejected appeals by staunch anticommunists to turn the young industry into a political weapon. In 1947 a commission dominated by Roosevelt and Truman appointees received "unsolicited" memoranda from the FBI regarding the alleged communist affiliations of some applicants for broadcasting licenses in California. Skeptical and territorial, the commissioners asked J. Edgar Hoover for specifics. After all, they reasoned, even rejected applicants were entitled by law to a hearing. The FBI explained that this would be impossible, given the confidentiality of its informants. When the FCC investigated on its own, it discovered that the claims were groundless. Commissioner Clifford Durr became so incensed at the FBI's infringement on civil liberties that he went public. An irate Hoover threatened to smear the FCC. During oversight hearings, congressmen noted the fact that Durr's assistant had cowritten the FCC's "Blue Book"—a telltale sign of progressive thought—and scolded the FCC "thought police" for its "misuse of power" and liberal regulation.[50] Ultimately, the other FCC commissioners rebuked Durr. Nonetheless, the FCC did not buckle under to outside pressure nearly as quickly and willingly as it would do in the years to come.

The National Association of Broadcasters (NAB), a professional association not unlike the Motion Picture Association of America in Hollywood, took its cues from the FCC when it issued its own standards of practice for the industry. But unlike the FCC, the more conservative

NAB hoped to establish rules that tightly controlled content. "No dramatization of controversial issues should be permitted," the NAB flatly ruled. In particular, it hoped to eliminate profanity, promote the institution of marriage, and reject "material tending to break down juvenile respect for parents, the home or moral conduct." In short, given the Cold War environment, the NAB urged networks to downplay, if not avoid altogether, controversial themes such as these.[51]

One World Television

The networks quickly responded to the NAB's proposed standards. "As you know," an NBC vice president wrote a director at the NAB in October 1947, "I have thought from the beginning that it may not be prudent of us to attempt to ban dramatization of controversial issues. I know, of course, the excesses which we are attempting to avoid but I do feel that any such prohibition may have a stultifying influence on this very important type of program." The networks believed that broadcasting could educate the public responsibly.[52]

NBC president Niles Trammell giddily detailed television's powerful promise. The new medium, he wrote, "exceeded the dreams of all of us" by marking "the greatest forward step in mass communication" in history. It is "the most potent tool ever developed for man's education," he trumpeted. "The entertainment world hails it as a revolutionary force that will raise the standards of every phase of the amusement business," but beyond amusements, Trammell noted that physicians, the military, clergymen, the police, and others had "found that this new medium can add immeasurably to the effectiveness of their work." Aside from content, "wrapped in a single package and dropped into your living room," Trammell declared that the medium would protect the postwar economy by facilitating consumerism and creating thousands of new jobs.[53] Far from the "vast wasteland" that FCC chairman Newton Minow would label it a decade later, television promised to be the great product of scientific achievement, appropriate for modern America in the atomic age. Like the early dreams for radio, television held inexhaustible promise to elevate, to educate, and to democratize.

Realizing they must control their programming before others did it for them, NBC executives issued their own broadcast standards the following year. Titled *Responsibility*, this statement of rules was intended to revise policies first established in 1934. Although it adopted much of what the NAB wanted, NBC also claimed responsibility for policing its own program content, much as other media had earlier. "All continuities, including the words of all songs or spoken lines as well as the wording of commercial copy, must be submitted for clearance and distribution" to the network bureaucracy before broadcast. In other words, "continuity acceptance," as NBC called its role as censor, was in the network's domain, an area populated in the late 1940s and early 1950s by men who were open—for the time being at least—to controversial subjects.[54]

Executive Sylvester "Pat" Weaver took up the FCC's public interest challenge by promising to uplift viewers. Weaver had worked in radio, joined the Young & Rubicam (Y&R) advertising agency, and later managed advertising for the American Tobacco Company, which produced Lucky Strike cigarettes. Only weeks after departing Y&R for NBC, the old ad man promised "to bring more class to the mass." A navy veteran, he labeled his programming strategies with martial monikers: "Operation Frontal Lobes" and "Operation Wisdom." One NBC executive pitched the network policy to a potential corporate sponsor in this way: "to attract as many viewers as possible, and to educate, in the *broadest* possible sense of the word." Weaver favored "genuine talent" over "cheap filler," and shows such as *Philco Playhouse* over lowbrow wrestling. He believed that entertainment, social progress, and profits were all compatible and appropriated the national "public interest" discourse when the network programmed educational, relevant, and controversial shows. "With television," Weaver wrote enthusiastically, "another step in the grand design of the liberals, making *all* people members of privilege, is taken."[55]

Weaver passionately believed that television could inform and unite Americans during the Cold War. He hoped to provide "strength of character, inner discipline, basic fortitude to meet a continuing crisis" by programming current events and documentaries for postwar audiences. But Weaver also hoped to show Americans these ideas through drama. "For it is our belief that television is a medium of reality," he preached to the Advertising Club of New York. "Television can help our people face the real world and cast aside ancient prejudices, fictions and reactions. Television must be in the vanguard of new adult hope that must come to all our people." He saw the industry as an instrument for social change: "We must use television to make every man a member of his own times, understanding its issues, facing its challenges. When the people know, the people respond—and we will let them know.[56]

Despite this initiative, Weaver understood that his plan faced potential problems as well. "On snob appeal," he wrote, "there is the danger of

losing the key to TV's greatness"—mass appeal. Also, he courted controversy. One Philco drama showed Weaver that there was a fine line between "new adulthood" and "*over-adult*." Censorship should remain
"positive," even though NBC "should not schedule *too much . . . too
early* or *too hot*." Still, Weaver granted wide latitude to progressive-
minded producers of anthology dramas, such as Fred Coe. He gave them
the power to shape network programs for an audience they imagined.
"The major responsibility must lie with the producer," Weaver explained
in 1949. "He knows what time he's on, what audience is likely."[57] Granting autonomy to his stable of producers proved invaluable for presenting
themes that ran counter to the dominant Cold War consensus. Such
power sharing would come back to haunt Pat Weaver in the coming
years; for now, though, Weaver and his staff showed a commitment to
"highbrow," progressive, and realistic programming. He voiced trust in
producers to create quality television and maintained faith in network
censors to monitor the situation.

Unlike the image of the disapproving prude, network censors were
instrumental in preserving early television as a rare public site open to
dissent. NBC relied on Stockton Helffrich and his staff of forty editors,
researchers, and other specialists at the network's Office of Continuity
Acceptance in New York City and in Buffalo, Chicago, Hollywood, Philadelphia, San Francisco, and Washington, D.C. Helffrich started his career
with NBC in 1933 and served as a navy lieutenant during the Second
World War before returning to his job as network director for Continuity
Acceptance, a job that he held until the late 1950s. Even as Helffrich controlled content censorship for the network, he viewed himself as the
citizens' representative in the RCA Building. Therefore, he consciously
sought out public opinion in order to decipher the meaning behind "the
public interest." Beginning in the fall of 1948, the guardians of television's
"Golden Age" issued weekly continuity acceptance reports (CARTs) from
their offices.

At first the networks employed censorship as a tool to satisfy their
commitment to progressive television. In early television one can see
many of the very same positions advocated by Wendell Willkie and the
Hollywood Left. Like these earlier voices of progressive politics, individuals working in early network television also promoted humane capitalism, urged decolonization and self-determination, rejected racial and
ethnic stereotypes, demanded respect for civil liberties, and aimed for
impartiality in dealing with the behavior of other nations, including the
Soviet Union.

The four separate sets in NBC studio 8-G, all broadcasting simultaneously in 1948, underscore the experimental nature of early television. The atmosphere allowed for progressive themes and critical commentary about Cold War America. Courtesy Library of Congress, Prints & Photographs Division, LC-USZ62-89816 / NBC.

Despite being situated in a solid corporate structure, in a cycle of growing prosperity and consumer confidence, during an age of the communist threat, NBC policed program content in order to moderate unfettered capitalism. Pat Weaver even suggested in one memo, "It is possible that television will not develop as an advertising supported medium."[58] Of course, as television followed the radio model, advertising did become standard, but that did not keep the network from constantly seeking to reject exaggerated advertising claims and to prevent some products from being hawked at all. NBC's censor labeled one ad "completely commercial" before rejecting it outright. In 1949, a series of interdepartmental memos circulated about which products to allow as advertisers on NBC. Although alcohol and cigarette companies frequently sponsored shows, the network considered deodorants, laxatives, and undergarments unacceptable unless "discreetly presented." "Let's hold the line on this," Weaver told Helffrich. Although radio had traditionally regarded such personal products as profitable—consider "soap operas" for example—television executives determined that no matter the profit, the dignity of television called for special care.[59]

Even when products were accepted, NBC questioned the sponsors' claims. In one case, the network reexamined a pain reliever that claimed to "stop the devil of ache and pain" associated with rheumatism and arthritis. Rather than "stop," the network demanded the use of the word "curb" to describe its truthful effect on symptoms. NBC also tested the claims of a toothpaste sponsor to "guarantee" the end of tooth decay. After analyzing the results, NBC eliminated the term and reasserted its "essential" role as arbiter of the public interest. The network also acted in the "public interest" when censors expressed their desire for Alka-Seltzer to be more positive in its ad campaign; the sponsor proved too negative when assessing its competitors.[60] Initially, at least, television executives believed they had a duty to curb the excesses of capitalism.[61]

They also followed the public's lead in promoting international organizations. One citizen in California wrote to NBC requesting that the network program with a One World conscience. "This is an awesome time in history and it is going to be decisive," she explained, and "it would be a good idea to think about World Government as a solution to future war." She added, "We cannot let the younger generation inherit our messes this time because this is the Atomic Age and there very possibly may not be a younger generation." One NBC affiliate forwarded the message to New York with the words, "There may be something in her suggestion."[62]

In the late 1940s the networks competed to televise the United Nations. Paley's CBS began daily broadcasts of General Assembly sessions in 1949; NBC executives admitted to a CBS "coup" and initiated a similar plan. Because of this "extensive public service," David Sarnoff complained that NBC "has been made to look disinterested in public service and has been made to appear ridiculous in a competitive commercial sense." On the other hand, he fumed, "CBS, who has done practically nothing for the UN in the past, now emerges—by a single gesture—as both enterprising and public spirited!"[63] The public appreciated the United Nations, and the networks responded by telecasting its sessions. This sentiment influenced program content in dramatic shows as well.

With an eye on American foreign policy and the developing struggles for decolonization and self-determination, the networks promoted a more realistic portrayal of people of color. Network censors were undoubtedly influenced by America's wars against fascism and authoritarian communism. America's vulnerability to international criticism for civil rights abuses at home also influenced Helffrich and his associates at NBC. Helffrich urged his staff to "keep as alert as possible to avoid not only clichés but those caricatures and exaggerations which tend to annoy some parties and hence work against audience good will towards NBC and its clients." These stereotypes are "lacking in humor" and are "potentially malicious," he wrote. In one instance, Stockton Helffrich took the *Philco* show to task for its portrayal of South Americans as "naive." Dialogue about whether Peruvians could be classified as "dark," "white," or "light" was stricken for insensitivity. "All of this chit chat," Helffrich hastened to add, "was in no way essential to the plot and seemed to us very undiplomatic" given "these days of the Marshall Plan." After the Korean War began, Helffrich informed his staff that the use of the term "Gooks" offended America's "Asiatic" allies. One particularly tactless executive complained, "Very largely in time there would be no humor left, no more Irish jokes, no more Italian jokes, no more Chinese jokes, no more Negro jokes." His opinion was in the minority, though, as NBC executives firmly believed they had a responsibility to broadcast with racial and ethnic sensitivity because doing so served both national and network interests.[64]

This consciousness figured into casting decisions and other hiring practices as well. On the afternoon of October 25, 1950, NBC executives invited members of the National Urban League and black newspapermen to the Johnny Victor Theatre in the RCA Building to discuss these matters. Lester Granger, the executive director of the National Urban League, began his remarks by showing demographically why networks should ignore, rather than appeal to, African Americans: their population had been until very recently, he said, primarily centered in the rural areas of the South, hardly television's audience. Granger admitted that *his* constituents were almost exclusively wage earners who lived "on their earnings and on their savings rather than on the dividends of investments" and therefore offered little incentive to the sponsors who were developing programs. Yet despite this lack of obvious appeal, Granger urged network executives to use the medium to push a progressive civil rights viewpoint. African-American leaders hoped to use television for their own purposes.[65]

NBC vice president Sidney Eiges agreed and told the gathering that although the issue has been "somewhat overlooked," television should offer examples of "colored policemen and colored icemen" and other jobs "which would be very true in real life." Further, showing blacks as businessmen, teachers, and newspapermen—indeed, the very jobs held by the audience members Eiges was addressing—might open up those same opportunities in the real world. Television could play a pivotal and unique role in promoting civil rights and economic equality, Eiges claimed. "We have been trying to advance that pace a little bit through that device" because television, unlike radio, offers "the visual opportunity to see the character taking that step without having to characterize it by voice and dialect and stereotype."[66]

This outreach marked a reversal for networks. Stephen Foster's antebellum song "Little Brown Gal" had been featured on NBC and CBS in the late 1940s; by 1950, however, public opinion dictated a change. Such "unacceptable" songs had to be "suitably revised" or face rejection, Helffrich explained. The networks acknowledged their earlier complicity in accepted racial attitudes and practices, but now censors recognized that "segregating the Negro" works "against our interests."[67] NBC admitted erring by approving or ignoring far too many racial and ethnic stereotypes from reaching the screen. For example, censors used their blue pencils repeatedly to omit Irish drunks and Italian gangs. "So sensitive have we become to this entire problem," one network executive declared in 1950, "that I think it is not the least bit difficult for me to say that, of course, the same thing applies where the Negro Community is concerned."[68]

The wartime contributions of African Americans certainly altered the racial sensibilities of many Americans by emphasizing their citizenship as defenders of democracy. The intersection of international affairs and domestic civil rights reduced the acceptability of old racial views. One noteworthy casualty of this new thinking was what did *not* appear on television. At a time when networks sought to transfer the most successful radio programs and stars of the time—Jack Benny, *Fibber McGee and Molly*, Fred Allen—they overlooked one of the most popular: *Amos & Andy*. Apparently, they did not consider blackface a welcome addition to their slate of progressive programs. The Cold War State Department held a different view and endorsed the export of minstrelsy. Of course, offenses and oversights continued even in early television. One black actor refused to audition for the role of a "typical Negro drunk" and complained to a newspaperman. Soon thereafter, however, the actor discovered that an Irishman had been paid ten dollars to take the job. Even so, one could see serious self-restraint on the part of programmers who did not wish to use their new medium to perpetuate old racial attitudes.

Network censors took the issue of self-determination even further by encouraging programs to relinquish other outmoded stereotypes. Early programs attempted to show women in realistic situations and with emotional depth. Although they handled it delicately, networks did not necessarily shy away from exploring sexuality in a complex manner. Even when the news programs did not cover the groundbreaking Kinsey Report on American sexuality, anthology dramas did. On April 19, 1949, a *Fireside Theatre* drama referred to the controversial report and, according to NBC censors, kept it "on a serious and mature plane." In another teleplay, *Philco*'s "Street Scene," audiences heard the cries of a woman in the throes of labor. Acknowledging the audience's shock, Helffrich defended the production by arguing that the presentation was "totally acceptable and in no way jarring to the sensibilities of a family audience." In still another drama, no attempts were made to hide or ignore the condition of a pregnant actress.[69]

Even when a stereotype met with popular and critical acclaim, network executives questioned the portrayal. Judy Holliday's "dumb blonde" in *Born Yesterday* won her an Academy Award, but NBC's advertising department revised the trailer by deleting its last line: "The story of the dumbest broad who ever lived and the man who kept her in mink." Although she might be entertaining in Cold War Hollywood, the archetypal dumb blonde appeared little more than a prostitute to the censors in network television. The term "broad," moreover, came under increasing scrutiny, having been seen by NBC and ABC as synonymous with "whore" and therefore rarely employed. Helffrich advised sensitivity, deciding that "the word is crude and might better be avoided" altogether.[70]

Typically, a sexually aggressive woman character would pass the censors, but her presence was duly noted as "some pretty sophisticated material." In one case "a pretty girl propositioned" the male lead but was *not* a prostitute or a vamp. Helffrich's office strove to maintain the integrity of the script and only deleted what it considered gratuitous. Therefore, a "mature" production of Alexander Dumas's *Camille* avoided "any prudish skirting" of one character's past but rejected a camera shot that featured another character's "great expanse of bosom." Likewise, censors deleted some accompanying narration because they considered that it objectified women.[71]

Stockton Helffrich raised his eyebrows more than once while observing Milton Berle's raunchy antics. Despite the program's high ratings, Berle's cross-dressing proved a particular annoyance. "We have had to cover the dress rehearsal and most of the preceding rehearsal time" just to monitor the situation, Helffrich noted, but recognizing the desire to allow free artistic expression, NBC rarely stepped in. This is not to say that there were no limits. In the case of one *Kraft Television Theatre* script concerning a female impersonator, censors "carefully checked the producer and [were] assured there [was] no pansy treatment inserted anywhere"; they also deleted crass dialogue for "obvious reasons."[72] Cross-dressing could be considered good humor but could also be considered in poor taste. Still, with regard to exposing the nation to gender-bending of all types, network censors were not nearly as rigid and prudish as Berle's frequent jokes suggested.

The common values shared by a cadre of writers, directors, producers, and network executives allowed for the proliferation of multilateralist themes in anthology dramas. But when the Cold War expanded after 1950, the network's sensibilities weakened, and executives altered their views to reflect the Cold War entrenchment. The writers' views remained remarkably consistent, however. Unlike their counterparts in Hollywood, TV writers and directors were unrestrained by organizational ties that tagged them as radicals and subversives. Still, though anthology dramas continued to present Cold War dissent, Progressives experienced many frustrations throughout the 1950s.

6

Guardians of the Golden Age

Cold War Television and the Imagined Audience

ED SULLIVAN began his television career in 1948 as a host of his long-running variety show, *Toast of the Town*. Late the next year he booked dancer Paul Draper and harmonica aficionado Larry Adler to appear. Both men had been targeted by anticommunists, but Sullivan gave them a stage nonetheless. Anticommunist columnists George Sokolsky and Westbrook Pegler, though, pressed Sullivan's sponsor, Ford Motor Company, to pull out. After discussing the matter at length, Ford executives sided with Draper and Adler. Sokolsky and Pegler, not to be outdone, appealed to the public to vent its ire at Ford. Almost 1,300 letters and telegrams later, Ford pressured Sullivan to pull the plug. In January 1950, anticommunist vigilantes successfully prosecuted the two performers in the court of public opinion. Adler was blacklisted; Draper moved to Europe. With hindsight, this can be seen as an obvious conclusion for a situation that appeared in the same month that Joseph McCarthy took the stage in Wheeling, West Virginia, to claim communist infiltration of the State Department.

In many ways the Draper-Adler incident appeared as a microcosm of things to come. One should note Sullivan's early support for the two accused. While damaging, the charge of communism in television did not carry the same weight as it had in Hollywood at the same time. Television provided an outlet of relative freedom even after 1950, when obstructing progressive talent and content became more common. But just as Sokolsky and Pegler did to Ford, throughout the 1950s anticommunists played the "cash card" and threatened corporate sponsors and ad agencies that refused

143

to promote the Cold War consensus. Many times Cold Warriors made direct appeals to the public, inviting them into the cultural arena as deputies patrolling the airwaves. In a hyperpoliticized climate, individuals connected with the television industry (whether producer, writer, sponsor, or viewer) imagined the American audience in different ways and redefined the meaning of the "public interest" doctrine. Did audiences thoroughly absorb the message of the anthologies? Perhaps. But actual audience reception mattered less than how individuals used the "imagined" audience to advance their political agendas.

After 1950, broadcasters who valued their own careers were loath to risk anything for tainted talent. That year marked the outbreak of war in Korea, just as the National Security Council (NSC) envisioned a global communist threat, a danger soon perceived to be more broad and more deep than first realized. The NSC dramatically reworked containment policy to reflect an ideological contest in which popular culture would play an important role. Policymakers adopted a cultural weapon to unite Americans, to unite the West under exceptional American leadership, and to infiltrate and undermine the Soviet bloc. The Cold War government used cultural outlets to express this new mission and to offer a sanitized image of the nation. Increasingly after 1950, regulators and television executives walked in step with the NSC and enforced a blacklist designed to silence dissenting voices in television.

NSC 68 and Deployment of the Cultural Weapon

From the summer of 1949 to the summer of 1950, the communist issue profoundly altered both American foreign policy and the domestic scene. Just as the events of 1946 had done to Hollywood, these later Cold War crises threatened to stifle the progressive worldviews expressed in the television industry. The aftershocks of the fall of China, the detonation of the Soviet atomic device, the discovery of the Claus Fuchs spy ring, the delivery of McCarthy's Wheeling speech, and the invasion of South Korea left policymakers reeling, especially in the State Department. Containment policy, it seemed, had failed to prevent communist strides in Europe, in Asia, and at home. Initially, Progressives dismissed the magnitude of these events. In time they witnessed firsthand the significance when their political standing in the country declined. As Arthur Miller later explained, "If our losing China seemed the equivalent of a flea's losing an elephant, it was still a phrase—and a conviction—that one did not dare to question; to do so was to risk drawing suspicion on oneself."[1] Cold

Warriors understood that perceptions of weakness could alter realities. As historian John Lewis Gaddis explained, "World order, and with it American security, had come to depend as much on *perceptions* of the balance of power as on what that balance actually was."[2]

Diplomats and policymakers worried that they were losing the Cold War and that containment policy was a sieve that inadequately restrained communism. Given the series of damaging events, Theodore C. Achilles, the State Department's director of the office of West European affairs, called for a close association of the free world. Sounding much like an early advocate for multilateralism, Achilles explained, "We need to unite and dismiss nationalism." But he was no advocate for universalism; he viewed the issue with bipolar glasses. A multitude of national identities had become an obstacle to containment. Achilles argued that "a world of wholly unregulated national sovereignties is not adequate to deal with modern conditions."[3] The West, he thought, needed to transcend national sovereignties and tighten its global bonds. Washington should provide the necessary guidance to secure the West against the further advancement of communism. Achilles had helped construct the North Atlantic Treaty Organization (NATO) the prior year, but his training and experience as a journalist would help him conceive of other institutions to unite the West under American leadership. Like Achilles, the new assistant secretary of state for public affairs, Edward Barrett, complained in April 1950, "There is not enough unity within the non-Communist world."[4] With events in China, Korea, and even the United States spiraling out of control, and a perception that the West was crumbling from within, diplomats believed that American security concerns had to trump the independent desires of other Western nations. Their worries fed a reevaluation of American foreign policy.

Having worked at CBS, as an editor at *Newsweek*, and then in the Office of War Information (OWI), Barrett embodied the government's solution: bringing media sensibilities to redraft official policy. The result was NSC 68 (officially titled "United States Objectives and Programs for National Security"), written and adopted in 1950. By using NSC 68 as a window into the mind of Cold War policymakers, one finds the general belief that monolithic communism had to be confronted by monolithic Americanism. While analysts have noted the document's prescription of steep increases in military and economic commitments to containment, few have emphasized the multitude of references to ideological and cultural considerations. State Department officials believed that the events of 1949–1950 called for more than merely augmenting the methods that already

existed. NSC 68 marked a turning point from which to revisit the fundamental rationale for the growing Cold War conflict and to evaluate the
shortcomings of the strategic methods employed up to that point. NSC 68,
moreover, heralded the deployment of the government's cultural weapon: a
collection of formal and informal foreign policies that included an idealized
national image, anticommunist dogma, civil defense preparations, and the
funding of many State Department cultural programs abroad.

Policymakers recognized that the nation had passed a watershed
moment. In some respects they viewed 1950 as the beginning of a new era,
just as Pearl Harbor had been. At one meeting in 1950, for example, President Truman looked around the table and expressed relief that he could
rely on the counsel of those present who "had gone through the travail" of
the Second World War. Vice President Alben Barkley warned of another
Pearl Harbor. George Marshall discussed "full mobilization" under the
new Cold War circumstances. "In 1940 we didn't know how to do these
things, but we do now," Truman added. To them, the events surrounding
appeasement of the late 1930s looked similar to the "shocks" of 1949–1950
and called for fresh thinking. Their conclusions would touch the nation's
communications industries.[5]

In his memoirs George Kennan, the director of the State Department's
Policy Planning Staff, recalled that "by and large, the moderate Marshall
Plan approach—an approach aimed at *creating* strength in the West rather
than *destroying* strength in Russia—seemed to have prevailed." But two
years later, Kennan added,

> All this was rapidly changing. A number of disturbing trends were now
> detectable, as a result of which I found myself increasingly concerned over
> the course of American opinion and policy precisely in the area where I
> was thought to have, and fancied myself to have, the greatest influence. . . .
> [Policy planners] could not free themselves from the image of Hitler and
> his timetables. . . . They viewed the Soviet leaders as absorbed with the
> pursuit of something called a "grand design"—a design for the early de-
> struction of American power and for world conquest. In vain I pleaded
> with people to recognize that this was a chimera: that the Russians were
> not like that; that they were weaker than we supposed; that they had
> many internal problems of their own; that they had no "grand design" and
> did not intend, in particular, to pursue their competition with us by means
> of a general war.[6]

Kennan was right. Although the architects of NSC 68 built their strategy on a foundation of containment, it marked a substantial change from

Kennan's original blueprints. Many scholars view NSC 68 as a document "of seminal importance" in the history of American national security policy. John Gaddis has likened it to the United States Constitution, a written law for containment.[7] As such, it is open to interpretation. Indeed, historian Ernest May has recommended going back to NSC 68 "again and again, much as a literary critic goes back to a novel or a poem." One can read NSC 68 as a cultural document, a script of sorts for American foreign policy; such a reading reveals the degree to which policymakers saw communism not only as a threat to American military and economic capabilities but also as a threat to "our values."[8] The discussion of values was not just hyperbolic filler; it was the thesis. In 1950, policymakers came to view the Cold War as a contest over values; therefore, they would seek to fashion cultural programs to reflect the anticommunist "public interest."

Written by Paul Nitze, Kennan's eventual successor as the director of the Policy Planning Staff, the document addressed the rationale and means of American foreign policy in the 1950s and beyond. Nitze's chief contribution to containment was to frame the contest in ideological terms, a move that made sense, given his background. Nitze had headed the nation's Strategic Bombing Survey team at Hiroshima and understood the obvious devastation there, but he also coldly noted that parts of the city regained electric power within a day and public transportation within two, and that victims survived in shelters. Nitze seemed to carry away the lesson that nuclear weapons alone would not necessarily dictate the victors and vanquished in future wars.[9] Later, as an official with the European Recovery Program, Nitze saw firsthand how Europeans feared the expansion of the Red army. Any preparations for "total war" had to acknowledge the limitations of physical force and the reach of psychological instruments.[10]

According to NSC 68, the United States had to expand its scope to touch every part of the globe, not just to defend the perimeter of Soviet influence. When the Soviets detonated their atomic device in 1949, America's lost atomic monopoly reduced the importance of physical borders and increased the need to emphasize, define, and export ideology. Nitze reasoned that the United States had to convey perceptions of American strength in a variety of ways to audiences ranging from policymakers to "mass opinion, foreign as well as domestic, informed as well as uninformed, rational as well as irrational."[11] So, the document also went beyond petitioning for military buildup, covert operations, and economic sacrifices to adding cultural weapons to the nation's arsenal. The willingness of Washington to combine foreign policy and cultural affairs would have a critical influence on the direction of television and other media.

The latest crises convinced many Americans that the double-edged sword of containment was ineffective. The military blade, NATO, had dulled after the Soviet detonation of an atomic device and because of what many foresaw as "eventual parity." Likewise, policy planners doubted the potential of the economic blade, the Marshall Plan, as well. Cold Warriors including Nitze understood that poor economic conditions, as could be found in postwar Europe, "are among the fundamental determinants of the will and the strength to resist subversion and aggression" at the hands of communism. But even after inaugurating the Marshall Plan and Point Four (which included aid to nations outside Europe), after providing special economic assistance for Asian allies, after endorsing loans and credits to Indonesia, Yugoslavia, and Iran, and after imposing trade restrictions on the Soviet bloc, Nitze concluded that solutions lay "not so much in the field of economics as in the field of politics" or political culture. After all, how potent were economic policies of containment after Stalin pressured his satellites to reject Marshall Plan aid? Of course, they were not intended to penetrate the Iron Curtain at all, just to build a bulwark against Soviet expansion. By 1949–1950, though, with parts of the anticommunist alliance "falling" or failing, Truman, Nitze, and others believed that new goals and methods must be formulated.[12]

The Soviets were only one sphere to consider. Even among American allies, the economic arm of containment produced as much indignation as appreciation. India's Jawaharlal Nehru, a leader in the nonaligned movement of nations that rejected Cold War bipolarity, warned that the United States must convince people that democracy could "deliver the goods," both materially *and spiritually*.[13] Though still urging stronger military and economic measures, such as the construction of a hydrogen bomb and increased taxation, essentially Nitze called for the development of cultural weapons based on the ideology of a sanitized national image. The ability to sell America could bring a "closer association of free countries in harmony" along the lines of the Allies during the Second World War. Nitze concluded flatly, "The United States must take steps now to shore up non-military and non-economic power."[14]

Nitze articulated what communications theorists have called cultivation theory, the belief that people are active consumers of culture, "whose interaction with the media comes to cultivate a world view or set of attitudes."[15] Applying this idea to the context of the 1950s, Cold Warriors believed that ideas reinforced constantly in the media could cause people around the world to align their thinking with that of the State Department. Although a military presence and economic assistance certainly fulfilled America's strategic goals, the export of cultural programs would go a long way toward framing people's view of their world, and the super-power contest.

Declaring that a point of "fateful decisions" had arrived, Nitze outlined the nation's "fundamental purpose" for policymakers. His profile of the nation was shared and adopted by like-minded cultural producers in television and other media. The idealized America represented independence and individualism, social equality, civil rights and civil liberties, a free market, and a multiplicity of opinion. Nitze ignored the domestic fascisms and domestic imperialisms that troubled many progressives. Rather than arguing that these scars could best heal in a democracy, Nitze proudly claimed that the nation enjoyed a "deep tolerance" for its "marvelous diversity."

Just as the Second World War promoted the image of a diverse America united in a single purpose, Nitze adopted that image for the Cold War era. At the precise time in 1950 that the Hollywood Ten reported to prison, Senator Margaret Chase Smith publicly rebuked Joseph McCarthy, and UCLA fired 157 employees for refusing to take the loyalty oath, Nitze underscored American unity: even though a democracy is, by definition, made up of competing voices, "essentially, our democracy also possesses a unique degree of unity." Critics noted that Cold Warriors manufactured and even coerced this "unique" consensus. By using the term "unique" as he did, Nitze intended to suggest that the nation was exceptional, compared with its allies, and an obvious leader of weaker-willed democracies against totalitarian communism.[16]

He clarified the incomparable nature of America in another manner, too. Because the national identity could be defined by its antithesis, Nitze characterized the "fundamental design of the Kremlin" in equally stark terms for policymakers. "Animated by a new fanatic faith," the monolithic Other posed a broad threat to the security of the world. If the Kremlin represented oligarchy, the United States emphasized the democracy inherent in its rhetoric. If communism promoted a "perverted faith" in Stalin as its deity, Nitze saw the United States as a beacon of religious toleration. Americans were thoughtful, compassionate, and intelligent; Russian leaders were cold, calculating, and illogical. Nitze's Russian communist was strong, inhuman, rigid, doctrinaire, scientific, cohesive, and united by dictatorial force.

By employing terms such as "evil" and "catastrophic," Nitze cast the new Cold War as an ideological binary: a contest waged between dystopia and Utopia. He summarized the new view of the Soviets in the most stark terms possible: "No other value system is so wholly irreconcilable with ours, so implacable in its purpose as to destroy ours, so capable of turning to its own uses the most dangerous and divisive trends in our own society, no other so skillfully and powerfully evokes the elements of irrationality in human nature everywhere, and no other has the support of a great and growing center of military power."[17] Policymakers relied on the wartime experience to instruct them on how to view the Cold War enemy. They had once drawn distinctions between Germans and Nazis and noted the elementary evil of the Japanese "race." If Kennan viewed the enemy as bad Russians, Nitze viewed them more fundamentally as immoral people espousing a cancerous ideology.

What must be done? "We must make ourselves strong," Nitze wrote. He echoed the complaints of diplomats who worried that the United States appeared "irresolute and desperate." All too often, Nitze added, Americans see Soviet "strength" amid European "disorder." To counteract this harmful perception, influential Americans had to demonstrate "the integrity and vitality of our system" and "the attributes of the nation to the free world."[18] In other words, the United States must present the world with cultural productions that show the moral fortitude of the nation just as they see American economic and military might.

Aside from cultural programs designed to unite Americans, Nitze called for American leadership and hegemony over the Free World. "The absence of order among nations is becoming less and less tolerable," Nitze wrote. The "shocks" of 1949–1950 imposed on the United States "the responsibility of world leadership." Policymakers believed they could deploy a cultural weapon abroad—just as the economic and military weapons had manifested themselves in the Marshall Plan and NATO—with the purpose of managing the "free world" through the export of cultural representations that emphasized virtuous American ideals. Nitze assumed much by referring in the document to the goals of the United States, Germany, Japan, Britain, and France as "our objectives." But he had faith that his vision of the American national identity could be "translated into terms relevant to the lives of other peoples—our system of values can become perhaps a powerful appeal to millions who now seek or find in authoritarianism a refuge from anxieties, bafflement, and insecurity."[19]

For those nations in the developing world, authoritarianism appeared not necessarily in the form of communism but rather in the forms of

West European imperialism and the segregated American South. Indeed, as historian Penny Von Eschen explains, "The Truman administration saw racial discrimination as its Achilles' heel in a propaganda battle with the Soviet Union to win the allegiance of Africa and Asia." Leaders in Washington hoped to lure them under the "free world" banner by accentuating the positive: America's democratic promise with regard to issues of race. Von Eschen has argued that the "politics of symbolic representation" many times superseded any real commitment on the part of politicians to domestic civil rights or anticolonialism abroad. But the "free world" rhetoric illustrated the desire to draw allies closer together, under American leadership, and to draw distinctions between democratic-capitalism and monolithic communism.[20]

Nitze wanted to project American strength internally and to the noncommunist world. Even more ambitiously, he believed that the proliferation of a sanitized American ideal could ultimately "foster a fundamental change in the nature of the Soviet system" itself. Ideology and culture could succeed where military and economic might had failed to disentangle the oppressed people of Eastern Europe (and China, some would add) from their Soviet taskmasters. "The greatest vulnerability of the Kremlin lies in the basic nature of its relations with the Soviet people," Nitze reasoned in the document. By adopting advertising strategies, particular American values could cause a rift between the leaders in the Kremlin and the people outside Red Square, leading in time to the deterioration of communism. According to NSC 68, "If we can make the Russian people our allies in the enterprise, we will obviously have made our task easier and victory more certain." Although this idealistic goal probably met with some skepticism inside the State Department, it certainly bore fruit over time. In sum, policymakers believed that drawing ideological distinctions with the Soviets could fortify anticommunism in the United States, sway opinion in the West and in nonaligned countries toward supporting American leadership in the cause, and even destabilize the Soviet regime.[21]

President Truman and his national security team adopted virtually all the proposals contained in NSC 68. More important, they embraced completely the spirit of its analysis by acknowledging the ideological contest and pursuing the cultural weapon. Even though the Truman and Eisenhower administrations interpreted some passages differently, NSC 68 remained their common handbook.[22] By viewing the threat in global terms, policymakers expanded containment policy in practical terms, by defending more ground and by allowing for a much broader response. This ideological rationale guided them as they developed internal security and civilian defense programs. They waged "overt psychological warfare calculated to encourage mass defections from Soviet allegiance and to frustrate the Kremlin design in other ways." While continuing to confront the Soviet Union with military and economic weapons, they sought to "expose the falsities of Soviet pretensions" and to "foster the seeds of destruction within the Soviet system." Therefore, by 1950 the foreign policy establishment recognized the need to encourage cultural productions based on an ideology favoring the Cold War consensus, to create static for provocateurs peddling multilateralism, and to transmit that sanitized message with the purpose of uniting Americans, uniting the West under American leadership, and undermining the Soviet bloc.[23]

Truman's belief that a revamped containment policy had to be undertaken became "more rather than less urgent since the Korean development" in the summer of 1950.[24] Dramatic events signaled to observers that a new day had dawned for the nation's foreign policy. President Truman inaugurated a worldwide "Campaign of Truth," and Congress increased appropriations for the United States Information Agency (USIA), the Voice of America, and other government-sponsored cultural programming.[25] The moderate brand of containment and its architect, George Kennan, had been swept aside in favor of Nitze's far-reaching vision of confronting the communist menace. Questioning Nitze's approach, George Kennan wrote with dismay in *Life* the following May that by overreacting to the Soviet menace at home and abroad, the nation might become "rather like the representatives of that very power we are trying to combat; intolerant, secretive, suspicious, cruel and terrified of internal dissension because we have lost our own belief in ourselves and in the power of our ideals."[26]

The nature of American diplomacy changed in 1950. One significant recommendation made in NSC 68 was to embrace the view that direct diplomatic negotiations with the Soviet counterparts had become "unacceptable, if not disastrous, to the United States and the rest of the free world."[27] Summits proved comforting to the public and to allies, but Nitze found them fruitless. In the absence of traditional diplomacy, the United States welcomed a new definition of diplomacy, one that included American culture. The government expressed a heightened interest in cultural production and attempted to make it consistent with U.S. military and economic aims. Washington came to understand the potency of the new television medium as a weapon to be waged in the Cold War. To diplomat George V. Allen, who served as assistant secretary of state for public affairs and as director of the USIA, television was not simply an instrument for domestic entertainment; it was indeed a *weapon* in the war against the Soviet Union. Diplomacy, he told one audience, was no longer conducted among diplomats who were "supplied with a pair of striped pants and a top hat," who "dwelt in foreign capitals and dealt with a small group of people in the foreign office of that country." Ambassador Allen understood that the structure of diplomacy had changed in such a way as to incorporate every aspect of each American's life. Diplomatic "negotiations" were just as likely to take place in a textbook or on a television screen as in a palace or on a warship. Instantaneous television transmission, then, became critical to American strategic policy. The portrayal of America and representations of unity were no small considerations. Such illusions could be even more important than the reality.[28]

Static: Interrupting Televised Dissent

The cultural weapon prompted congressional Cold Warriors to take a closer look at television after 1950 with an eye toward cleansing the medium of controversy, alternative visions, and dissent. Members of HUAC drew parallels between their earlier foray into Hollywood and the planned investigation of "un-American activities" in television. According to their annual report for 1951, "The committee hopes that its investigation of Hollywood will have a far-reaching effect and prevent a large-scale future Communist infiltration of the television industry. It is logical to assume that the Communists will endeavor to infiltrate television on a large scale because it is rapidly becoming an important entertainment medium in the United States."[29]

After 1950, the FCC redefined the "public interest" in such a way as to legitimate existing social institutions and to extol the virtues of capitalism. This effort was facilitated by a number of Eisenhower appointments to the commission. In particular, the president won senate confirmation for John C. Doerfer and Robert E. Lee, two friends of Senator Joseph McCarthy and FBI Director J. Edgar Hoover. Although FCC regulators had become notoriously ineffectual, the one weapon in their oversight arsenal was the threat of nonrenewal of broadcast licenses, which allowed commissioners' rhetoric to take on meaning beyond their real power. Doerfer used the transmission of McCarthy's speeches by affiliates as a litmus test of loyalty to country and anticommunism. Commissioners undertook an information campaign, preaching their gospel to businessmen, sponsors, and television affiliates around the country in the mid-1950s.

President Eisenhower confers with NBC executives David Sarnoff, Sylvester "Pat" Weaver, and Robert Sarnoff, 1954. Courtesy Wisconsin Historical Society Image 44104 / NBC / By permission of Sigourney Weaver.

One commissioner likened the public to "shareholders" who owned the American airwaves, the national ether. Another commissioner called upon "Mr. and Mrs. United States" as he deputized them into the anticommunist crusade. The receptive elements in the industry and the public became media watchdogs, encouraged as they were to "lend a hand" in reforming "bad taste programming."[30]

Although audiences may not have concerned themselves with the inner workings of the FCC, several columnists and organizations responded with zeal: American Business Consultants, the American Legion, AWARE, Inc., White Citizens Councils; even Harvard's Conservative League, the Queens College's Intercollegiate Society of Individualists, and Yale's Conservative Society cast eyes on the media. Anticommunist activists promised to patrol the airwaves for fellow travelers, inform the public of their findings, judge the loyalties of transgressors, and organize boycotts against "soft" sponsors. Together these consumer-enforcers made it difficult for network executives to ignore the fact that anticommunism made good business sense. As Tom Englehardt has written,

"The guardians of television were few in number . . . and they guarded the gate fiercely against apostasy of every sort. Anything appearing on screen was to be vetted for the aberrant, impure, or un-American. Inside that screen, fortress America fought back, defending itself against the ambushes of the forces of evil."[31]

Within months, anticommunists issued the famous 200-page report titled *Red Channels: The Report of Communist Influence in Radio and Television*. With little regard for whether performers were innocents, dupes, or outright "Reds," anticommunist vigilantes condemned an industry that allowed communist sympathizers to "boost" more than 150 subversives "to stardom." The list published in *Red Channels* included many members of the old Hollywood Democratic Committee (HDC) and its many incarnations: HICCASP, ICCASP, and ASP-PCA.[32] It also included two who figure prominently in the next chapter: playwrights Lillian Hellman and Arthur Miller. The blacklist had arrived in the television industry.

Although Chayefsky, Serling, Rose, and many other writers of anthology dramas were not blacklisted outright, networks did "graylist" them in some ways. That is, networks tried to balance the concerns of anticommunist activists with the sustained popularity of anthologies among the silent majority of viewers, and even though none of these high-profile writers held direct ties to radical political organizations worthy of blacklisting, networks limited their involvement in the production process to a remarkable degree. Even the most prolific and successful writers felt forced into the tedium of revisions; networks often created distance between the writer and his original script, a buffer populated by a committee of proxies. Chayefsky complained that his work was "frequently mangled" by others without his knowledge.[33] Writers were kept away from rehearsals, left to learn what had happened just as "their" words went out on a live broadcast. Director Delbert Mann explained that networks blithely requested "more conventional" material and "some different kinds of stories."[34] These routine frustrations prompted many writers to seek work in other venues, including overseas.

Aside from employing both blacklist and graylist, the networks redefined the "public interest" ethic in terms that turned artistic presentations into commodities. The networks came to view the industry in even greater business terms and saw themselves as middlemen between the sponsor's product and the consumer's eyes. Once, RCA chairman David Sarnoff explained his company's role as that of "a plumber laying a pipe. We're not responsible for what goes through the pipe." The government, the public, sponsors, and broadcasters all understood their new roles as coproducers of television content. Sarnoff argued in 1950 that "[we must] convert [our] *products* into the necessary *weapons* of war."[35] If executives viewed cultural productions as weapons, they also came to view talent as technicians. Networks checked virtually all talent before allowing such people to work on a project. Those uncleared seldom knew why, because blacklists, as common as they had become, remained extralegal.

The threat of boycott and public shaming convinced many a sponsor and ad company to take charge of programs. Director Arthur Penn remembered the sponsor's transformation from benign neglect to malignant interference: "In the beginning, the dramatic shows were not of any great interest to the advertising agencies. Philco had a benign agency until the end of 1953 when they discovered people were indeed watching, and, lo and behold, we felt their hot breath. It started with, 'Oh, God, is she going to say that?' or 'Can you get her not to have such a dirty nose?' The pressure got worse and worse."[36]

General Electric, for example, in 1953 entered the growing field of sponsors producing anthology dramas. That same year Joseph McCarthy announced plans to investigate GE's 131 defense plants for subversives and security risks. In December 1953 the corporate board announced plans to cleanse itself by firing all "Reds" and suspending anyone who refused to testify. A few months later the board hired a new host for its weekly program, someone who could lend an air of anticommunist respectability to the proceedings: Ronald Reagan. In its eight years on television, *General Electric Theater* became known as something of a departure from other anthologies for producing biopics, bible stories, melodramas, and westerns. Unlike so many others, this show catered to those viewers wishing to avoid the educator.[37]

Timid censors who had once used routine censorship to allow creativity and realism soon stifled controversial dialogue and themes. Serling remembered one *Kraft Television Theater* teleplay that presented a minister in an unsympathetic light. The network reaction, he recalled, "was violent, quick and frightening." Even the most trite and annoying revisions (those that prompt guffaws in hindsight) were notable for their routine nature. Paddy Chayefsky observed that the writer was becoming "treated with a peculiar mixture of mock deference and outright contempt." Sometimes words such as "hell" were replaced with "Devil," and "damn" with "blast you!" Serling considered it a victory when he traded censors two "damns" for a "hell." Not surprisingly, Reginald Rose was less successful when he pleaded, "Look, I'll take out the second 'son of a bitch' if you give me one 'fuck you.' "[38] With the pretense of protecting the imagined audience for the "public good," censors at first dickered over dialogue and then expanded the realm of the unacceptable to include wholesale thematic changes.

In a new atmosphere that glorified capitalism, many revisions came at the corporate sponsor's request. Serling liked to tell the story of how one play for the CBS show *Appointment with Adventure* had to be revised: he was instructed to change the word "lucky" to "fortunate" because the cigarette company sponsoring the show did not want the original word to call up its competitor, Lucky Strike, in the minds of the audience. Serling was saddened to find out that they were *not* kidding. Another time, the American Gas Association, sponsor of *Judgment at Nuremberg*, allowed reference to sexual sterilization and images of graphic concentration camp footage but prohibited mention of the lethal use of gas during the Holocaust. In yet another case, executives at Westinghouse urged the producers of *Studio One* to change the title of Rudyard Kipling's age-old *The Light That Failed* to *The Gathering Light* because Westinghouse relied so heavily on its production of light bulbs. What went under the radar of the sponsor was the theme of lesbianism in the script. Director Wellington Miner recalled that Westinghouse was "so consumed with anguish over that failing bulb, they had no time to notice that they had, at one and the same time, given their stamp of approval to a blaringly homosexual love story." Even when sponsors did not overtly seek to change the content, in Serling's opinion, the ads they inserted into the programs "hurt the flow, the continuity and the build" to the point that commercials "dilute the effect of any play."[39]

The original argument for habitual censorship had been turned upside down. Where once Stockton Helffrich used the "blue pencil" to protect progressive themes, to promote the "unsponsorable," now the network called on him to accept the new decree. By the mid-1950s, Helffrich framed his job in terms of protecting the family. Just as he had earlier defined censorship in vague terms, Helffrich now proclaimed with surety, "It's a common-sense flagging of problems that come along in scripts or films." He admitted that he held wide, arbitrary power to decide "what is, and what is not, good taste." Ignoring the contradiction between changing definitions of "good taste," he demanded that problems "meet the requirements of family audiences."[40] White, nuclear families, one could be assured, were the norm he was trying to protect. Instead of using the medium's position in the home as an opportunity to explore controversial issues and to represent a diverse nation in a realistic manner, network executives were arguing that television's special place in the private sphere served as a potential threat to the very families they had once promised to uplift.

Despite the changing environment, amid all this meddling there was compromise. Certainly it frustrated many writers: Serling wrote that television had gone from "a medium best suited to illuminate and dramatize the issues of the times" to a "product pressed into a mold, painted lily-white," and one that had had "its dramatic teeth yanked one by one." But some writers became satisfied with simply raising certain issues when they could. Their willingness to compromise, to blunt some edges in their scripts, allowed the dramas to continue, albeit in a neutered form. Playwright Reginald Rose admitted later, "I was surprised I got away with the stuff I did. Television was so sensitive to criticism, and the criticism almost always came from the right. The network people were really petrified for their jobs. Yet, they were also afraid of being that way, so sometimes things got through."[41]

Playwrights and screenwriters attached a public purpose to their Cold War scripts. Of course, scripts can be read in different ways. They wrote about personal concerns to be sure—a son's relation to a distant father, a disillusioned wife, a worker nearing retirement—but even such personal issues took on a political dimension during the Cold War.[42] In many cases writers expressed their political views through the mouths of their characters; individuals in government, business, and the arts—in the West, behind the Iron Curtain, and around the world—politicized private behavior. Instead of endlessly searching scripts for political commentary, the harder task may be to locate scripts totally devoid of such content.

Rod Serling's *Patterns* (1955), for example, pits a young, up-and-coming executive against the aging, sickly, naive businessman he hopes to replace. After the old man literally works himself to death, the guilt-ridden young man declines his promotion with a lecture for his corporate boss. Serling was questioning a capitalist system that undervalued loyalty, ethics, and the individual while it overemphasized ruthless competition. The play sardonically attacked Defense Secretary Charles Wilson's notion that "what was good for our country was good for General Motors, and vice versa." At a time when comparisons between capitalism and communism had become routine, anthologies presented American audiences with a view that challenged acceptance of even the most elementary American creeds.[43]

Another tenet of universalism, one that Wendell Willkie and Hollywood writers had espoused years earlier, was a double-barreled attack on colonialism, regardless of the colonizing country's strategic relationship with Washington. Such was the case with Reginald Rose's 1959 drama, *The Cruel Day*, which appeared on *Playhouse 90*. The story explored the precarious French-Algerian situation as it played out in one family. A dutiful French captain joins an assault force searching for Algerian rebels and cooperates in the bloody massacre of an entire family. Filled with regret, the captain then doubts the morality of maintaining empires. When he returns home and spies his fifteen-year-old son plucking the wings off a defenseless butterfly, he launches into a violent rage and slaps the boy because he realizes that the colonial mentality has taken root in the next generation, right under his own roof. Originally titled "The Atrocity," the play showed colonialism beyond the patriotic platitudes and the supposed "need" for violence when controlling an "inferior" people. It shifted the debate away from sympathizing with colonial people—which Rose surely appreciated—and forced viewers to understand that such enterprises wear on the consciences of colonizers as well. Democracies lose their meaning when they engage in or support these endeavors. As embarrassing as this program was to the French, Rose hoped that viewers would ultimately question America's increasing involvement in the affairs of Latin America and Southeast Asia.[44]

Writers also illustrated America's "domestic imperialisms" as diplomats fended off similar embarrassing reminders abroad. How difficult it must have been for foreign service officers in the summer of 1955 to press France on its dealings with its North African colonies in the very same week that a young African American named Emmett Till was lynched in Mississippi. Civil rights leaders linked their struggle with colonization, a tie that *Time* recognized when it reported, "Today's drive of the U.S. Negro toward equality is as strong as any social tide in Asia or Africa or Europe." Confronting the race issue was difficult but necessary in the minds of television writers, in part because the subject was actually part of the much larger global issues of anticolonialism and self-determination.[45]

Both Reginald Rose and Rod Serling drafted outlines based on the notorious Till lynching, and both earned a remarkable public response. Even before it was telecast, news of Serling's *Noon on Doomsday* (1956) prompted 15,000 threatening letters, written primarily by members of southern White Citizens Councils, to flood the producers' offices in New York City. Scared producers ordered modifications. When Serling refused, thirty sober editors immediately went to work on revisions in over a dozen different meetings. In the end Coca-Cola products were removed because they were so strongly identified with the South. The word "lynch" was completely omitted from the script. And the killer became "just a good, decent, American boy momentarily gone wrong." Editors went so far as to take the episode out of the South altogether and place it in a small, bucolic New England town. Serling grumbled, "The agency would've placed the play at the North Pole if it hadn't been for the necessary inclusion of Eskimos, which would prove still another minority problem." Similarly, Rose's *Tragedy in a Temporary Town* (1956) courted controversy, endured adjustments, and enjoyed critical success from liberal groups.[46]

Several anthology dramas more directly targeted American foreign policy. Writers scolded U.S. allies for their colonial activities, promoted pacifism, and portrayed nuclear hysteria. Given the potential for atomic disaster, the government counseled preparation, whereas television expressed anxiety. The Federal Civil Defense Administration and the Office of Civil and Defense Mobilization struggled to offer a consistent, coherent civil defense plan to meet the atomic threat. Debates among competing institutions, responding to the dictates of different administrations and constituencies, severely limited its success. From the government's perspective, atomic testing could be portrayed as routine, scientifically important, and a search for knowledge that would be used to allay fears rather than heighten them. Historian Paul Boyer writes of ideas "ranging from the merely unrealistic to the totally bizarre, that quickly took on a formulaic, almost hypnotic quality, as if the entire nation were caught up in a kind of collective trance about the nuclear Utopia ahead." Government spokesmen buried reporters under reams of statistical data: tonnage, distances, radiation levels, numbers of potential victims.[47]

Atomic tests also confronted the artistic community. Just before sunrise on February 2, 1951, an eight-kiloton bomb exploded over Frenchman Flat, Nevada, and brought the first dawn of the day. It's safe to say that most citizens saw their shadows on that Groundhog Day in Los Angeles, a mere 300 miles away. Other tests throughout the 1950s reminded Americans on a daily basis about the possibility for imminent doom.

While Serling wrote a script on atomic testing, the Atomic Energy Commission (AEC) took pains to reassure Americans by arguing that atomic testing enhanced personal security; it did not necessitate panic. After the atomic test at Eniwetok in May 1951, General James Cooney announced, "The immediate radiation hazard from [an] air burst disappeared after the first two minutes. Rescue . . . work can begin immediately in any area where there is life." The disappearance of danger and the preservation of life were appealing themes amid testing. Yet the AEC went further by essentially domesticating the bomb: in March 1951 it made a public announcement to the American Institute of Architects that "special efforts would be made to gain information useful to architects trying to design atom-resistant buildings." Westinghouse was a pioneer in the development of products to fill those architects' creations. Westinghouse president Gwilym Price declared, "I believe that we are within five years of the beginning of commercial atomic power." The company envisioned a day in the not too distant future when its television spokeswoman Betty Furness would showcase a Westinghouse atomic toaster in what *Time* referred to as her "electrified Utopia."[48]

But Serling's fear of proliferation outweighed his sense of security in 1952 when the British detonated an atomic bomb and the United States successfully tested the hydrogen "Super," a nuclear fusion device immensely more powerful than previous weapons. The following March, Americans learned that diligent Westinghouse workers toiled on the *Nautilus* nuclear submarine project as well as atomic elevators. In all, the government conducted over 100 atmospheric tests at a surreal "doomtown" in Nevada's Yucca Flats, where suburban mannequins clothed in neckties and aprons stood beside household appliances and full pantries. When he put pen to paper, Serling questioned bomb tests and concluded that such events were destabilizing forces, not instructive exercises.[49]

Given the bureaucratic rivalries within government and the mixed messages emanating from government, anthology writers stepped in to interpret civil defense for Americans. They encouraged full disclosure of nuclear tests and questioned the government's ability to promote preparation without unleashing hysteria. In *Nightmare at Ground Zero* (1953), *Mr. Finchley versus the Bomb* (1954), and *Forbidden Area* (1956), Serling squarely placed the consequences of "brinkmanship" and "rollback"— terms associated with accepted American foreign policy—before the audience. He personalized atomic testing and showed it as something volatile and potentially catastrophic for ordinary Americans.

Soon after the Yucca Flats tests, Serling's *Nightmare at Ground Zero* (1953) appeared on the CBS program *Suspense* as a dark comedy challenging the government's portrayal of the atomic threat. It's a warm September evening in the Yucca Flats of Nevada. Amid the preparations for another atomic test—they occur every two weeks—the audience enters the home of George and Helen. George is a nebbish mannequin-maker who builds "dummies" that permit the military to gauge the destructive force of their tests. Helen, however, is tired of her absent, atomic-obsessed husband and nags him to the breaking point. Finally, she screams in terror at the possibility of enduring another frightening test without him and demands to accompany him to the next one. George manages to place his sedated wife, disguised as one of his "dummies," into the test house before the blast. The audience hangs in suspense over whether she will be saved from the explosion. Ultimately, the audience has been persuaded into caring about the survival of a single stranger. How could they *not* care about the potential of many more innocent victims in a real explosion?

While atomic bombs proliferated and the government sought ways to domesticate the bomb in the minds of Americans, Serling thus confronted the issue head on. In the contest between atomic security and atomic fear, Serling placed himself on the side of fear. The teleplay opens with the picture of a gate that bears a sign: "Restricted Area—Keep Out"; on the inside are armed guards. In effect, he is saying that the bomb is off limits and can never be contained or used by citizens in the beneficial ways the government and business had promised. Rather, Americans are reduced to the nonthinking "dummies" the military has carefully placed inside a home. Indeed, military planners in the teleplay and in the real world became fixated on superficial realism for their tests: a father complete with smoking jacket and slippers; a mother in a dress and stockings. One painter complains to another, "Even dummies yet. And not just any place. Father here. Mother there. An' for what? At four a.m. they drop an A-bomb on it—an' there ain't nothin' left anyhow." The other painter responds, "Kinda creepy, ain't it? Looks like a house. Furnished like a house. But it ain't a house. At four in the morning—*it's Ground Zero!*" Serling explains to audiences that George and the advocates of atomic testing are so caught up with individual tests that they "don't care that I'm frightened to death!" And yet, as real as the mannequins are, they are not human. How bad can the results be if they kill objects that only "bleed plaster-of-paris," Serling wonders.

Serling addresses radioactivity as well. A military officer in charge whispers to the mannequin "father" with a smirk, "Well old man, this is it! By morning you'll be just so much dust. Dangerous dust I'll wager, too," he winks. "Radioactive, you know." It is the secret that few openly discuss or understand. Later, after having placed Helen in the house, George, filled with guilt, comforts himself with the knowledge that his comatose wife "won't feel a thing. They tell me it's so quick." The audience knows, of course, that if she survives the blast, this is a false promise indeed. In the end, he spares her life.

The next year Serling returned to ground zero with *Mr. Finchley versus the Bomb* (1954) on NBC's *Kaiser Aluminum Hour*. It is the story of a lone elderly man who temporarily halts an atomic test. Why return to the topic? For Serling, the issue only grew in importance. By 1954 the nuclear stakes had changed dramatically. In January, John Foster Dulles explained to the Council on Foreign Relations, "Local defense must be reinforced by the further deterrent of massive retaliatory power. . . . The way to deter aggression is for the free community to be willing and able to respond vigorously at places and with means of its own choosing." By mentioning "more security at less cost" (a phrase famously bastardized as "more bang for the buck") Dulles calmly explained the reliance on weapons of mass destruction. This message was made only more clear by the launching of the first nuclear submarine, the *Nautilus*, less than ten days later. The doctrine of massive retaliation was accompanied into American homes by Serling's drama. The government's continuing test schedule convinced Serling that he had to reach audiences once again. This second script, coming as it did on the heels of the first, confirms the political nature of his cultural product. Months later, Serling joined and became an active member of the Hollywood chapter of the national Committee for a Sane Nuclear Policy (SANE), which pushed the Eisenhower administration toward adopting a testing moratorium and a comprehensive nuclear test ban treaty.[50]

Aside from anticolonialism and atomic testing, TV writers also emphasized the ambiguity of American involvement in the Korean War. To be sure, unheroic portrayals of soldiers courted controversy, but perhaps the fact that so many of these writers and directors had served in uniform made them immune to the most blistering attacks by the American Legion. In *The Strike* (1954), Serling showed an American soldier's anguish at being forced by his superiors to fire on fellow Americans. His teleplay expressed his opposition to the war, as he explained a few years later: "*The Strike* for example was written in 1953 when the Korean situation in the American mind *was* an emotional problem. Its politics were muddled and unclear; its morality was questionable; its point and purpose lost from view."[51] (Notably, *The Strike* aired on the tenth anniversary of D-Day.) Likewise, the *U.S. Steel Hour* debuted in November 1953 with *P.O.W.*, a teleplay one critic praised for its "competent acting, adult themes and an intellectual daring not common on television." Similarly, in *The Sergeant* (1952), Serling took viewers inside the mind of an American soldier confined to a prisoner-of-war camp.[52]

As the Korean belligerents had agreed to Panmunjom as the site for truce talks the previous fall, Serling focused on the human element within the unfolding drama. Negotiations bogged down on the nettlesome POW issue, and amid reports of communist "brainwashing" of American captives, Serling considered the novel notion that a handful of American soldiers might not wish to return home.[53]

In *The Sergeant*, as news circulates around the camp that prisoners will be released, the youngest among them, Ray, sits in silent apprehension. Why is he not jubilant? his friend Rosie asks. Although tormented, tortured, and starved, Rosie wonders who would dare "crack" and stay with the Chinese? Ray's father, a back-slapping ward boss preparing to run for governor, had sacrificed his family for his ambitions. The politician proudly talked up the mythical exploits of his son in Korea, the courage and success, characteristics Ray knew were not his. Serling showed how American policymakers had sacrificed their sons for a bogus victory. Even though Ray came home—he was no traitor or coward—both men had learned from the experience and grown closer. As Serling concludes, "Men who can conquer fears and can destroy hatreds—they are the brave ones." Teleplays touching on the Korean War allowed audiences to conclude that such brutal conflict opened emotional wounds as much as physical ones. Serling showed that this ambivalent war created victims even as it valorized those victims as heroes.

Indeed, writers cast skeptical eyes at hero worship, especially during the McCarthy era. Writers fought to preserve treasured American civil liberties, abuses of which were made most apparent by Joseph McCarthy. Serling spent nineteen months, more time than on any other script, crafting an attack on anticommunist excesses in *The Rack* (1955). "I took an agonizing national problem, the root of which dug deep into the morality and conscience of a country," he remembered immodestly, "and treated it honestly, fairly, and effectively." Like Serling, Reginald Rose attacked McCarthyism in *An Almanac of Liberty* (1954). Rose explained, "Issues that bother me are issues concerning people who want to impose their beliefs on others. . . . In a way, almost everything I wrote in the fifties was about McCarthy." Together, Serling and Rose showed that Stalinist-styled "show trials" were hardly alien to Americans.[54]

Writers excoriated as hypocrites those who undermined the very democratic principles they espoused, but also questioned subtle notions of American exceptionalism. Portraying the United States as the world's leading democracy fulfilled the designs of NSC 68. By planning "to build and maintain confidence among other peoples in our strength and resolution," Nitze and his successor, Robert Bowie, hoped the West would unite under American leadership. As historian Reinhold Wagnleitner put it, "In an effort to solidify the political claim to leadership, it was essential to prove that the United States was no longer in its infancy and that it had reached cultural and artistic maturity." Defense against Soviet treachery provided one rationale for nations to fall in line, but emphasizing American distinctiveness, uprightness, and historical destiny offered another.[55]

Cold Warriors valued themes of unity and conformity, especially on the race issue. In the spring of 1954, millions of Americans tuned in to CBS's popular anthology drama program, *Studio One*. On one night viewers watched Reginald Rose's original teleplay *Thunder on Sycamore Street*. In the two weeks preceding that broadcast, the State Department rejected playwright Arthur Miller's passport application to tour Europe; Puerto Rican nationalists shot five Congressmen in the House of Representatives chamber; journalist Edward R. Murrow chastised Senator Joseph McCarthy on his nationwide broadcast; and the Vietminh assaulted the French installation at Dien Bien Phu. Amid these events, and just weeks before the Supreme Court announced its landmark *Brown v. Board of Education* decision, the audience watched Rose's racially charged drama.

The play began after Betty Furness seduced her viewers into buying Westinghouse kitchen appliances from her "electrified Utopia."[56] Rose's story dealt with the quiet community of Eastmount, where an angry mob gathers to remove by force an ex-convict who has just settled in their neighborhood. At a critical moment the protagonist is literally stoned while standing on his front porch. Rose's main characters, however, are not the man and woman seeking to reside in Eastmount, but Phyllis and Arthur Hayes, two conscience-bound neighbors who undoubtedly represent the viewers at home.

PHYLLIS. We're going to be just like everybody else on Sycamore Street.
ARTHUR, *shouting*. Phyllis! I've told you. I'm not going to be a part of this thing!
PHYLLIS, *after a pause*. Listen to me, Artie. We're going out there. Do you want to know why? Because we're not going to be next.
ARTHUR. You're out of your mind!
PHYLLIS, *shouting*. Sure I am! I'm crazy with fear, because I don't want to be different. I don't want my neighbors looking at us and wondering why we're not like them. . . . They'll look the other way when we walk the streets. They'll become cold and nasty. We can't be different!

We can't afford it! We live on the good will of these people. Your business is in this town. Your neighbors buy us the bread we eat! Do you
want them to stop?

ARTHUR. I don't know, Phyllis. I don't know what to think. I can't throw
a stone at this man.

PHYLLIS. You can! You've got to, or we're done for here.[57]

Given the restrictive times, it may come as little surprise that Rose's
original script detailed what occurred when an African American family
moved into a northern white town. Fearing public criticism (which they
received anyway), sponsors and network officials forced Rose to replace
the black man with a parolee. The theme, however, remained substantially intact as Rose challenged conformity and prejudice.

His views elicited a nationalistic backlash. The network switchboard
lit up that night. "You *Studio One* Commies! If you don't like this place,
why don't you get out?!" a viewer reportedly barked to an unsuspecting
operator. By invoking a political epithet to characterize the cultural exploration of racial issues, viewers situated popular culture within a Cold
War context. Almost immediately television had become a political instrument in the eyes of the writers, the sponsors, the government, and
the audience. In many cases viewers considered what they saw on television as representative of themselves, their neighbors, and their enemies.
As Americans sat comfortably in their living rooms, they accepted, rejected, and adapted themes into what can be considered an emerging Cold
War national identity.[58]

Racial disharmony directly challenged Nitze's belief of a democracy diverse in opinion but united in purpose. Paddy Chayefsky's *Holiday Song*
(1952) undermined the crusade against "atheistic, godless communism" by
showing three-dimensional Americans who have reason to question their
religious convictions from time to time. In this case, a cantor cannot sing
for the Jewish New Year services because the Holocaust has shaken his
faith. The drama is notable for three reasons: it is based on a true story; it
spotlights a minority group; and it questions the existence of God. When
pitching the idea to producer Fred Coe, the self-proclaimed "WASP from
Mississippi," Chayefsky purposely identified the main character as a Meth-
odist minister. Coe, who had already learned of the untraditional subject
matter from the newspaper, reminded his Jewish writer that the character
was also Jewish and insisted on producing the play as originally intended.

Complex or dark themes stood in contrast to standard portrayals of
Americans, especially those exported by the USIA, which distributed

films including *The Life of President Eisenhower*, religious epics, and the musical *Oklahoma!* to over eighty countries in twenty-seven languages. Government and business, in this case Hollywood studios and distributors, worked closely to cleanse the image of America. Government-sanctioned cultural exports detailed economic assistance programs, dispensed anticommunist propaganda, extolled the virtues of capitalism, hailed the melting pot, and promised the freedoms of consumer choice. Meanwhile, Europeans favored more subversive offerings such as Brando, jazz, and *Marty*.[59]

Paddy Chayefsky's *Marty* (1953) is a celebration of American mediocrity over the heroic. In the boy-meets-girl story, the boy is a middle-aged butcher who falls in love with a girl regarded as a "dog." Marty is constantly nagged by his mother and neighbors about getting married. "Why don't you find somebody?" they all ask. Marty explains sheepishly, "I'm a little, short, fat, ugly guy." He would rather wallow in pity surrounded by his buddies. "What do you want to do tonight?" one asks another. "I don't know. What do you want to do tonight?" he responds. "I don't know," and so it goes. They are directionless and apathetic, a group of followers devoid of leaders. Finally, Marty summons the courage to go stag to a dance and reaches out to a gangly loner, only to find out that his mother disapproves of her.

Calling *Marty* "the most ordinary love story in the world," Chayefsky rebelled against what he called America's "shallow and destructive illusions" by delving into the Oedipal relationship, virility, and homosexuality. Marty lacks ambition and is satisfied with his working-class status. His most satisfying loves are relationships with his best friend and with his mother. He seeks out a girlfriend reluctantly, and only then at the insistence of his neighbors. Chayefsky reacted against a cinematic history full of robust masculinity and glamorous femininity. He rejected the notion "that love is simply a matter of physical attraction, that virility is manifested by a throbbing phallus, and that regular orgasms are all that's needed to make a woman happy. These values are dominant in our way of life and need to be examined for what they are." Many of Chayefsky's protagonists were not witty, suave, or classy; they were weak, troubled, sensitive, hesitant, and effeminate. Their dialogue was written "as if it had been wire-tapped."[60] Tight studios, rudimentary sets, poor lighting, and the absence of editing led directors to employ close-ups, allowing the human face to become, in Barnouw's words, "the stage on which drama was played."[61] The effect let audiences see Americans like themselves with physical and emotional scars—hardly the typical fare from Hollywood.

Emotive acting contributed to the unique character of the anthology drama. It emphasized realism over a more sanitized illusion and looked remarkably like European (especially Russian) performance techniques. "Method acting" was sweeping the New York artistic community. The Actors Studio, founded in 1947 in the United States, was based on the teachings of the Soviet actor and director Konstantin Stanislavski. Teachers such as the blacklisted anthology director Martin Ritt called for actors to perform "naturally, to so infuse one's own self with the thoughts, emotions and personality of the character that one became the character." Actors were to draw upon personal experiences in order to understand their characters and thereby make their performances more real. Rod Steiger's interpretation of *Marty* is but one example of a method actor filling the screen with a realistic portrayal. "I tried to make it like it was happening to me. I think the thing that worked with me in *Marty* was the loneliness I had in my childhood."[62]

Delbert Mann, who directed *Marty*, remembered the outpouring of audience emotion. "That show brought more phone calls and letters than any show we ever did," he recalled. "They were universally, 'My God, that's the story of my life. How could you have played it so truly?' People were crying on the phone." What resonated with the public was that, in Chayefsky's words, "the main characters are typical, rather than exceptional." By contrast, state-sponsored cultural offerings appeared banal.[63]

At the same time, foreign policymakers hoped to raise confidence among Americans, strengthen leadership over the West, and instill fear in the Kremlin. Was Marty the exceptional American man who could achieve these goals? No, according to some quarters inside the government. Recently released House Un-American Activities Committee documents show that *Marty* raised eyebrows all along the anticommunist front. "I don't know what Chayefsky's present orientation is," one investigator wrote in a memo. "A few years ago, he was the subject of heated discussion in the Communist press . . . and in Communist circles in New York. . . . The motion picture for which he is chiefly famous, 'Marty,' is very highly regarded in the Iron Curtain countries."[64] Just as the American government sought to sanitize national identity for domestic and global consumption, anthologies appeared to focus on nagging social problems. By formulating themes to spotlight the "ordinary" and make them acceptable, these writers challenged Cold War America's developing self-image.[65]

By the late 1950s, the anthology drama was in steady decline for several reasons. In 1955 David Sarnoff commissioned a consulting firm to study NBC from the top down for mismanagement and inefficiency. Anthology drama programs—fiefdoms of progressive thought—came under scrutiny. As media scholar Vance Kepley Jr. has found, "Weaver's policy of autonomous production units might have been useful when the company needed to develop new shows quickly, but it provided few mechanisms for holding down costs." New middle managers and profit-minded executives, "which Weaver had purged or bypassed," now held great influence over the direction of the company and its programming schedules. During Christmas week that year, David Sarnoff removed Pat Weaver—the man who had proved so instrumental in supporting the "unsponsorable"—in favor of Robert Sarnoff, the chairman's son. Their agenda included instituting a corporate structure and cutting costs. The anthology drama was a casualty of this new thinking. The emphasis on corporate thinking rather than on a democratizing medium doomed televised dissent. Anticommunists and capitalist cost-cutters combined to stifle progressive teleplays.[66]

The American Broadcasting Company (ABC), a weak competitor of NBC and CBS, helped to change the face of television as a whole. In 1953 the FCC commissioners disregarded any worries they may have felt over all-powerful media conglomerates by agreeing to a merger between ABC and United Paramount Theatres. Of all companies, Paramount symbolized the old Hollywood abuses that the *Paramount* antitrust decision had intended to address. As Balio concluded, the FCC believed "combination might improve ABC's programming and [its] ability to attract sponsors and affiliates."[67] Although perhaps unintended, the "improvement" of programming increasingly included favoring affordable, old, acceptable Hollywood films over topical, controversial, live television plays.

The marriage between Hollywood and television was consummated the next year when ABC signed a contract with Walt Disney to produce a weekly promotional program titled *Disneyland*. Here the great entrepreneur blended his motion pictures, his theme park, and his television program for American eyes. Disney's achievement is largely credited with persuading other Hollywood studios to follow suit, but one cannot overlook that Disney's idealized America played a significant role in his success.[68] Disney took a nostalgic look back at "Frontierland" and had many smiling children (and presidential candidate Estes Kefauver) don coonskin caps. Disneyland's "Main Street" was the vision of clean, white picket fences in small-town America. Even "Tomorrowland" romanticized the future by portraying the nuclear family gathering around the glow of its electrical consumer goods. As blacklisted director Martin Ritt explained, Disney productions "were considered totally without message. That's childish. They certainly weren't without message. They were selling a different parcel of food, which the American public and the world public was prepared to buy." To Fred Coe, the prominent producer of anthology dramas, networks "lowered television" by introducing "their *Disneyland* public relations shows." He grumbled, "They didn't care about anything but the ratings."[69]

The same month that *Disneyland* premiered, another independent producer showed Hollywood how to make it in television: the master showman, David O. Selznick. On Sunday, October 24, 1954, Selznick produced a spectacular titled *Lights Diamond Jubilee* for simultaneous transmission over all four major television networks. Simply put, Selznick bludgeoned the audience by extolling the virtues of Cold War America. To entertain viewers at home for two hours, he spent over $300,000, hired some fourteen celebrities, relied on filmed sequences from five units and six directors, and included two orchestras. More than 90 percent of televisions tuned in to see the exceptional nature of America, replete with an appearance by President Dwight Eisenhower himself, then recuperating in Denver from his heart attack. Selznick had offered Albert Einstein the chance to appear playing his violin over the laudatory label "The man who launched the atomic age." With the image in his mind of fiddling while Hiroshima burned, Einstein refused. The humanitarian did not wish to be a part of a national celebration that remembered him for shepherding his one world into a Cold War.[70]

Nevertheless, Selznick was thrilled to revive his post–*Gone with the Wind* career in an emerging television age. He breathlessly dictated a wire to his friend the publishing magnate Henry Luce, trumpeting his success and urging Luce to report the glory in one of his many magazines. Selznick's was the first commercially sponsored show on which any president of the United States had appeared, "the first to weave editorial content into an entertainment pattern" with "a single theme throughout," and "the first to present in entertainment terms the story of private enterprise's contribution to the building of America in anything like these terms." For his efforts, Selznick received "gigantic mail from the public," proving to him that his program "had a tremendous impact on them in terms of their faith in the future, their faith in God and their feeling as Americans. These were my objectives and the hope of achieving this was my motivation in the concept and execution of the show." Disney and Selznick blended showmanship and salesmanship. They and others sold an idealized vision of the nation that suited American foreign policy at the time.[71]

Prestige dramas increasingly became network "specials," offering serious discussion of social issues as something extraordinary rather than something customary and acceptable. In 1954–1955 these "specials" consumed only forty-one hours of airtime for the season. In 1959–1960, however, live dramatic "specials" accounted for 246 hours of programming.[72] In other cases, socially conscious themes became encoded in seemingly harmless science fiction programs such as *Star Trek*. Beginning in October 1959 on CBS, Rod Serling used his new show *The Twilight Zone* as an outlet for his views on war, atomic testing, race, capitalism, and anticommunism. By the end of the 1950s, anthologies gave way to what one media critic has called "Eisenhower *Walden*"—programming genres extolling the virtues of placid domesticity: the situation comedy and quiz shows.[73]

The domestic situation comedy proved to be a genre well suited for portraying the ideal America. There were close ties between nation and family in the 1950s. Both required corporate organization, sturdy leadership, and obedient citizenship. Both also required vigilance to ensure security. As television producer Norman Lear recalled, the televised family of the 1950s was portrayed "as a protective shield, warding off external forces. Home was happy, secure, serene. If tempests arose, they would ultimately be calmed there as well, and nothing ever suggested that the security could fail." A plethora of such programs promoted placid domesticity as well as racial and gendered conformity in this era. Women were homemakers, uniformly attentive to the needs of their husbands, children, and nation. They happily wore cosmetics, jewelry, and aprons surgically attached to their petite waists.

Guilt and manipulation were used to enforce compliance to society's rules in these "family melodramas." This marked a change from similar programs prior to the mid-1950s which depicted working-class families (*Life of Riley*, *The Honeymooners*). The older programs "lacked an emphasis on familial love and relationships, moral transgression, and lessons learned." That emphasis "was to come . . . [in] the mid-to-late 1950s."[74] This shift toward "living room lectures" coincided with the initial decline of the anthology drama.

One value imparted to viewers was that of consumption. Whereas advertising annoyed writers and distracted viewers of anthology dramas, household consumption was heartily embraced in the domestic comedies. Harriet Nelson, the female lead in the wildly successful *Ozzie and*

Harriet series, turned toward the camera to plug her modern kitchen appliances. She blurred the lines between character and neighborly actress as she promised simple answers to everyday concerns.

Likewise, under the steady hand of the patriarch, simple problems met commonsense solutions. On *I Love Lucy*, Lucy Ricardo (Lucille Ball) created charming anarchy for Ricky (Desi Arnaz), but "at the end," as David Halberstam concluded, "there was Desi embracing her, understanding her. All was forgiven, and everything came out all right."[75] Wise parents on *Ozzie and Harriet*, *Father Knows Best*, and *Leave It to Beaver* diffused the anger of burgeoning juvenile delinquents with "a good hardy talk."[76] The backstage social problems of alcoholism and infidelity behind many of these shows only emphasized what a false image had been perpetrated.

Happy families also were ethnically and racially uniform: white and Protestant. Network executives felt the most intense pressure from anticommunist activists, questioned progressive definitions of the "public interest," and promoted a sterile national image. At the same time, their programmers resorted to showcasing vicious racial and ethnic stereotypes. From the summer of 1951 to the summer of 1953, over the loud objections of the NAACP at its summer convention, minstrelsy appeared on postwar televisions in the form of those radio schemers, *Amos & Andy*. Complaining that black doctors appeared as quacks and black lawyers as crooks, the NAACP went so far as to seek a court injunction against the show's first broadcast, but to no avail.

From 1950 to 1953, ABC brought *Beulah* to television. That producers hired Butterfly McQueen and Hattie McDaniel, two African American actresses who had portrayed house slaves in David O. Selznick's *Gone with the Wind*, to play modern-day mammies suggests the racial perspective of the show. Beulah helped the Hendersons, a suburban white family, persevere through many a domestic crisis: Mr. Henderson burned the steaks at a picnic; he fell into a river while fishing. In one situation, Beulah's maternal instincts took over as she comforted son Donnie after he ran away from home. Meanwhile, Beulah had no family of her own, only the love of her work-shy boyfriend Bill. White audiences accepted this version of the African American experience.

Similarly, *Life with Luigi* appeared on CBS from 1952 to 1953. A cast that included few Italian Americans interpreted the experiences of an Italian immigrant man, fresh off the boat, struggling to assimilate.[77] Another ethnic show, *The Goldbergs*, enjoyed a longer run. Beginning in 1949, creator and star Gertrude Berg showed Molly Goldberg's middle-class Jewish family living in the Bronx, struggling with typical middle-class problems. In 1951 Berg publicly defended Philip Loeb, the actor playing her husband, against charges of communist sympathies. Only after General Foods threatened to pull its sponsorship did Loeb go. (Blacklisted, he committed suicide four years later.) By 1953 Molly had become a caricature of her former self. "Yoo-hoo, Mrs. Bloom," she would yell to her new neighbor, signaling to audiences that Molly had some good gossip to spread. She had turned from a mother solving her family's middle-class problems to a meddling yenta involving herself in the affairs of others. The following season, the program's last, Berg tried to freshen the show by moving the Goldbergs to the suburbs. Sadly for her, few wanted to see these stereotyped ethnics move out from their urban shtetl.

Amos & Andy, Beulah, Life with Luigi, and *The Goldbergs* not only illustrate the desire on the part of network programmers to transfer popular radio comedies to television; they also suggest the Cold War tendency to forgo progressive notions of race and ethnicity in favor of the familiarity and nostalgia that stereotypes offer. This may be of little surprise, given the environment of the 1950s, when anticommunist hysteria peaked and when anxious Americans sensed disorder in their world. Domestic fascisms, social class differences, and "our racial imperialisms" were simply too controversial at times to be highlighted. When that hysteria had subsided somewhat, by 1954, all these shows were off the air. For a time, though, programmers had trapped certain groups in representations of the distant or imagined past.

Another genre that fit well with Cold War ideology was the quiz show. These and other shows "eased the transition from a depression-bred psychology of scarcity to an acceptance of spending."[78] Quiz shows emphasized the acquiring of goods and money and flaunted the image of the smart, acquisitive American. The games became lessons in democratic capitalism: while their countrymen watched, contestants from a variety of backgrounds competed for unimaginable wealth. Typically, winnings were supposedly based on knowledge rather than on mere chance. The meager rewards of *The $64 Question* on radio in the 1940s had been replaced with *The $64,000 Question* on television in 1955, allowing some contestants to win over $250,000. And winners usually stayed on for many weeks, developing notoriety.

Such was the case with Herb Stempel, an ordinary working stiff from New York City, who mastered *Twenty-One*. When public interest in Stempel waned, however, the producer pitted him against Charles Van Doren, an intellectual from Columbia University and the son of poet

Mark Van Doren. Behind the illusion of fair capitalism lay the reality of a fixed system as producers fed both contestants the answers and ordered Stempel to take a dive. Coincidentally, the question Stempel "missed" had to do with the name of the movie that won the 1955 Academy Award for Best Picture. How poignant that a real "Marty" of a man from New York City had "forgotten" *Marty*, and so publicly spurned the patron saint of television realism. Afterward, the young, telegenic Van Doren sweated and stammered his way to winning over $100,000 and enough of a following to put him on the cover of *Time* and in a chair at NBC's *Today* show.

After the scandals broke in 1958 revealing inappropriate shenanigans on many such shows, humorist Art Buchwald labeled the conspirators "quizlings." As grand juries convened and Congress held hearings into the quiz shows in 1959, investigators began to point fingers at overzealous sponsors. Indeed, earlier in the decade, single-sponsor advertising had dominated Cold War television, a trend that did not mesh with the anthology drama. Consumers "helped to make television an indispensable medium," Barnouw writes. "Few people now dared to be without a television set, and few major advertisers dared to be unrepresented on the home screen." But products that "sold magic solutions" were not always consistent with progressive themes presented in the very anthology dramas they sponsored. Paddy Chayefsky's awkward lovers, Rod Serling's greedy businessmen, and Reginald Rose's modest humanitarians did not fit well with the dominant national image that urged confidence, consumption, and ambition. In the midst of grave, complex issues, anthologies screeched to a halt so that sponsors could flog their wares: the latest fix-it for "serious problems" such as bad breath or a dirty floor could be administered easily for a quick resolution. Historian Elaine Tyler May explains, "Commodities would solve the problem of the discontented housewife, foster pride in the provider, . . . and allow the children to 'fit in' with their peers." Products promised finality, whereas anthologies underscored ambiguity.[79]

In an age not only of anticommunism but also of corporate culture, perhaps inevitably, network television became increasingly guided by business concerns. This mind-set coincided with Cold War consensus ideology and ran counter to the multilateral attitudes evident in anthology dramas. When most television productions moved from New York to suburban Los Angeles in the mid-1950s, one element responsible for making the anthology drama more "real" was lost: the fact that teleplays had been performed live. The difference between live transmission and tape is the difference between reality and illusion. Audiences understood that anthology dramas drew them into a production in a way that telefilm never could. Actors and directors, working without the benefits that the filming process allowed, gave the viewer the impression that the action was happening right then, that the themes the characters explored were pertinent in a way that breaking news was pertinent. Bigger-budgeted telefilms produced in Burbank "duped" the audience in some way. Even the well-known flubs and bloopers of live transmission had added to, rather than detracted from, the reality of what the audience was viewing.[80]

Technology limited the live anthology drama's reach as more studios moved from irrepressible live telecast to the more manageable telefilm. In 1953 over 80 percent of telecasts were live; just a half-dozen years later the trend toward film and tape was irreversible. By 1960, only 36 percent of telecasts were performed live; the other two-thirds of programs were filmed or taped. Of course, filmed programming had commercial appeal, primarily because it was profitable. Replayed programs cost virtually nothing to produce; once the actors were paid and the product was in the can, a show could be played for pure profit in perpetuity. One of the anthology dramas' greatest assets, its live quality, had been replaced more and more by the benefits the new technology promised. As a result, new writers and directors emphasized action and location shooting. Dialogue, one could argue, became another element of a script, not the key component it had been for the live telecast.

For all these reasons—the blacklist, censorship, increased sponsorship, changing programming strategies, new technologies—anthology writers became frustrated. As the Cold War gripped domestic television content, many writers found an outlet for free expression in Europe. One London screenwriter informed a CBS producer that television was "on the point of exploding here." By 1960, *Weekly Television Digest* estimated that almost 100 million television sets existed worldwide, receiving signals in millions of homes in Britain, the Soviet Union, Japan, and Brazil. Television also reached such distant places as Sweden, Honduras, and Nigeria. Viewers in Taiwan, Kuwait, and Aruba did not have long to wait.[81]

At the height of its popularity, the anthology drama had provided a safe form of protest for a segment of the population even amid heightened Cold War tensions. When conventional arenas of politics remained closed or inhospitable to political dissent, television furnished the artistic community with a site for the articulation of their fears and frustrations about American foreign policy. Communications technology conveyed an alternative message, one that ran counter to the Cold War consensus, which valued American exceptionalism, benign capitalism, and atomic security. At the same time, the government recognized the importance of playing cultural politics: it invited the audience to help fashion foreign policy through the polling booth, the boycott, the letter campaign, and the box office.[82] Television networks did their part by swamping the airwaves with a sterile image of the nation in a variety of programming genres.

Taken together, these genres amounted to the embodiment of the Cold War consensus, but they also contributed to the "vast wasteland" of which FCC chairman Newton Minow spoke in the early 1960s. If NSC 68 set out a revamped strategy that was designed, in part, to contain America, the television industry went a long way toward achieving that goal.[83] A few popular genres and their repetitive themes reinforced the idea that Cold War America was orderly, united, prosperous, and gifted. These programs and their advertisements suggested that when (their definitions of) trouble arose, it was solved swiftly and painlessly. By broadcasting in this manner, networks and sponsors normalized "moderation" and the status quo. Together, they implied a question: could the same be said of life behind the Iron Curtain? These "safe" programs had a great influence on the way Americans viewed their nation at a time when national identity took on great political significance. They stunted further social change and sacrificed the idealistic formulations of organizing the world as put forth by progressives in anthology dramas.

American culture during this time can be seen as not quite so conformist when one considers the popularity of anthology dramas. Writers were not merely victims of Red hysteria nor completely silenced by the blacklist and censorship. Looking at those screenwriters' worldview—one influenced by the ideology of multilateralism—shows that they sought to construct an alternative national identity, contrary to the one offered by the emerging Cold War consensus. This new vision questioned many fundamental principles and assumptions that the American foreign-policy-making establishment promoted. By noting the changing rationale for censorship, we see that the blue pencil and the blacklist were *tools* employed to hinder the reach of such universalist principles. We also see writers actively engaged in a negotiation, using their own weapons: unleashing criticism on public airwaves, compromising on the most unacceptable scripts, and encoding messages in science fiction. When the American cultural scene proved inhospitable to television writers, they joined Progressives who had been banished from Hollywood in a migration of dissent. Film, theater, and television talent found outlets for free expression in foreign lands. Once abroad, they continued their interactions with the government's Cold Warriors, individuals who sought to export a sanitized image of the nation in cultural productions of their own.

7

The Cultural Battlefield in Europe

ANTICOMMUNISTS EFFECTIVELY contained radicals in the motion picture industry during congressional hearings in the fall of 1947. Congress approved contempt citations against the Hollywood Ten, and studio moguls soon agreed to impose a blacklist on talent. A few weeks later, one member of the Hollywood Ten, a weary Dalton Trumbo, took a drag on his ever-present cigarette and examined his mail. "You're washed up in America, you smokey punk," one postcard promised him.[1] "And the Hollywood Ten went to prison," is the way studies of the cultural Red Scare end typically; but that moment marked only the midpoint of the story. So much of what had taken place in political culture up to this time—the crucible of the Second World War, the postwar progressive movement, the containment of Hollywood progressives, the movement of dissent to early television—all served as prelude for the contest over American cultural diplomacy. Given the political and financial price he paid, Trumbo agreed with his agitated correspondent that he was "washed up in America." But very soon, after great difficulty reestablishing his career in Hollywood and to his own surprise, Trumbo found other outlets for his views on American identity for foreign audiences.

Histories of the period show that many blacklisted individuals found work by adopting pseudonyms and by using politically pure friends to make financial arrangements for them. Producer Frank King later joked, "There are more ghosts in Hollywood than in Forest Lawn" cemetery.[2] Dalton Trumbo used at least nine different names to write no fewer than thirty-five scripts. He caused a sensation when, writing as "Robert Rich," he won the Academy Award for best original story for *The Brave One* (1956). Despite the Academy's imposition of a resolution intended to prevent tainted talent from receiving nominations, the blacklisted writers Carl Foreman, Michael Wilson, and Nedrick Young also embarrassed the

Academy by winning awards during the 1950s. Years later, Woody Allen romanticized the system's intrigue in *The Front* (1976).[3] What appeared in retrospect to be madcap adventures often obstructed the broader truth: when anticommunists silenced individuals in America, those articulating views contrary to the dominant political culture moved their dissent underground and overseas.

After experiencing frustration at home, many blacklisted artists, including Dalton Trumbo, found outlets for free expression in Mexico and in Europe. Trumbo may have appeared "washed up" in America but not so in the rest of the world. The story of what happened to the Hollywood Left and to those who shared their worldviews in theater and television continued beyond the borders of the United States. Once abroad, these American expatriates became unappointed, roving, cultural ambassadors with progressive portfolios. Equipped with an alternative vision to that of the State Department, they formed a band of illicit diplomats who negotiated a national identity on the front lines of the Cold War.

At the same time that artists plugged into the world, the government increased its presence abroad. Congressional investigators policed the cultural battleground, patrolling for signs of dissident talent; the State Department deployed the cultural weapon with countless radio broadcasts, art exhibitions, and motion picture exports; and Washington carefully examined the impact of these programs in Europe. Studies show how mass communications "emerged as integral components to statecraft" and allowed residents of the Soviet empire a window into the West, arguably resulting in a form of American "cultural hegemony."[4] But to understand the development of American public diplomacy in the 1950s, one must look beyond the Congress, White House, State Department, United States Information Agency, Voice of America, and other key institutions. Independent cultural producers and European audiences, though holding no official status, influenced the direction of American cultural programming around the world.

During the 1950s, many individuals who cared deeply about representations of the American nation were drawn to Europe, thereby expanding the contest over public diplomacy. When visions collided overseas, as they often did, one finds that no single entity—including the government— could claim control over the cultural weapon. Not only were there too many cultural producers involved in this contest, but the outlets available to these producers grew substantially during the 1950s. Foreign audiences, moreover, reminded Washington that they were unique constituencies, unwilling to accept an American cultural empire wholesale.

Artists Plug into the World

The Cold War drew cultural producers, businessmen, and government officials to Europe for a variety of reasons, but the first Cold War artists to plug into the world did so because they were frustrated in the domestic market. At first in the late 1940s, institutionalizing the blacklist proved awkward and inconsistent. Lawyers for Loew's (MGM) fought off lawsuits brought against the studio for breaking labor contracts with members of the Hollywood Ten, including Albert Maltz. At the same time Daryl Zanuck, the mogul behind the progressive themes in *Wilson* (1944) and *One World*, purchased the film rights to Maltz's latest novel, *The Journey of Simon McKeever*. Zanuck quietly sent John and Walter Huston to San Francisco with a skeleton crew. Only when the *Hollywood Reporter* made "such a stink" about the transaction, did Zanuck announce that he had scrapped the deal.[5] The promise of public scrutiny prevented progressives from working openly in Hollywood.

Still years before the famous breaches were made in the blacklist, blacklisted talent felt acute financial burdens. Having earned $2,000 a week from Twentieth Century-Fox in 1947, Ring Lardner Jr. had purchased an elegant estate for his wife and five children in Santa Monica when the subpoena from HUAC arrived in his shiny new mailbox. During the appeals process, Lardner worked for "cut rate costs" but soon sold his house at a $9,000 loss and moved his family into rentals.[6] Other members of the Hollywood Ten—Adrian Scott, Lester Cole, and Dalton Trumbo—claimed to have lost $150,000 each in broken studio contracts. With little income and mounting legal bills, blacklisted artists looked for any outlets open to them. Trumbo made deals with other Progressives who remained active in filmmaking, the business he knew best. For example, he worked steadily on a script for producer Sam Spiegel at a scale lower than usual; when Spiegel withheld the sums owed to Trumbo altogether, Trumbo could do little except feel the sting of frustration. He contracted to write a script for actor Larry Parks, but it pained the proud writer to have to request a small advance. Yet when doors closed in Hollywood after 1950, even these contacts with Progressives disappeared. Parks found himself blacklisted when Congress appeared in Hollywood for another round of investigations in 1951. Markets for controversy dried up in the Cold War environment. "They're going to have to figure out new ways of blacklisting before they starve me out entirely," Trumbo told his agent with defiance.[7]

At the same time, Trumbo pursued quick cash from magazine writing and from some sympathetic friends but soon found the work dissatisfying and fruitless to someone accustomed to recognition. When editors requested that he cut his piece for *Theatre Arts Magazine* in half, he curtly told them, "Do with it as you wish: the waste-basket, the scissors or the rewrite."[8] Though *New Yorker* editors liked much of his article, the board notified Trumbo that, suspiciously, the vote simply "went against this story."[9] The fiction editor of the *American Magazine* returned his material, calling it "too glum," and he suffered similar humiliations at *Women's Day* and *Today's Woman*, two publications he already considered of low prestige. In a letter asking his agent to pull his work from circulation, Trumbo expressed the pain of "continuous rejection" and wondered to what extent his sullied name had caused those rejections.[10]

Desperate for work, blacklisted artists turned to Broadway, thinking that traveling the many miles and dealing with new personnel would help. Before exhausting his legal appeals, Dalton Trumbo prepared *The Biggest Thief in Town* for the stage in 1949. "We are delighted to welcome you to the New York Theatre," agents Audrey Wood and William Liebling wrote to Trumbo, "and hope this will be the first of many successful plays." Unfortunately, critics lambasted Trumbo for political reasons, and the show closed after only thirteen performances. "I bleed for you," Albert Maltz wrote to Trumbo. "Write another play. Screw them all." Instead, Trumbo admitted to leaving town in a hurry, "like a startled grouse" during hunting season. He concluded rightly that his political notoriety stood in the way of his future success. Not to worry, Trumbo's agent told her client, reminding him that Albert Maltz recently had sold his work to Fox for $25,000. She suggested that Trumbo could salvage his work, "if you would do it under a different title and with a different name in order not to prejudice the first night audiences" against his play.[11] Warily, Trumbo returned his play to the theater scene under a new title and new name. When Progressives were squeezed out of Hollywood and Broadway in the late 1940s, blacklisted talent constructed a front in order to make a living.

At the moment of these mounting frustrations, opportunities opened abroad. While awaiting verdicts, both professional and legal, Trumbo received a letter from Cecil Madden, a London writer who had seen Trumbo's play in New York and told him that "you have an amusing idea there." Madden then advised Trumbo to adapt his script for the London stage. What a revelation: forget the hundreds of Americans and focus on the millions of people outside the United States. Trumbo's agent hastily prepared copies of the script to mail to London, even making some typographical errors in the process. When a similar opening came from Eastern Europe, Trumbo responded with amusement, "By all means penetrate the iron curtain with anything they wish." Maltz agreed with exploring these new avenues and even suggested a proactive effort to send their work to East Germany.[12]

The domestic front did work for some, but its failure for others prompted the search for reliable outlets abroad. This situation undoubtedly struck many of the blacklisted talent as familiar: veterans from Hollywood in the 1930s who had seen firsthand the flood of German talent escaping Hitler, including Billy Wilder and Fritz Lang. For a group that routinely employed the rhetoric of "domestic fascism" to excoriate their anticommunist opponents, it made sense to draw the parallels and look overseas. As one writer found out, "The [American] blacklist in Europe tended to be less bitter, less beaten down," than in the United States. "The blacklistees in Europe remained idealistic" even in the face of global containment.[13]

Frustrated American talent thus found temporary work, supportive communities, and artistic freedom outside America. Many nations opened their doors to these Progressives and welcomed their representations of Cold War America. Director Lewis Milestone, one of the "unfriendly" witnesses at the HUAC hearings in 1947, used Paris as his base but traveled extensively throughout Europe, finding work with many national film industries. Likewise, even though director Edward Dmytryk's name became contaminated as a member of the Hollywood Ten, he parlayed his success with the award-winning *Crossfire* (1947) into work in London. Dmytryk took the script for *Salt to the Devil* (1949) to British motion picture magnate J. Arthur Rank, a man working hard to rebuild the postwar British film industry. Despite worries that his political views had spoiled his career, Dmytryk discovered that Rank would produce the movie. Rank, moreover, allowed (even expected) that blacklisted screenwriter Ben Barzman would begin rewrites and advise on sets in February 1949. For the lead they cast blacklisted actor Sam Wanamaker. Set during the Depression, the movie showed capitalism at its ebb: desperate and hungry people competing against one another for work. Given the postwar devastation and rationing in Europe, the film resonated with audiences, especially members of the working class, and won prizes at film festivals in Venice and in Czechoslovakia. Dmytryk and Barzman believed the American blacklist could be dealt a heavy blow, even broken, if tainted talent could find work in Europe. Progressive themes, furthermore, threatened as they were in America, could apparently proliferate abroad.[14]

The opportunities outside Cold War America prompted many leftists to trade their temporary trips for permanent homes in Europe. After six weeks in London, Barzman went to Cannes with friend Adrian Scott, the producer of *Crossfire* and another member of the Hollywood Ten. Scott, on a final vacation before heading back to America to serve his prison sentence for contempt, was living proof to Barzman that "things were getting worse in Hollywood, and we would never be able to get work if we returned."[15] By moving to Paris, the Barzmans joined a long tradition of political opponents seeking asylum in foreign countries. Ultimately, the Paris community included scores of writers, producers, directors, agents, actors, musicians, and technicians, all collaborating on new projects—in other words, a complete film colony of Hollywood itself. In London, known American communists and fellow travelers continued to work in Britain's film industry. They also helped orient recent arrivals to their new lives as expatriates in Europe.

Another site where Progressives flourished was closer to their Southern California homes. Mexico in the 1940s had become a refuge for many political opponents, especially those who had escaped Adolf Hitler, Joseph Stalin, and Francisco Franco. By the 1950s, American dissidents were arriving as well: academics, reporters, bureaucrats, and members of the motion picture industry settled in Mexico City, Cuernavaca, San Ángel, and other locales. Many times, they sought out the comfort of one another's company. Despite the difficulties involved in reestablishing careers and enduring harassment, one expatriate concluded that "the richest, most wonderful years of our lives were in Mexico."[16]

Progressive George Pepper, the blacklisted former executive of the radicalized Hollywood Independent Citizens Committee of the Arts, Sciences, and Professions, moved to Mexico. Soon thereafter came screenwriter Hugo Butler and his wife, Jean, who had both been Communist Party members in the 1930s. The Butlers moved to Baja and then Mexico City, where they continued to work, now for two language markets. "Pepper became our producer," Jean recalled, setting up a small production company for which she and Hugo wrote the occasional feature and many Spanish-language docudramas.[17] Further, Pepper consolidated affairs as de facto studio chief, talent agent, recruiter, and promoter. Screenwriters John Bright, Bernard Gordon, Julian Zimet, and Gordon Kahn joined the others;

after their release from prison, Dalton Trumbo and Albert Maltz arrived to restart their stalled careers.[18]

Meanwhile, Hollywood became more restrictive in the early 1950s and encouraged increasing numbers of Progressives to seek opportunities beyond the borders of the United States. The events of 1949–1950—the "fall" of China to Mao Zedong's communists, the detonation of the Soviet atomic bomb, the discovery of a domestic spy ring, the rise to prominence of Senator Joseph McCarthy, and the onset of the Korean War—encouraged the government to view the Cold War globally, as an ideological contest whereby culture became a vital weapon in the war against communism. This all-consuming approach brought grave consequences for the American stage and screen, and progressives perceived imminent danger. Ring Lardner Jr. recalled that "the Hollywood we returned to from prison in 1951 was a much more hostile environment."[19]

Indeed, HUAC revisited Hollywood for a new round of investigations lasting six months; the Independent Citizen's Committee of the Arts, Sciences, and Professions was labeled a communist front, and the Supreme Court rejected an appeal by Communist Party leaders arrested for subversion. Some witnesses before HUAC, like director Elia Kazan, screenwriters Budd Schulberg and Clifford Odets, and actors Sterling Hayden and Lee J. Cobb, willingly named names of alleged communists and fellow travelers before continuing their own careers. Others, like actress Judy Holliday, admitted sheepishly that they had been "duped" into attending subversive meetings and signing membership cards. Director Edward Dmytryk, claiming that the Korean War had changed his views, underwent a jailhouse conversion and sought to cleanse himself by naming names before committees in Congress and in Hollywood, much to the distress of the remaining Hollywood Nine.

Playwrights Lillian Hellman and Arthur Miller were prominent members of this new round of blacklisting in the years 1951–1953. Like the Hollywood Ten before them, Hellman and Miller used their typewriters to engage in the political debate of their times and, frustrated in America, found outlets overseas. In May 1952, writer Lillian Hellman famously told HUAC that she "would not cut my conscience to fit this year's fashions" and refused to cooperate. Though she was not held in contempt, her Hollywood career suffered. In 1952, just a few weeks after her testimony, Hellman revived her old play *The Children's Hour* for theater audiences. She demanded control over the production, took on the role of director, and cast prominent method actors in the leads. The play deals with a girl's accusation that two female teachers at her school have been carrying on a homosexual relationship. The sexual subject matter was provocative, taboo even for the 1950s, but Hellman was drawn to the revival for its theme of false accusation. She showed that Red-baiters, much like the student in her play, seized power for their own purposes with little regard for their victims or for the truth. As Hellman told a gathering at her midtown Manhattan home one night in December 1952, she wanted audiences to see the play as a statement "not about lesbianism, but about a lie."[20] Characteristically, Lillian Hellman did not mince words, regardless of the consequences.

In similar fashion, Arthur Miller saw his play *The Crucible* open on Broadway weeks later, on January 22, 1953. A frustrated Miller had abandoned Hollywood to return to the New York theater, where he couched his concerns about contemporary hysteria in a play based on the Salem witch hunts. On the day of the opening, New York newspaper headlines trumpeted, "All 13 Reds Guilty" for "conspiring to teach and advocate the duty and necessity of forcible overthrow of government."[21] The opening night's reviews from New York theater critics Brooks Atkinson and Walter Kerr were harsh: "Arthur Miller is a problem playwright" whose writing is "cruder" in this play.[22] Though Miller won a Tony Award, the show closed after only five months. Meanwhile, Kazan glorified the role of informer in his classic *On the Waterfront* (1954) and enjoyed great success. When anticommunists silenced Hollywood, they quieted Broadway as well. Within the year, Hellman and Miller joined the growing community of artists already working overseas.

Once abroad, expatriates resumed their activities, even political ones on occasion, and were largely unmolested, though they remained cautious. When several English-language newspapers published the names of people "named" in congressional hearings, there were few noticeable effects on expatriates. Director Bernard Vorhaus panicked when he was "named" and proceeded to buy up as many copies of the *Rome Daily American* as he could find within a hundred miles.[23] Still, a film he was working on continued right along into production in Italy. The exile community in Paris, growing substantially throughout the 1950s, joined the French political left and the French film scene. They went to Ciné Action, a leftist film club populated by actors such as Yves Montand and Simone Signoret, but were careful to remain unaffiliated with any political organization. Even in countries lorded over by dictators, exiles found opportunity. Writer Leonardo Bercovici, who had worked with David O. Selznick before he was blacklisted, enjoyed work in Tito's Yugoslavia and Franco's Spain. Screenwriter Allen Boretz found less repression as a communist in fascist Spain than he had found in Cold War Hollywood. While admitting that some censorship existed, Boretz remembered that "I personally felt no repression of any kind. Nobody bothered me in Spain." In fact, many cultural bohemians from France "drifted down" to Madrid during the 1950s.[24]

Waves of blacklisted artists who experienced frustration in the domestic setting found themselves virtually forced into the global marketplace. With them they brought their progressive ideology. At the same time, U.S. foreign-policy-makers thought the Cold War demanded that the nation increase its engagement in world affairs. After 1950 the government became ever more committed to viewing the contest with the Soviets in ideological and cultural terms. Consequently, although Progressives enjoyed much relative freedom to produce overseas, expatriate havens also came under attack by the most dedicated American anticommunists, intent on managing the cultural battleground in Europe as well as in the United States.

The Cultural Weapon at Work

Even before the 1950s the United States government engaged in European cultural affairs, albeit in a limited way compared to the years thereafter. By the early 1950s, a consensus within the Congress, White House, and State Department tried to project national power by deploying a cultural weapon. In some respects, the decade-long experience as an American occupation force in Germany and Austria served as a model for how the cultural weapon could work in the rest of Europe. In the ideological contest with communism, the government's cultural weapon was designed to unite the West under American leadership and to penetrate the Iron Curtain.

Germany and Austria became laboratories for testing American hegemony. The important, complex, and ultimate goal of denazification—that of ideological reform and reeducation—led American leaders to favor a plan of occupation-by-culture. In other words, Washington held the belief that rehabilitation would come when former enemies demilitarized, wrote democratic constitutions, rebuilt economies, and adopted American culture. With this last purpose in mind, the United States government inaugurated radio broadcasts and exported motion pictures, books, and music. The State Department established America Houses in many European capitals and major cities; there were twenty-seven in western Germany alone. Diplomats filled rooms with concerts, art exhibitions, plays, and lectures. Their libraries and reading rooms offered novels, magazines, newspapers, and other printed material, all with the express purpose of interpreting *America* to the people of Europe.[25]

The government consistently preached the benefits of democratic-capitalism, but efforts to eliminate Nazism transitioned into anticommunism. Looking at the Austrian case, historian Reinhold Wagnleitner explains that the need for political reeducation led to general reforms in the nation's education system, such as promoting English-language classes and American Studies curricula. As a result, Wagnleitner shows, these reforms were "highly important for the long-term securing of a positive climate of reception for U.S. culture." While the government used occupation for purposes of containment, many enterprising businessmen also benefited. Indeed, the two worked together, as Wagnleitner concludes: "The activities of U.S. cultural officers had opened unimaginable possibilities for the U.S. culture industry." Because the United States completely dominated local media operations in occupied territory—it licensed newspapers, promoted articles on daily life in America, and censored radio programs—American publishers could break into the European market. American "books followed the jeep" after the Second World War, and that "guaranteed the U.S. publishing system a dominating position" in the 1950s.[26] In Europe during the late 1940s and throughout the 1950s, the goals of foreign policy and the interests of business coincided. Anticommunism made good business sense, and the expansion of consumer products made good foreign policy.

For filmmakers possessing the proper anticommunist credentials, there were great opportunities in the occupation zones. This partnership between Hollywood and Washington, forged in occupied territory, replicated itself elsewhere in Europe in the 1950s. An examination of the independent producer David O. Selznick illustrates the synergy between public and private cultural efforts in Europe in those years.

Selznick had moved from supporting Hollywood's united front against HUAC's interference in 1947 to supporting the break with perceived radicals and instituting the blacklist. Believing that the Marshall Plan held so much promise, he put his filmmaking career on hold and traveled extensively throughout Europe after the HUAC hearings. "For a long time Selznick has been thinking in . . . international terms," one showbiz magazine informed readers in Britain. "He has spent almost as much time in Europe as in America during the past two years."[27] He clipped public opinion surveys, trying to take the pulse of the audience. Finally, in 1950, Selznick ordered his staff to speak to a State Department contact about entering the German market with a backlog of twelve of his films that he was "especially anxious to distribute." After a frank meeting they reported to Selznick in a confidential memo that the State Department was "highly enthusiastic over the possibility" of Selznick's advising the American High Commission on its overall motion picture program. They also discussed the possibility of Selznick's producing several "semidocumentary" features to further the cause of denazification. The State Department representative assured Selznick that the government would encourage the German ministry of economics to increase imports of the American films.

At a time when American policy was to help German industry to its feet, and despite "a good bit of antagonism in Germany" toward American competition, Eric Johnston's Motion Picture Export Association looked to reap the benefits from its allegiance to American foreign policy. Beginning in February 1948, about eight weeks after studio executives issued the Waldorf Statement that started the blacklist, the American High Command in Germany allowed the MPEA to distribute films in the occupation zones. Representing ten studios and independent producers, the MPEA called for the export of at least 180 films over the next year, and Selznick hoped to be a part of that project. In time, the MPEA took advantage of the fact that antitrust restrictions, which threatened the domestic market, did not apply overseas. As the program of cultural diplomacy expanded outside occupied territory during the 1950s, Selznick, the MPEA, and other Hollywood producers "followed the jeep."[28]

The same year that Selznick traipsed through Europe, the Truman administration unleashed a "Campaign of Truth" in its propaganda war against the Soviet Union. It marked a starting point for the government's deployment of the cultural weapon. In April 1951, while reorganizing the national security apparatus, President Truman institutionalized the government's propaganda efforts. He centralized authority over cultural diplomacy in the Psychological Strategy Board (PSB), a group representing several national security agencies that formulated policy and reported directly to the National Security Council. In January 1952, Secretary of State Dean Acheson formed the International Information Administration (IIA), a semiautonomous agency housed within the State Department. Like the PSB, the IIA was charged with developing foreign information activities. Its administrator, Wilson Compton, reported directly to Acheson. After the initial bureaucratization, the "Campaign of Truth" got under way.[29]

On March 4, 1952, Acheson and Compton joined President Truman aboard the Coast Guard cutter *Courier*. The ship made waves in more ways than one as it sailed the seas. It created radio waves when the three men broadcast their speeches in forty-five languages with the help of thirty-seven transmitters in relay stations around the world. It also made waves in Moscow, signaling Washington's debut in a global propaganda war. "I am speaking to you today from a ship," Truman explained, "and it will perform a very special mission. This vessel will not be armed with guns or with any instruments of destruction. But it will be a valiant fighter in the cause of freedom. It will carry a precious cargo—and that cargo is Truth." At the end of Truman's term, the ship of state carried an emerging cultural weapon. In time, the government exported its definition of American ideals to all parts of the globe.[30]

In many ways the Eisenhower administration's "New Look" foreign policy bore a remarkable resemblance to Truman's old foreign policy.[31] Where Eisenhower disagreed with Truman was in domestic matters. In place of a Fair Deal, Eisenhower urged corporate conservatism; he applied to governance the business practices of streamlining and efficiency. This model, which had served him well in the military and when organizing his presidential staff, also guided his thinking on foreign policy. While accepting the outlines of NSC 68, Eisenhower favored nuclear weapons over expensive conventional forces with the promise of "more bang for the buck." Volatile rhetoric also played an important part. Secretary of State John Foster Dulles preached "rollback" and practiced "brinkmanship" with the singular purpose of demonstrating strength to other nations. In reality, Eisenhower and Dulles showed great restraint during Khrushchev's crackdown on Hungarians seeking liberation from Soviet domination in 1956, implying that "more bang for the buck" was more bark than bite. In fact, Eisenhower worked toward what historian Melvyn Leffler has called "a preponderance of power," which rested not only on nuclear deterrence but also on the notion of undermining the Iron Curtain by other means.[32]

The rhetorical war was part of larger plans for psychological warfare, an aspect of national security policy that Eisenhower strongly supported. As the president told Senator Styles Bridges, "I want to wage the Cold War in a militant, but reasonable style, whereby we appeal to the people of the world as a better group to hang with than the Communists." Therefore, Eisenhower's psychological warfare initiatives fit with his corporatism in that they encompassed programs that staged the war on the cheap, anything "from the singing of a beautiful hymn up to the most extraordinary kind of physical sabotage."[33]

Four short days into his term, Eisenhower organized the President's Committee on International Information Activities and appointed William Jackson as its chair. The Jackson committee interviewed over 250 witnesses, examined classified materials, conferred with members of Congress, and concluded that all American diplomatic, economic, and military actions had a psychological dimension to consider. In June 1953 the committee recommended that Eisenhower consolidate all American international information programs under the new United States Information Agency, whose administrator would report directly to the National Security Agency. The president budgeted over $100 million to fund the project. For example, with this level of commitment, the USIA had sponsored overseas libraries in more than 160 cities around the world by the late 1950s. These libraries allowed some 80,000 visitors each day to peruse more than 2.2 million volumes of Americana.[34] Eisenhower believed big changes in the balance of power could come from the smallest of schemes. That general thinking led him to rely on elite units trained for covert operations in Iran, Indonesia, and Guatemala, but the same thinking led the Eisenhower administration to use the global media to win friends and influence people.

Cultural warfare allowed the government to satisfy many goals. The favorable representations of the nation that made up this cultural weapon drew basic distinctions between the consumer abundance of capitalism and the apparent emptiness of communism. Attempts to manage the cultural scene in Western Europe served the larger purpose of binding allies under American leadership. The ideological and strategic objectives of the government fused nicely with the economic motivations of the business community. After all, normalizing and valorizing consumption strengthened the domestic economy. Corporate executives, advertisers, and media titans—an army of cultural producers in the private sector—bankrolled much of the cultural weapon, something that fiscal conservatives certainly appreciated. Furthermore, private initiatives helped considerably when Congress slashed public funding for the USIA during the brief recession of 1953. Finally, by using cultural exchange programs, the administration could appear to make peace and promote "understanding" with the Soviet bloc while still waging a Cold War. The cultural weapon was attractive for all these reasons.

If New York and Hollywood became producers for the government, Washington served as promoter, distributor, and exhibitor. For example, in November 1951, just a year after exploring occupied territory, Selznick responded to a request by the State Department to tape two radio interviews for the *Arts and Letters* show on the Voice of America (VOA). "I think such a recording used by the State Department, would be helpful not only to the cause of good will and understanding among free peoples," an associate wrote to Selznick in a memo, "but also to call attention to our productions, for which so many thousands of moviegoers are waiting in the free areas." The cash-strapped Selznick had not made a motion picture in some time but always hoped to raise enough cash to finance his return to the big screen. Leasing his old films for foreign exhibition provided an enticing option. Additionally, using the platform of state-sanctioned international radio virtually put the stamp of approval on his product. Selznick beamed at the potential to "more or less blanket Europe." He had in his hands the ability to use the government to publicize his motion pictures not only in controlled markets such as Germany, Austria, and Japan but also in free markets in Europe, Asia, and Latin America.[35]

The impetus for selling motion pictures abroad came both from the government and from its partners in Hollywood, such as David O. Selznick. In 1953 Selznick informed William Jackson, the new chairman of Eisenhower's International Information Activities committee, that Hollywood needed more government assistance in securing foreign markets. As if to demonstrate his Cold War qualifications to Eisenhower's new man, Selznick pointed to the Golden Laurel Awards, his initiative, that recognized "films which serve the democratic cause" to counter "the festivals and awards sponsored by the Russian Government."[36]

Selznick and other producers did receive much-needed government assistance in filming overseas. In 1956 he and his partners at Twentieth Century-Fox entered into delicate negotiations with the Italian government for use of the military during the filming of *A Farewell to Arms* (1957). Soon enough, Selznick enjoyed some "fine cooperation" in the persons of Ambassador Clare Boothe Luce, the former actress-congresswoman, and Frank McCarthy, the former assistant secretary of state who had since become a vice president at Fox. The revolving door of filmmakers and diplomats, along with their shared ideology, helped Selznick make his much-anticipated return to the big screen.[37]

Selznick got his movie, but Luce got help for her political agenda as well. Since her appointment to Rome, she had set about to rehabilitate Italy's postwar reputation and to continue the American presence in a key Cold War site. A confidential State Department "country plan" for

Italy revealed that Washington and Luce were deeply concerned about Italy's status in the Western alliance. In Italy, "unlike other Western European nations, communism still has the practical possibility of coming to power by legal means"; therefore, "an extraordinary United States Information Service (USIS) effort is called for." An alliance with Hollywood represented the ideal: "to reach every Italian, repeatedly and effectively," and to concentrate on media "that can carry our message to broader audiences."[38]

While shepherding Premier Mario Scelba on his springtime tour of the American East Coast in 1955, the *New York Daily News* reported, Luce "seized every opportunity to press for an enlargement of our cultural program abroad." In Washington, she accompanied Scelba to the White House for a state dinner and urged Eisenhower to "pick up the tab" for American symphony concerts and other cultural exhibitions.[39] In New York, she arranged for an American theater company to premiere *Porgy and Bess* in Italy. Reportedly "weary of Red strutting about the superior Russian ballet," Luce hoped to use productions of the musicals *Showboat* and *Oklahoma!* "to counteract Communist claims that the only plays and movies Americans can produce reek with crime." Indeed, *Showboat* and *Oklahoma!* were hugely successful foot-tappers that reimagined and sentimentalized American slavery and the American West, respectively. These love stories viewed the domestic "race problem" in terms of steady progress for a diverse but united democracy and incorporated them into a collective memory of an idealized American history.[40]

At the same time as Ambassador Luce facilitated Selznick's production, she worked hard to purify the important Italian cinema, which overtook France and Germany to become the leading European film center in the 1950s.[41] Luce explained, "Embassies have learned (sometimes the hard way) that certain groups of private citizens can be very important in forming American public opinion." She urged Premier Scelba to begin "cracking down on Red efforts to control the motion-picture industry and to infiltrate Italian cultural fields."[42] She also threatened to cancel government contracts with Italian companies that relied on communist-dominated trade unions, which would leave tens of thousands of Italians in dire economic circumstances. Luce reportedly told Eisenhower, "If it is ever a choice between spaghetti and a union card, Giuseppe will choose the spaghetti."[43]

Concerted action by so many individuals in government had an impact on American cultural exports. Because of this close connection between Washington and Hollywood, much of what Europeans saw in their theaters represented familiar aspects of containment ideology: anticommunism, bi-polarity, the benefits of capitalism, and notions of American exceptional-ism.[44] Several westerns, with clear lessons about good and evil, took Ameri-can mythology to Europe. *Oklahoma!* (1955), one of Hollywood's rousing musical epics that splashed vibrant color across screens, was an idealized version of the American West, one that remembered the frontier more for enterprising pioneers than for diversity and exploitation.

Consistent with this American image, and in an attempt to bolster the civil rights profile of the nation, the State Department exported film shorts about the extraordinary lives of notable blacks such as Ralph Bunche and scores of athletes, rather than focus attention on the real, dif-ficult experiences of average African Americans.[45] In another case, the USIA distributed a documentary *Life of Eisenhower* while withholding one on the life of Franklin Roosevelt because it showed too much poverty at home and cooperation abroad with Stalin. The catalogue of approved exports included many Disney animated features, religious epics such as *The Ten Commandments* (1956), the "sexploits" of Marilyn Monroe and Jayne Mansfield, and menacing subversives from the "Red" planet in *Invaders from Mars* (1953). Films that did not meet these thematic stan-dards were banned.

European audiences in the mid-1950s consumed a complex blend of American culture—at times laudatory and idealized, at times serious and critical. Despite the best efforts on the part of members of Congress, dip-lomats, and compliant producers to export *America* to Europeans, expa-triates continued to work and to express their progressive ideology on the screens and behind the scenes. When anticommunists competed with these alternative voices throughout the decade of the 1950s, European au-diences helped to influence the future of American public diplomacy.

Audience Feedback and American Foreign Policy

The proliferation of progressive themes abroad prompted a backlash by anticommunists, beginning in 1953. That year the Soviets detonated their first hydrogen bomb, and Senator Joseph McCarthy became a committee chairman, two events adding fire to the passion of anticommunists and their never-ending search for subversives in movie studios, television net-works, and overseas.

In 1953, anticommunists followed the activities of Lillian Hellman in Hollywood and on Broadway. Despite her stage triumphs, Hellman was getting little work. As with others before her who found job prospects dwindling and bill collectors calling, therefore, she resorted to Europe. There, the independent producer Alexander Korda offered her a deal. During her extensive tour of Europe that summer, Hellman expressed relief because it was "the first time in a good two years that I have felt the lifting of burdens." In a letter to her secretary, Hellman recalled that her play *The Little Foxes* had been produced in Rome during the war "and everybody thought it was wonderful."[46] Why not, she wondered, take her plays to the friendly environment in Europe? The events of the early 1950s led many Progressives who held to their beliefs to explore their opportunities in foreign lands. But just as HUAC had followed Hellman's trail to New York, so too would it track her to Europe.

Unsatisfied with the search for communists at home, Joseph McCarthy became a cultural martinet who searched for domestic subversion by inspecting the activities of America's artistic "ambassadors" overseas. In 1953, with the help of his staff assistants, McCarthy turned to the 30,000 "communist books" inside the overseas America Houses and demanded that the State Department pull many of them from their shelves. In this latest of his many hastily made lists, McCarthy lumped radical and liberal authors together willy-nilly: Charles Beard, Arthur Schlesinger Jr., Henry Wallace, Reinhold Niebuhr, Upton Sinclair, Albert Einstein, Leonard Bernstein. His list of banned writers also included Pearl S. Buck, W. E. B. Du Bois, Howard Fast, Dashiell Hammett, Ernest Hemingway, Langston Hughes, Archibald MacLeish, Norman Mailer, Arthur Miller, and Lillian Hellman.[47] That so many odd pairings should appear on the same list illustrated the eccentricities of McCarthyism. The USIA's overseas libraries became places to showcase a sanitized representation of America, but when European readers looked at the face of the ideal America, what they saw was the face of Joseph McCarthy.

This situation embarrassed President Eisenhower, who had just taken office and found himself fielding many questions by reporters about McCarthy's "book burnings." Following the advice of assistants such as C. D. Jackson—a man who worked closely with Henry Luce at Time-Life—the president urged moderation within the anticommunist camp. Eisenhower condemned the practice of censoring books in a commencement address at Dartmouth in June 1953. America should fight communism "with something better," he told graduates, "not try to conceal the thinking of our people." With an interest in how the nation looked in the eyes of world opinion, Eisenhower said that to do otherwise "isn't America." In a press conference a few days later, he urged restraint, "because if we go too far," the president warned, "we are not advertising America."[48]

After a month, though, it was apparent that the senator had wrested attention from the new president. The headlines continued, and reporters inundated Eisenhower with more questions, not fewer. Now there were reports of State Department evasions over who made the book lists, who appeared on the lists, and who pulled the books from the shelves. Finally, after a long exchange with one reporter, Eisenhower admitted that some staff members in the overseas libraries were undoubtedly "frightened" when anticommunists presented them with a list of works by "subversive" authors.[49] Something had to be done. But even though Eisenhower disparaged Red hysteria, he did not do so on the grounds of decency or as a principled stand for civil liberties. Rather, he knew the situation *looked* bad. Therefore, reasonable Cold Warriors came to realize the need to soften some edges while still redoubling their efforts in the area of cultural export.

There is much evidence to suggest that Europeans disregarded the officially sanctioned image of America in favor of another. At the very same time that McCarthy's aides were scouring the shelves of overseas libraries, Europeans packed theaters to see *The Crucible* (1953). Arthur Miller used Puritan Salem to expose the crimes of anticommunist hysteria with his witch-hunt parable. In the process, he showed Europeans that the leading democracy was enduring a great test of its civic values. Amid the grumblings of some American audiences and anticommunists in Congress, Miller expressed worry and frustration, but he soon found solace as *The Crucible* toured throughout Europe. With satisfaction, he informed an editor in 1954 that his play was "a Great Success" in Munich, Berlin, Amsterdam, Oslo, Copenhagen, and Brussels. *The Crucible* opened in Paris later that year with two prominent French actors in the leads. "Over there, you see they appreciate me," Miller explained in a letter to a friend, "Unlike here."[50]

Other writers enjoyed similar successes. Lillian Hellman toured London again in the spring of 1955. While there, she attended a play about Joan of Arc and was immediately moved by the story of another woman bullied by the state into disavowing her beliefs. That Hellman saw herself as St. Joan probably said as much about her ego as about her political troubles, but her adaptation, called *The Lark*, fired up audiences on Broadway just as *The Children's Hour* had. A few years later France provided another source of material for a Hellman adaptation: Voltaire's *Candide*. Like her other projects during the blacklisting years, this one poked fun at authority figures; Hellman looked at the absurdity of routine inquisitions and the sanctioned tortures and executions of heretics. In common cause, she and composer Leonard Bernstein joined forces to produce the show. Despite its impressive pedigree, *Candide* (1956) fell flat in America; it ran only two months. But when Hellman took it to the London stage, it thrived. Undoubtedly, her international celebrity made the connections between *Candide* and HUAC all the more clear in the minds of Londoners.

The activities of Miller, Hellman, and others provoked staunch anticommunists to redouble their efforts to purify American cultural production abroad in the 1950s. The American Catholic War Veterans urged the army not to allow any of Miller's productions to see stage lights in occupied Europe. But Miller later quipped that his *Crucible* played well "wherever a political coup appears imminent, or a dictatorial regime has just been overthrown," such as in Greece, Czechoslovakia, and parts of Asia and Latin America.[51]

Miller's expression of that point of view led anticommunists to monitor the movements and activities of expatriates. Despite having no formal jurisdiction, congressional investigators arranged for meetings with Mexican officials in Mexico City. The American embassy kept tabs on the writers there, sometimes forcing the expatriates to hold meetings during ostensible picnics in the countryside. Despite the occasional harassment and withheld mail, however, the Mexican government knowingly or unknowingly shielded the community of blacklisted talent within its borders: to some extent, government intrusions kept these most political of people out of politics. "If we had indulged in any political activity we could have been expelled [from Mexico] without a trial," an expatriate explained. "Everybody was scared to death, and we did everything we could not to be political."[52]

At other times, the ones "scared to death" were foreign governments that relied on American support. Three members of one exile community in Europe who inquired of the Israelis whether they would welcome "a Dassin-Berry-Barzman moviemaking kibbutz" were told by the Israeli cultural attaché that Israel had too much to lose from such a venture.[53] Even so, such contacts between foreign governments and cultural critics proved worrisome to officials in Washington. That people who interpreted the American character in ways wholly unacceptable to the U.S. government could make inroads on the cultural battlefield of Europe had to end.

The State Department found a surefire way to disrupt the activities of Progressives roaming abroad: withholding passports. The government had employed this tactic earlier against a handful of prominent citizens with clear ties to radical politics, such as the singer and actor Paul Robeson in 1950. During an era when anticommunists feared a globalized threat, the government turned its attention to restricting the movement of many more artists, especially those already abroad.

A Mexican lawyer handling a residency application for screenwriter Julian Zimet requested his passport. Because some years had passed and the passport had expired, Zimet approached the American embassy for a renewal. After delays, an embassy official explained that the passport would come only after cooperation on other matters. "What sort of cooperating do you have in mind?" Zimet asked. The embassy official produced a list of expatriate artists in Mexico. "Tell us what you know about these people. It'll be confidential," he promised Zimet. "Nobody outside the embassy will know that you've been talking to us." Even though Zimet declined, his application went through, but the government clerk typed on Zimet's passport registration receipt that the document was not proof of American citizenship, and that the privileges granted to American citizens need not extend to Zimet.[54]

Other passport disputes played out on a more public stage. In the mid-1950s the State Department revoked the passport of one of the most prolific expatriates, the Cincinnati-born director Jules Dassin, whose well-publicized successes angered many Cold Warriors in Washington. When Dassin prepared to shuttle between France and Italy on a coproduction, his French producer took him to the Quai d'Orsay for a French passport. "The only passport we can give you is one which says you belong to no country," the official said, but he quickly added that even this option was closed to Americans, under pressure by the American State Department. After many pleas, the weary officer agreed to sign a *titre de voyage*—with his eyes closed, and with the promise that Dassin would tell no one when he reached Italy. Upon his arrival in Rome, Italian authorities ordered Dassin to leave the country, an act insisted upon by American ambassador Clare Boothe Luce. The Italian writer with whom Dassin was to collaborate angrily appealed to his foreign minister, at one point asking if his nation had become a colony of America. As the controversy continued, however, bureaucrats wore down the producers, and the producers abandoned Jules Dassin.[55]

Ambassador Luce went beyond facilitating productions by compliant producers such as David O. Selznick and pressuring the Italian government to purge leftist unions from the Italian motion picture industry. She also tried to prevent popular American expatriates from contaminating the Italian cultural scene. But her activism angered many Americans, including MGM president Arthur Loew. "Ambassador Luce has absolutely no right to interfere in this matter," Loew declared. Producer and well-known liberal Dore Schary, who had once worked with Selznick, called her actions "outrageous" and "a flagrant political censorship."[56] Influential *New York Times* columnist Bosley Crowther complained that Luce wanted films to be "unblemished mirrors of the favorable aspects of American life," whereas "some of our strongest motion pictures have been those that have searchingly observed some of the ugliest and most tragic aspects of conditions that prevail." A government waging the Cold War for democratic principles, Crowther concluded, should know better.[57] One who came to the ambassador's aid was producer Arthur Hornblow Jr., who produced the film version of *Oklahoma!* He reminded critics that "the smell of anti-Americanism and communism in Italy is no joke, and Mrs. Luce lives with it daily."[58]

In 1955, Jules Dassin found that his work could set him free from his purgatory. He wrote and directed *Rififi*, another in a string of his realistic *film noir* features about urban crime in America and Paris. Although the genre had been popular in Hollywood in the late 1940s, the image hardly fit the requisite themes of Cold War ideology. Nevertheless, in Europe the film was such a critical and box office success that the French ministry of culture submitted *Rififi* at the Cannes Film Festival, where it won for Dassin the prize for best direction. But *Rififi* caused an incident when organizers revealed the American Dassin's name under a French flag in the international competition.

Hoping to avoid a similar sensation at the Venice Film Festival three months later, Ambassador Luce pressured organizers to pull from the program the critically acclaimed, gritty urban drama *Blackboard Jungle* (1955), with its major themes of juvenile delinquency and racial prejudice in the United States. Richard Brooks, who had unmasked American anti-Semitism when he penned *Crossfire*, wrote and directed *Blackboard Jungle* to expose the reality under the surface of the 1950s suburban ideal: cynicism, tension, antisocial behavior, and teen rebellion. Luce and the festival organizers replaced it with a predictable western love story, *The Kentuckian*.

In 1957 Dassin directed *He Who Must Die*, written by the blacklisted writer Ben Barzman. Again, the French ministry of culture submitted the film at Cannes. The French press pestered the Americans about what many Europeans viewed as a senseless blacklist, and whether the customary embassy reception would include invitations for Dassin and Barzman. With the hour of the reception at hand and the foreign press in attendance, an invitation was quietly slipped under Dassin's door. Dassin recalled making his way along the receiving line populated by nervous Hollywood elites. One embassy official visited him, hinting that his passport could be returned to him if only he cleansed himself in America. He refused. The fight for Jules Dassin, symbol of two nations, came to an end when he concluded that his best opportunities remained in hopscotching around Europe.[59]

The passport case involving Arthur Miller also revealed how fanatical anticommunism could hurt an American foreign policy that dictated presentation of the nation only in the best possible light. The case started when the State Department denied Miller's application to attend the premier of *The Crucible* in Brussels in 1953. The writer of the *The Crucible* thus became a character in his own play. Members of HUAC questioned Miller's donation of royalties to postwar relief efforts in Poland and in Czechoslovakia. They wondered why he had signed an amicus brief for the Hollywood Ten. They castigated him for calling the FBI "peeping Toms" who practiced "fascism, American style." But a surprising amount of time was spent on his progressive views and his scripts. After all, most could see that he had been called to testify because of *The Crucible*. One committee member questioned Miller on whether he would put artists "in a preferred class." Another inquired if writers have "special rights" to explore alien ideas without bearing the consequences. Still another wondered if Miller believed "the artist lives in a different world from anyone else." In exasperation, a congressman finally asked the author, "Why do you not direct some of that magnificent ability you have to fighting against well-known Communist subversive conspiracies in our country and in the world? I mean more positively?" Miller calmly explained to the committee: "I am not a fictionalist. I reflect what my heart tells me from the society around me. We are living in a time when there is great uncertainty in this country. It is not a communist idea. You just pick up a book review section and you will see everybody selling books on peace of mind because there isn't any."[60]

After being cited for contempt of Congress, as the Hollywood Ten had been, Arthur Miller entered a lengthy appeals process. Meanwhile, his passport troubles reverberated through the artist community. If the government could restrict the free movement of such a prominent writer, other writers believed any one of them could be targeted for similar past political activity and contemporary writing. Lillian Hellman kept up with the case religiously.[61] So did Tennessee Williams. "The news that Arthur Miller lost his passport is shocking and disgusting," Williams wrote to his agent. "It is also frightening to me, since I have not yet had any news of mine. Do you think they'll refuse it?" Although he was apolitical, Williams drafted a letter of protest to the State Department, for he knew that he could be next. "If I lost my passport, I would just curl up and die!" he explained with desperation. "I have to get out of this country at least once a year, the way things are now."[62]

With the ascendancy of Republican control of the White House, McCarthy's tactics, once seen as a necessary evil, became seen as less necessary and more evil by thoughtful Republicans attempting to make a cogent foreign policy. In the meantime, though, Miller's trials continued until August 1958, when, by a unanimous decision of the Court of Appeals, he was acquitted of contempt of Congress. Miller labeled the government's intrusion "inhuman."[63] Many Americans had to agree.

As the U.S. government tried to silence progressive voices and attempted to woo (if not outright Americanize) Europe by exporting a sanitized national identity abroad, Europeans balked. Scholars have shown how Europeans accepted, adapted, and rejected American cultural export on the basis of their own needs and desires. While schoolchildren in Germany and Austria dutifully learned English, they also absorbed slang: "sex appeal," "pin-up girl," and "boogie-woogie."[64] While they read Henry Luce's *Time* and *Life*, they also acquired novels by Norman Mailer and Gore Vidal. While Europeans listened to Aaron Copland and George Gershwin, they also loved improvisational jazz, rebellious rock-and-roll, and other so-called "Negro music." They may have viewed *Life of Eisenhower* one week, but they enjoyed a gangster film set on the dark, rain-soaked streets of San Francisco the next.

The producers of progressive culture were important because they articulated an alternative to bipolarity, challenged American exceptionalism, and sparked a backlash that unmasked the viciousness of extreme anticommunism. But progressive ideology was only part of the appeal. Europeans were attracted to the works of Hellman, Miller, and others for many reasons. Although some enjoyed viewing lavish Hollywood spectacles, many others did not and delighted instead in works they considered more serious. It would be an overstatement, however, to suggest that European audiences wholeheartedly endorsed the progressive ideology contained in the cultural productions they viewed. The fascination with dissent can be explained another way. Aside from offering a novel approach to the United States and the world, alternative themes "also satisfied apolitical curiosity."[65] This was just the point that the Eisenhower administration came to realize: American culture served the national interests, regardless of political intent.[66]

Nationalistic flag-waving did not appeal to European tastes. In time it did not appeal to American tastes much either. George Kennan warned back in 1951 that such fanaticism tended "to rivet attention upon ourselves" rather than on the international scene.[67] In other words, the most zealous anticommunism was bad not just because of its crude opportunism and heavy-handed tactics but because it worked against American foreign policy interests, for in their attempts to show the best of the nation, zealots showed the worst of America. It also turned the focus away from any real threat of Soviet expansion and put the spotlight on false enemies. The actions of progressive artists overseas had at once prompted McCarthy's shameful actions and highlighted for Europeans the hypocrisies inherent in a garrison-state democracy. Many Cold War liberals, such as the Americans for Democratic Action, joined the fight against communism at the same time as they fought to protect civil liberties. After all, lawyer Joseph Rauh, a leader of the ADA, had represented both Lillian Hellman and Arthur Miller.

Some Cold Warriors regretted the embarrassment that the overseas libraries and the passport cases brought to the national profile, but they were still committed to the original purpose of the cultural weapon: to promote an idealized image of the nation and to draw distinctions with the Soviet Union in the hope of winning the hearts and minds of just about everybody. Even after McCarthy's swift fall in 1954, the Eisenhower administration still believed it could work closely with business to promote a positive impression of the nation, this time in the emerging medium of European television.

As early as the late 1940s, some officials involved in the Voice of America had spoken with members of private industry about the need for the United States to beat the Russians in the area of international television. This "space race" for global television never materialized but showed the desire on the part of both government and business to extend television to the world. If any single event sparked the growth of international television, surely it was the 1953 coronation of Queen Elizabeth II. For over seven hours, television proved itself as a political instrument when for the first time an estimated twenty million Britons came together to watch their monarch crowned. The occasion was replayed for eager television audiences in the United States as well, where millions of viewers watched. The popularity of the transatlantic transmission impressed Americans in government, business, and at the networks, all of whom were looking to expand their TV operations in Britain and in other countries. Over the next two years, the number of television sets abroad grew from 3 million to almost 11 million.[68]

The year after the coronation, the seven congressional members of the International Telecommunications Commission met in Washington to discuss the potential for global television. One member, Senator Alexander Wiley (McCarthy's Republican colleague from Wisconsin), saw an opportunity "to improve trade, to increase understanding."[69] Indeed, he understood that selling both television sets and programs would "improve trade," while conveying positive messages about America would "increase understanding." Nowhere was this more clearly possible than in English-speaking countries. The same year in Britain, Parliament passed the Television Act of 1954, allowing for an independent, commercial television network to compete with the state-sponsored British Broadcasting Corporation (BBC). There was much opposition to commercial television in Britain. Before the Television Act passed Parliament, Labour politicians and distinguished English actors joined forces, claiming that their nation would be swamped by American culture. They warned, furthermore, that what happened in Britain would serve as a model for continental programming decisions. They were right; the USIA examined ways to encourage commercial television in many European countries, thereby opening the airwaves to American content.[70]

Media scholar Kerry Segrave argues that Americans were in part responsible for this result, explaining that

> the strategy for achieving the commercialization of British television was masterminded by the London branch of the American J. Walter Thompson ad agency, working with a group in Parliament. Their well-financed campaign did not emphasize commercial advantages but shrewdly attacked the BBC at its most publicly objectionable point—its monopoly status. That commercialization of British television opened a crucial market for U.S. advertisers and their agents. Equally important was the idea that the British example would be followed by other European nations, increasing the outlets for U.S. television fare, U.S. advertising, and U.S. goods.[71]

At the very moment when Americans knocked, Europeans opened the door. By 1954, thirteen nations claimed commercial television systems; fifteen had state-run systems; and another twenty-seven were developing industries based on the American standard.[72]

Commercial television came to Britain in September 1955. Soon thereafter, Americans looked to trade over the waves of this *other* English channel, and before the year was out, American distributors already had sold twenty-five productions worth $3 million. That cache included the domestic situation comedy *I Love Lucy*, the classic western *Gunsmoke*, and the blackface antics of *Amos & Andy*. Within the first eighteen months of commercial television in Britain, American advertising agencies, including Young & Rubicam and J. Walter Thompson, reaped hundreds of millions of dollars from their clients in the foreign markets. Many of these agencies and sponsors opened foreign offices and fine-tuned their techniques. To representatives attending the first World Congress on Commercial Television in London, pharmaceutical giant Johnson & Johnson provided lessons on making advertising pitches to diverse audiences. Screen Gems, the television division of Columbia Pictures, opened an office in London. With all the American activity in overseas television, *U.S. News & World Report* suggested in 1956, "an American visitor watching television in Britain might almost think he was still back home."[73] The cultural weapon was well at work.

The government contributed to these trends. The USIA kept detailed statistics on television operations overseas and provided this information to American distributors and advertisers. Despite the ability to produce and distribute enough material to fill the needs of emergent television industries, the USIA made it a policy not to compete with Hollywood. The government fed documentaries and other "informational" programs free of charge to hungry stations but allowed American producers to supply the rest. The government also played a role in trade agreements, especially as nations constructed barriers to their American imports. As early as 1956, American television executives discussed forming their own export association, like Hollywood's MPEA/MPAA. The proposed "state department" for the television industry would work the middle ground between American trade negotiators and foreign governments. By 1959, the Television Program Export Association (TPEA) had become a reality and negotiated deals on its own. Columnists for the trade paper *Variety* likened all this fevered interest in foreign television to a "colonial policy" for American media.[74]

As it happened, this was a colonial policy that the Eisenhower administration encouraged but did not control. In theory, television screens that exhibited American programs accomplished many things at once. The programs could convey the image of the nation that Cold Warriors so valued but also situate an important icon of consumer capitalism—the television set itself—inside millions of European homes. An assortment of American businesses profited from the sale of RCA receivers, a backlog of Hollywood films, network programs, and advertisements.

Ironically, though, the success at opening foreign television markets for Americans also proved invaluable to Progressives who articulated an alternative vision of America. From the beginning, commercial networks such as Britain's independent television network (ITV) relied on purchasing American programs to fill its schedule. That television was new and that ardent Cold Warriors overlooked much of its content allowed many blacklisted writers to work for Britain's small screen. In one instance, two members of the Hollywood Ten wrote for the British series *Robin Hood*, weekly tales of the swashbuckling thief known for stealing from the rich and giving to the poor. Ring Lardner Jr. headed a group of writers in New York, and Adrian Scott headed a group in Los Angeles, all writing for overseas television. "Most of our scripts had either a progressive idea or at least something human about them," one writer recalled. Producer Hannah Weinstein tapped into the blacklisted community and signed television contracts with many American writers living in Europe.[75]

Many other writers gave the government few grounds for harassment. Television writers such as Rod Serling and Paddy Chayefsky had never had the connections to radical or suspect organizations that others once held, but they did share an ideology that challenged the views of the Cold War consensus, and their scripts reached an avid following in Europe.

Undoubtedly, anthology drama writers recognized the financial rewards of entering the European cultural scene. But many also understood the relative artistic freedom Europe offered. Although most writers exported their scripts to the European market, Rod Serling's experiences may serve as a representative sample. Serling was pleased to discover that the BBC had no commercial breaks to interrupt his teleplays. Furthermore, without a "sponsor problem," he could return original scenes and dialogue to European productions. Even more significantly, Serling was able to sell his controversial script about the Korean War, *The Strike*, to the BBC after MGM's rights elapsed with no production in sight.[76] To their credit, the BBC and ITV both went out of their way to present material as originally intended. When one BBC official learned that a production concerned itself with "Negroes not Mexicans[,] and sheriff suicided [*sic*] not killed," he requested Serling's original treatment because "compromise here unnecessary."[77] Other European countries also chose from American culture whatever they wished to exhibit. The fact that progressive messages continued unabated during the 1950s goes a long way toward explaining the U.S. government's difficulty of extending an informal cultural empire over Cold War Europe.

Serling's orientation to British television shows that despite their well-publicized attempts to stifle progressive artists overseas, ardent Cold Warriors failed to curb universalism. One force behind this breakdown came from the tenacious and enterprising writers who presented universalist ideology overseas. But Serling's situation also reminds us of the important role that receptive Europeans played. European audiences and programmers provided another force that changed the way Washington staged the Cold War.

European audiences and critics expressed how refreshing American realism appeared in light of state-sanctioned cultural productions. Paddy Chayefsky's *Marty*, for example, became an international sensation because it presented an inverted image of what Cold Warriors put forth. What in *Marty* appealed to Europeans? Dialogue rather than song-and-dance routines, black-and-white rather than Technicolor spectacles, small people with complex lives rather than prominent people living in abundance. A columnist for the *London Daily Mail* explained that *Marty*'s appeal lay "not in its story alone but the almost clinical exactness with which it lays bare the bankruptcy of life in a part of New York we have not seen before. And yet it is all too familiar to us." The *London Sunday Times* critic wryly noted that *Marty*'s rejection of "the cheap morality" so common to American cultural productions seemed "almost to constitute an un-American activity." Others appreciated the universality of themes, one noting that characters "are so real . . . they could just as truly be British." An edition of *Life International* labeled Chayefsky "the best ambassador the U.S. has sent abroad in years." Many Europeans accepted anthologies as best representing not only their flawed American ally but also universal truths.[78] They marked an art form far different from the garish displays that Europeans believed typical of America. Ironically, productions that challenged notions of American exceptionalism helped win the hearts and minds of Europeans, and unknowingly, Europeans invited American cultural export.

During the mid-1950s, after McCarthy's attempts to silence voices and after American allies reacted in disgust to those attempts, the Eisenhower administration came to see such brash efforts at content control as futile and embarrassing. Yet even after the Senate censured Joseph McCarthy in 1954, anticommunists continued the charge. Mississippi Senator James O. Eastland appeared on the *Face the Nation* television program in February 1955 to explain the potential hazard of allowing

American Progressives to find "left wing firms" abroad willing to produce and publish their work.[79] But Eastland, chairman of the Senate Internal Security Subcommittee, found himself in disagreement with the Eisenhower administration.

Moderate anticommunists in government increasingly viewed *any* American cultural export as valuable in the effort to define differences between democratic-capitalism and totalitarian-communism. In the mid-1950s the government eased its tight supervision over cultural exports when it realized that its representation of America could peacefully coexist with alternative visions. In 1956 President Eisenhower inaugurated the people-to-people campaign, which made "every man an ambassador," to represent the nation to the world. The forty-one committees that made up the campaign's foundation included poet Marianne Moore, novelist William Faulkner, cartoonist Al Capp, and CBS president Frank Stanton. As one government pamphlet explained to the nation's new negotiators, "It's a good idea to lay off preaching to the friends you make. People all over the world chide Americans about this tendency." Rather, the advice continued, "it's wise to try to get across the idea that your answers and those of other Americans may not always agree."[80] To paraphrase the subtitle of the film *Dr. Strangelove*, the government could stop worrying and learn to love expatriates.

The Eisenhower administration, in the last years of the 1950s, began to measure and evaluate European audience reception of American content. When the USIA relied on the Gallup organization to survey Europeans in four key NATO countries in 1958—Britain, France, Italy, and West Germany—they discovered that nearly all reported seeing a variety of American-made television programs, including anthology dramas, and that their generally favorable chief impression was that Americans were the same as or similar to Europeans. Though viewers did also note unfavorable American qualities, the USIA concluded that "the results make it seem probable that in the net the gains exceed the losses." Also noteworthy was the desire on the part of Europeans to learn more about the "life of ordinary people" in the United States rather than the sanitized and extraordinary images so common in official propaganda.[81]

On July 10, 1959, C. D. Jackson urged the president to convene a meeting of the top national security personnel to focus on the issue of psychological warfare. The president complied by inviting fifteen such leaders to a White House dinner discussion on September 10. Soon thereafter he appointed Mansfield Sprague to chair a committee assigned to consider American cultural programs in light of the current world situation. The

Jackson committee report of 1953 and the Sprague committee report of 1960 neatly bookend the Eisenhower administration's efforts in the area of public diplomacy.

The Sprague committee followed much the same investigative process as the earlier effort, but this later group insisted that the government should pay close, "systematic" attention to foreign audience reception when making decisions about American cultural exports. Public opinion mattered greatly, the Sprague committee argued, especially in the post-colonial world of Africa, Asia, and Latin America; indeed, recent events in the Congo, Vietnam, and Cuba only reinforced this recommendation. There were opportunities to undermine the communists as well, especially by broadcasting to the East. The committee members learned, for example, about East Germans and Czechs who had risked their lives by organizing television-watching parties in their homes. Armed with this evidence, the committee encouraged the Eisenhower administration to promote exchanges behind the Iron Curtain. The members specifically mentioned the utility of state sponsorship of private individuals in television and other media with the purpose of using the rapid proliferation of technology to accomplish national goals.[82]

With new weapons for an old purpose, the Eisenhower administration sought to use institutions such as the USIA and the VOA to extend American culture abroad regardless of an ideological litmus test. This effort moved beyond film, television, and other visual media; American-sponsored jazz tours became valuable weapons in the Cold War, starting in the mid-1950s. Though local officials suppressed jazz in the Eastern bloc, the music remained a popular form of youth culture and rebellion. To officials at the USIA, any American art form that could simultaneously promote rebellion in the right places and convey a message of racial diversity in America could not be all bad. This was the rationale for appointing Louis Armstrong, Duke Ellington, and Dizzy Gillespie as "jambassadors."[83] The VOA introduced its first jazz program in 1956. Jazz exhibits and concerts entered the America Houses in 1957. Even Red army soldiers stationed in Berlin liked jazz and smuggled it into the Soviet Union.[84]

On July 25, 1959, Vice President Richard Nixon opened the American exhibition in Moscow and showcased the works of many Cold War critics. The art fair included a sculpture by Jo Davidson, the burly leader of the "subversive" ICCASP syndicate. The State Department not only distributed Paddy Chayefsky's popular film *Marty* as part of a cultural exchange program but sponsored Chayefsky as a goodwill ambassador on tour, representing the United States. The head of United Artists, Arthur Krim, recalled that Soviet bureaucrats selected *Marty* "because they thought it would show the seamier side of American life" but soon discovered that common Russians "were absolutely enthralled that a butcher could have so much, his own house, a room for his mother and aunt, a phone that worked." When Chayefsky visited Moscow in July, he confirmed statistics about growing unemployment in America and the problem of censorship, but the curmudgeonly writer also chided his hosts by saying, "At least half of those four million unemployed Americans went around job-seeking in their own cars." Chayefsky condemned widespread censorship in the Soviet system and fumed about travel restrictions that delayed his visit to his mother's village in Kiev. After suffering "this saga of Communist manipulation and mendacity," Chayefsky told Arthur Schlesinger Jr., the Cold War liberal historian who joined the tour, that he would write a scathing and "wrathful" script about his experiences.[85]

Some zealous anticommunists rose in Congress to publicly protest these new ambassadors of American culture. That had little effect on Eisenhower administration policy. "I don't like jazz music," Nixon told Soviet premier Nikita Khrushchev. "I don't like it either," the premier replied.[86] Apparently jazz could bring enemies together one way or another. We don't know what Ike and Nixon thought about *Marty* and the artistic merit of works by blacklisted talent, but their administration did recognize the political value of exporting such works overseas.

Diplomacy occurred in surprising places and in unsuspecting ways. Nixon's famous "kitchen debate" with Khrushchev took place in front of David Sarnoff's RCA cameras. The vice president interrupted the premier: "I will not comment on the various points that you raised, except to say this: this color television is one of the most advanced developments in communication that we have." While Nixon and Khrushchev debated the merits of capitalism and communism, respectively, viewers watched on the modern marvel of which Nixon spoke. Milton Eisenhower, the president's brother, and Llewellyn Thompson Jr., the American ambassador to Moscow, witnessed the disgraceful spectacle. *New York Times* reporter James "Scotty" Reston reported that the two men "were standing outside wondering whatever became of diplomacy and why didn't somebody pull the plug on the whole thing."[87] Later, during Khrushchev's famous tour of America in September 1959, security concerns kept him from visiting that most sensitive of Cold War sites, Disneyland, but he did manage to attend a lunch at Twentieth Century-Fox studios.

Nikita Khrushchev and Richard Nixon act out for the television cameras in Moscow, 1959. Courtesy Library of Congress, Prints & Photographs Division, US News & World Report, LC-U9-2808, frame 33.

What appeared to be cultural exchanges leading to "further understanding" offered only a facade of real peace. Ironically, leaders in Washington and Moscow appropriated progressive rhetoric for unintended purposes. Eisenhower and Khrushchev marketed a "spirit of Camp David" and made gestures toward "peaceful coexistence," but both maintained bipolarity. The USIA considered "peaceful coexistence" to be a "communist line" designed to appeal to the anxious world.[88] An illusion of harmony served the purposes of the Cold Warriors.

At the end of the decade, Dalton Trumbo finally admitted that he was the blacklisted "Robert Rich" who had won so much notoriety for writing *The Brave One* (1955) from behind a front. In 1960 he wrote the screenplay for *Exodus*, based on the Leon Uris novel, and adapted Howard Fast's novel *Spartacus* for the screen. His name appeared on both, and the blacklist effectively ended. Ring Lardner Jr. joked about the epic length of the two box office hits: "In a three-month period last year more thousands of feet of film were released" under Trumbo's name "than

Like New Yorkers in 1939, here Muscovites gather around a television set at the American pavilion in Sokolniki Park, 1959. Courtesy Library of Congress, Prints & Photographs Division, US News & World Report, LC-U9-2868, frame 37.

any screenwriter has ever inflicted on the American public in a similar space of time in the history of the business." The comments were similar to ones made twenty years earlier about David O. Selznick's *Gone With the Wind* (1939). Perhaps the more amazing event involving Trumbo took place with little fanfare. An agent representing Paramount, Warner Bros., and RKO negotiated for the release of *The Brave One* in the Soviet Union. The deal was consummated in Moscow under a Soviet-American cultural exchange agreement and cleared by Turner B. Shelton, the chief of the USIA Motion Picture Service at the State Department. The bland bureaucratic nature of the moment emphasized how much American public diplomacy had changed in the previous twenty years.[89]

Blacklisted screenwriters such as Dalton Trumbo, harassed playwrights such as Arthur Miller, frustrated television writers such as Rod Serling, opportunistic producers such as David O. Selznick, and many representatives of the State Department all converged in Europe during the 1950s. The European theater of the Cold War provided the stage for an "Iron Curtain call" in which a diverse cast of cultural negotiators met. Their activities show that artists and the public sought to play active roles in shaping American foreign policy by articulating an alternative national identity at the same time that the government attached great importance to that identity. Progressive artists and their overseas productions triggered a reaction by anticommunists and devout Cold Warriors. The most zealous among them employed far-reaching practices—censorship, harassment, and limits on the free movement of those they opposed—with the stated goal of stifling progressive ideology. Ironically, these dubious methods were the very ones that Americans claimed most to abhor in their war with totalitarianism. Progressives proved tenacious, their ideology portable, and European audiences accommodating. By the late 1950s the reaction of America's allies contributed to softening the government's hard sell of Americanism. Europeans grumbled over anticommunist hysteria and consumed progressive productions. In many ways, the contest waged over America's Cold War national identity was as dramatic for its participants as the scripts they produced. In the end, staging the Cold War proved to be a difficult task for the United States government, something that would become even more obvious as the 1960s dawned.

Looking at Moscow in 1959, one could see that Progressives had achieved their goal: to create a community that tolerated diverse views. There is great irony in that U.S. government officials had for so long tried to silence progressive culture, only to realize that its proliferation actually served American foreign policy needs. Ultimately, the government co-opted progressive cultural products, using them with others to unite the West under American leadership and, in time, to undermine the Soviet bloc. Indeed, one world had been created by the global export of American culture.

Afterword

The Cold War Epic

GEORGE KENNAN was one of the policymakers present at the creation of the Cold War. Unlike most of his contemporaries, he lived long enough to witness the end of the Cold War as well. Writing the first volume of his memoirs in 1967, surrounded by the turmoil and turbulence of that era, Kennan looked back at his original advocacy for the firm and lasting containment of Russian expansion. Much to Kennan's dismay, after he left government for academia, American policymakers expanded his containment policy—ideologically and globally—and applied it to places like Vietnam. He must have been haunted by the fact that others purposefully misread his observations and used his words as the rationale for domestic witch hunts and foreign entanglements. When looking at the prolonged Cold War, how many observers have come to see continuity where there is complexity, and simplicity where there is nuance?

The Cold War was not a static set of events. Rather, the Cold War was a dynamic and multifaceted period in international history. Since its end, a false collective memory is in danger of forming, one confirmed by its repetition in textbooks and mass media, one that designates the half-century after the Second World War as generally a fixed period of time. While the distance of time provides perspective, it also threatens a more subtle understanding of the past. Already the public, removed as it is from the Cold War that dominated the world for fifty years, has come to view the conflict in fixed ways: two unified, conformist, and monolithic superpowers waged a bipolar contest for control and influence over the rest of the world. The foregoing chapters are intended to help other studies challenge that all-too-familiar memory. A history detailing the persistence of dissent in culture industries challenges a collective memory of the 1940s and 1950s as a period noted for domestic conformity and global bipolarity.

212

In truth, the Cold War was not a bipolar struggle. Europeans living on the front lines in battleground nations, like other citizens of the world, complemented and confounded Cold War policies made in Washington and in Moscow. Surely, the United States and the Soviet Union were superpowers, but just as certainly, they were not hegemons. The Truman and Eisenhower administrations worked hard to shape information programs that would appeal to the proverbial hearts and minds. The American bureaucracy—diplomats, the USIA, Voice of America, the Sprague Committee, FBI agents—measured European opinion on a daily basis during the Cold War and relied on such unofficial sources as Hollywood studios, the MPAA, television networks, Gallup polls, and advertising agencies for more data. All this suggests the importance of foreign opinion's effect on American foreign policy and public diplomacy. Policies aside, foreign audiences helped define the character and intensity of the Cold War.

Even at the American "pole" there existed a diversity of opinion within camps on the political left, right, and center. Although multilateralists loosely united to support the United Nations and civil rights, they diverged on accommodation with the Soviets. Cold War liberals fully split with radicals during the congressional hearings that revealed unapologetic fellow travelers in Hollywood. Similar divisions appeared on the right. After reading over his public statements advocating containment, Kennan admitted that critics "might suggest I was headed for a job as staff consultant to the late Senator Joe McCarthy or to the House Un-American Affairs Committee." Yet Kennan situated himself between the idealism of One World on the one hand—which he labeled "as innocent as six-year-old maidens"—and the "hysterical sort of anticommunism" on the other.[1] The Eisenhower administration came to recognize that the excesses of McCarthy and his associates harmed American influence in Europe. Political philosophies, moreover, did not always govern actions. After all, more than a few nimble Hollywood moguls used their motion pictures as propaganda to support the wartime government and the Soviet ally, then during the Cold War they recalibrated and helped define the Soviet enemy. In doing so they achieved public goodwill, government assistance, and opportunities for open markets.

A closer examination of the period reveals another truth: America in the 1940s and 1950s was not a clearly conformist prelude to a backlash of dissent in the chaotic 1960s and 1970s. This was especially true because anticommunists failed to silence American dissent completely during the early Cold War. Too often observers overgeneralize and note stark differences between the placid 1950s and the rebellious 1960s. Even when diplomatic historians note the opposite, how earlier Red hysteria gave way to later détente, they too see change rather than continuity between the decades. As this book attempts to show, Cold Warriors tried to construct a uniform and sanitized national identity with rigid lines between the Soviet and American spheres, but they failed when domestic dissent fashioned programs articulating an alternative vision of the nation and exported that vision overseas. There was robust and varied dissent in culture industries such as Hollywood, Broadway, and television. Talent promoted humane capitalism, anticolonialism, self-determination, civil liberties, and impartiality in dealing with all nations. When zealous anticommunists attempted to silence critics in one industry, dissenters found space in other places where they continued to express their views. In a period of relative conformity and repression, there was also much deviation. Themes of dissent foreshadowed vocal forms of protest in the 1960s and 1970s: the moratorium on nuclear testing, the antiwar movement, and the counterculture.

Whereas political calculations, economic programs, and military technologies helped wage the Cold War, cultural programs and commodities helped end it. This book supports others that show how the cultural weapon complemented these other strategies of containment. For example, some Europeans appreciated the American nuclear umbrella, but others believed the mere presence of nuclear weapons made Europe more vulnerable to disaster. Some Europeans welcomed Marshall Plan aid; others understood that assistance came with strings attached. Once the Cold War became viewed as an ideological contest with Soviet communism, only culture (as propaganda, as dissent, as neutral content, and as consumer products) could breach the Iron Curtain with regularity. And when zealous anticommunists patrolled Europe and policed content, Europeans embraced dissent.

In the mid-1990s George Kennan published another volume of his memoirs, which included his thoughts on the end of the Cold War. Looking back at the intense Red hysteria of the 1940s and 1950s—"an episode of our public life so disgraceful that one blushes to think about it"— Kennan condemned the most ardent anticommunists, who "seriously distorted the understanding of a great many Americans about foreign policy, implying as they did that our policy was always the decisive mover of events everywhere in the world."[2] George Kennan was right: Washington could not direct the Cold War because a large cast of characters stood on the stage at the same time and read lines from many scripts.

Notes

Abbreviations Used in the Notes

CART	Continuity Acceptance Reports, NBC, WHS
CBLP	Clare Boothe Luce Papers, LC
DDEL	Dwight D. Eisenhower Presidential Library, Abilene, KS
DOSB	*Department of State Bulletin*
DOSP	David O. Selznick Papers, HRC
DSP	Dore Schary Papers, WHS
DTP	Dalton Trumbo Papers, WHS
FRUS	*Foreign Relations of the United States*
HDCP	Hollywood Democratic Committee Papers, WHS
HRC	Harry Ransom Humanities Research Center, Austin, TX
HSTL	Harry S Truman Presidential Library, Independence, MO
HUAC	House Committee on Un-American Activities, NA
JRP	Joseph L. Rauh Jr. Papers, LC
LC	Library of Congress, Washington, DC
LHP	Lillian Hellman Papers, HRC
NA	National Archives and Records Administration, Washington, DC
NBC	National Broadcasting Company collections, WHS
NTP	Niles Trammell Papers, NBC, WHS
PNP	Paul H. Nitze Papers, LC
RG	Record Group
RSP	Rod Serling Papers, WHS
SEP	Sidney H. Eiges Papers, NBC, WHS
SISS	Senate Internal Security Subcommittee, NA
SPWP	Sylvester (Pat) Weaver Papers, NBC, WHS
TWP	Tennessee Williams Papers, HRC
USIA	United States Information Agency
WBP	William F. Brooks Papers, NBC, WHS
WHS	Wisconsin Historical Society, Madison, WI

Portions of this book were published in an earlier form as "Reading Between the Lines: Negotiating National Identity on American Television, 1945–1960," *Diplomatic History* 28, no. 2 (April 2004): 197–225, and are reproduced here by permission.

Introduction

1. David Gelernter, *1939: The Lost World of the Fair* (New York: Avon Books, 1995), 7.

2. Joel Engel, *Rod Serling: The Dreams and Nightmares of Life in the Twilight Zone* (Chicago: Contemporary Books, 1989), 78.

3. Robert Haddow, *Pavilions of Plenty: Exhibiting American Culture Abroad in the 1950s* (Washington, DC: Smithsonian Institution Press, 1997), 31.

4. Ibid., 36.

5. Ibid., 18–37; Paul Hoffman, *Peace Can Be Won* (New York: Doubleday, 1951), 34.

6. Rockwell painted Nixon on occasion, including for the cover of the *Saturday Evening Post* a few months later.

7. Haddow, *Pavilions of Plenty*, 213.

8. Untitled *Hollywood Reporter* clipping, December 30, 1959, SISS, box 113, Films and Plays file, RG 46, NA.

9. On earlier attempts at using culture to create an American national identity, see Eve Kornfeld, *Creating an American Culture, 1775–1800* (Boston: Bedford/St. Martin's, 2001); and John Kasson, *Amusing the Million: Coney Island at the Turn of the Century* (New York: Hill and Wang, 1978), among others. These historians have examined these processes and emphasize contestation.

10. The idea that the era is noteworthy for its general consensus is put forth in William O'Neill, *American High: The Years of Confidence, 1945–1960* (New York: Free Press, 1986). The historical literature on domestic communism and anticommunism is bountiful, especially since scholars gained access to the archives of the former Soviet Union. Although differences exist—and often become heated debates—most studies agree on certain premises: the American anticommunist movement encompassed more individuals than Joseph McCarthy; anxiety was based, in part, on legitimate concerns about the activities of domestic communists who maintained communication with Moscow; and too many political opportunists exaggerated the threat, promoted Red hysteria, and used their influence to harm many innocent victims. For example, see Les Adler and Thomas G. Paterson, "Red Fascism: The Merger of Nazi Germany and Soviet Russia in the American Image of Totalitarianism, 1930's–1950's," *American Historical Review* 75, no. 4 (April 1970): 1046–1064; Richard Fried, *Nightmare in Red: The McCarthy Era in Perspective* (New York: Oxford, 1991); John Earl Haynes, "The Cold War Debate Continues: A Traditionalist View of Historical Writing on Domestic Communism and Anti-Communism," *Journal of Cold War Studies* 2, no. 1 (2000): 76–115; Harvey Klehr, John Earl Haynes, and Fredrik Firsov, *The Secret World of American Communism* (New Haven: Yale University Press, 1995); Harvey Klehr, John Earl Haynes, and Kyrill Anderson, *The Soviet World of American Communism* (New Haven: Yale University Press, 1998); John Earl Haynes and Harvey Klehr, *Venona: Decoding Soviet Espionage in America* (New Haven: Yale University Press, 1999); David Oshinsky, *A Conspiracy So Immense: The World of Joe McCarthy* (New York: Free Press, 1983); Ellen Schrecker, *Many Are the Crimes: McCarthyism in America* (Boston: Little, Brown, 1998); and Jacob Weisberg, "Cold War without End," *New York Times Magazine*, November 28, 1999, 116–123, 155–158.

11. Ideology, public opinion, and popular culture appear to be vital components in any study of the Cold War. Indeed, historian Elaine Tyler May has explained that

"both foreign policy and culture in the United States rest largely on ideology." May, "Commentary: Ideology and Foreign Policy: Culture and Gender in Diplomatic History," *Diplomatic History* 18, no. 1 (Winter 1994): 71. See also Michael H. Hunt, *Ideology and U.S. Foreign Policy* (New Haven: Yale University Press, 1987), 3, 12–13, 15; Susan Jeffords, "Commentary: Culture and National Identity in U.S. Foreign Policy," *Diplomatic History* 18, no. 1 (Winter 1994): 93–94; Amy Kaplan, "Commentary: Domesticating Foreign Policy," *Diplomatic History* 18, no. 1 (Winter 1994): 103. For an earlier treatment of Cold War critics, see Thomas G. Paterson, ed., *Cold War Critics: Alternatives to American Foreign Policy in the Truman Years* (Chicago: Quadrangle Books, 1971). Also see Paul Boyer, *By the Bomb's Early Light: American Thought and Culture at the Dawn of the Atomic Age* (Chapel Hill: University of North Carolina Press, 1985). On the impact of domestic politics on foreign policy, see Kristin L. Hoganson, *Fighting for American Manhood: How Gender Politics Provoked the Spanish-American and Philippine-American Wars* (New Haven: Yale University Press, 1998).

12. According to George Lipsitz, "Culture can seem like a substitute for politics. . . . Culture exists as a means of reshaping individual and collective practice for specified interests." Lipsitz, *Time Passages: Collective Memory and American Popular Culture* (Minneapolis: University of Minnesota Press, 1990), 16–17.

13. See Brian C. Etheridge, "*The Desert Fox*, Memory Diplomacy, and the German Question in Early Cold War America," *Diplomatic History* 32, no. 2 (April 2008): 213, for a suitable definition of public diplomacy: "communication activities designed to shape, manipulate, or otherwise influence public opinion to achieve or facilitate the attainment of foreign-policy objectives." While there still remains disagreement on the precise definition of "public diplomacy," the Library of Congress concluded that the first reference of the term appeared in 1965 at the Edward R. Murrow Center for Public Diplomacy. On public diplomacy, American cultural export, and the culture of the Cold War, see Frank Ninkovich, *The Diplomacy of Ideas: U.S. Foreign Policy and Cultural Relations, 1938–1950* (New York: Cambridge University Press, 1981); Emily Rosenberg, *Spreading the American Dream: American Economic and Cultural Expansion, 1890–1945* (New York: Hill and Wang, 1982); Stephen J. Whitfield, *Culture of the Cold War* (Baltimore: Johns Hopkins Press, 1991); Christian G. Appy, ed., *Cold War Constructions: The Political Culture of United States Imperialism, 1945–1966* (Amherst: University of Massachusetts Press, 2000); and Liam Kennedy and Scott Lucas, "Enduring Freedom: Public Diplomacy and U.S. Foreign Policy," *American Quarterly* 57, no. 2 (2005): 309–333.

14. Several excellent studies examine American cultural export during the Cold War: Walter Hixson, *Parting the Curtain: Propaganda, Culture, and the Cold War* (New York: St. Martin's, 1996); Reinhold Wagnleitner, *Coca-Colonization and the Cold War: The Cultural Mission of the United States in Austria after the Second World War* (Chapel Hill: University of North Carolina Press, 1994); Uta Poiger, *Jazz, Rock, and Rebels: Cold War Politics and American Culture in a Divided Germany* (Berkeley: University of California Press, 2000); and Richard Pells, *Not Like Us: How Europeans Have Loved, Hated, and Transformed American Culture since World War II* (New York: Basic Books, 1997). All four authors show how American culture seeped into Europe but not always the way Washington had intended. Kenneth Osgood offers a comprehensive look at public information campaigns in *Total Cold War: Eisenhower's Secret Propaganda Battle at Home and Abroad* (Lawrence:

University Press of Kansas, 2006). In *Cold War Orientalism: Asia in the Middlebrow Imagination, 1945–1961* (Berkeley: University of California Press, 2003), Christina Klein shows how liberal-minded "middlebrow" culture—film musicals, magazines, and other media—adapted American racial thinking and prepared Americans to undertake paternalistic involvement in postcolonial East Asia. In *Television in Black-and-White America: Race and National Identity* (Lawrence: University Press of Kansas, 2005), Alan Nadel explains how television westerns, *Disneyland*, and other shows imagined "the West" and dealt with racial issues in sanitized ways for Free World audiences. This book moves beyond race to see how cultural programs also shaped American attitudes on a panoply of other issues related to American foreign policy. In *U.S. Television News and Cold War Propaganda, 1947–1960* (New York: Cambridge University Press, 1999), Nancy Bernhard notes how State Department personnel and network executives worked together to use television news and interview programs to support American foreign policy.

15. I am mindful that some readers might prefer more textual analysis of scripts in these pages, not just the documents that surround these texts. Although acknowledging its importance in cultural studies, I purposely have resisted engaging in more textual analysis because, as recent conference panels, plenary sessions, and journal roundtables will attest, traditional diplomatic historians have criticized practitioners of cultural history for finding in cultural texts whatever themes serve their purposes. Screenplays in particular are notoriously open to many interpretations because they are produced by collaborators who come to projects from many backgrounds and perspectives. Moreover, it is hard to detect audience reception, which further makes historical interpretations dicey propositions. In other words, who is to say that my readings of these texts are accurate, even if my analysis appears reasonable? Therefore, I have used private correspondence, organizational minutes, speeches, travel itineraries, legal testimony, and other sources to uncover evidence that corroborates the messages I see contained in screenplays and scripts. I seek to demonstrate the depth of political activity and the breadth of foreign policy dissent in culture industries. I believe that more textual analysis could alter the methodology significantly and might lead to a very different book, one that detracts attention from more quantifiable activities of well-rounded dissenters during the Cold War. In sum, I seek to balance traditional diplomatic history with cultural history. At the very least, I hope this approach provokes future studies and different interpretations.

16. Hunt, *Ideology*, 3, 12–13, 15; Terry Eagleton, *Ideology: An Introduction* (London: Verso, 1991), 12.

17. Panel commentary, "The State, Private Actors, and Anglo-American Relations in the Cold War," Society for Historians of American Foreign Relations annual conference, Washington, DC, June 15, 2001.

18. Kaplan, "Commentary," 103; Eagleton, *Ideology*, 5–6.

19. Eagleton, *Ideology*, 6; Geoffrey Smith, "Commentary: Security, Gender, and the Historical Process," *Diplomatic History* 18, no. 1 (Winter 1994): 80; Michel Foucault, *The Archeology of Knowledge* (New York: Pantheon, 1972).

20. See Benedict Anderson, *Imagined Communities: Reflections on the Origin and Spread of Nationalism* (London: Verso, 1983). Also see Eric Hobsbawm, *Nations and Nationalism since 1780: Programme, Myth, Reality* (Cambridge: Cambridge University Press, 1990), 9; John Breuilly, *Nationalism and the State* (New York: St. Martin's, 1982), 3; Matthew Frye Jacobson, *Special Sorrows: The Diasporic*

Imagination of Irish, Polish, and Jewish Immigrants in the United States (Cambridge: Harvard University Press, 1995), 17.

1. Hollywood in the Crucible of War

1. David O. Selznick, "New Frontiers in American Life," speech at the University of Rochester, May 9, 1940, DOSP, HRC, box 2367, file 6.

2. Ibid.

3. So-called Poverty Row studios included Monogram, Republic, and Grand National.

4. Thomas Schatz, *Boom and Bust: American Cinema in the 1940s* (Berkeley: University of California Press, 1997), 15–18.

5. Independent producers such as Sam Goldwyn, Cecil B. DeMille, Walt Disney, Charlie Chaplin, and David O. Selznick typically financed their own projects, signed their own talent, used their own production facilities, and then relied on studios for distribution. Independent talent included actors James Cagney, Gary Cooper, and Olivia de Havilland (after a renowned wartime lawsuit freed her from her studio contract); directors Howard Hawks, Alfred Hitchcock, Leo McCarey; and writer Ben Hecht and writer-producer Dore Schary.

6. Morrie Ryskind, "No Soap Boxes in Hollywood," *The Nation*, March 4, 1936. See Carl Bromley, ed., *Cinema Nation: The Best Writing on Film from* The Nation, *1913–2000* (New York: Nation Books, 2000), 116.

7. *Variety*, September 16, 1933, quoted in Larry Ceplar and Steven Englund, *The Inquisition in Hollywood: Politics in the Film Community, 1930–1960* (Berkeley: University of California Press, 1983), 54.

8. Morton Thompson, "Hollywood Is a Union Town," *The Nation*, April 2, 1938. See Bromley, *Cinema Nation*, 137.

9. For a good discussion of the complex Hollywood labor situation, see Gerald Horne, *Class Struggle in Hollywood, 1930–1950: Moguls, Mobsters, Stars, Reds and Trade Unionists* (Austin: University of Texas Press, 2001).

10. Lionel Stander oral history, in *Tender Comrades: A Backstory of the Hollywood Blacklist*, ed. Patrick McGilligan and Paul Buhle (New York: St. Martin's, 1997), 617.

11. Ceplar and Englund, *Inquisition*, 65. It is difficult to estimate party membership with any accuracy because of the underground nature of the organization. Moreover, some people who attended meetings never joined; others paid dues but never attended. Even more difficult to gauge is the strength of adherence. Radicals such as Lionel Stander never joined the party at all. Even the most radical individuals found "cell" meetings boring and time-consuming. Ultimately, it appears that the perception is what is most significant. While investigators for the House Committee on Un-American Activities (often referred to as HUAC) could count fewer than 200 card-carrying members, they certainly led the public into believing their numbers and influence were much more pervasive. I believe Communist Party membership is not the best way to define radicalism. Ideological convictions, especially those expressed by individuals in the name of the national identity, remain more important.

12. *New York Mirror*, April 14, 1940.

13. Stander oral history, 609.

14. Ibid., 613–614.

15. Neal Gabler, *An Empire of Their Own: How the Jews Invented Hollywood* (New York: Doubleday, 1988), 284. (Selznick further cut ties with Mayer when he and wife Irene divorced. Selznick later married the actress Jennifer Jones, best known for portraying a nun in *Song of Bernadette* in 1943.)

16. Ibid., 4. See also Norman Zierold, *The Moguls: Hollywood's Merchants of Myth* (Los Angeles: Silman-James Press, 1991).

17. Robert Abzug, *America Views the Holocaust, 1933–1945: A Brief Documentary History* (Boston: Bedford/St. Martin's 1999), 85–108.

18. Breen quoted in Schatz, *Boom and Bust*, 265.

19. "Willkie Engaged to Defend Films," *New York Times*, September 2, 1941, 19; Frederick Barkley, "Hits Columnists on Movie Inquiry," *New York Times*, September 16, 1941, 18.

20. Gov. Culbert L. Olson to Sen. D. Worth Clark, September 15, 1941, DOSP, HRC, box 2363, file 3.

21. Schatz, *Boom and Bust*, 38, 116–122.

22. Ibid., 21–27, 155–160.

23. David O. Selznick to Whitney, Altstock, Case, Calvert, and Cooper, September 27 and 30, 1940, DOSP, HRC, box 2367, file 6. When the Hays Office placed obstacles in his way, Selznick labeled the situation "untenable."

24. Gerald Mast, *A Short History of Movies*, 4th ed. (New York: Macmillan, 1986), 135–154, 168–169, 380, 399–400, 488.

25. Ibid., chap. 11.

26. Michael Sherry makes the point that New Deal–era economic and social reform focused attention on national unity for a common purpose. In this way domestic activism intertwined with foreign relations. Sherry, *In the Shadow of War: The United States since the 1930s* (New Haven: Yale University Press, 1995). On the origins of American cultural diplomacy, see Frank Ninkovich, *The Diplomacy of Ideas: U.S. Foreign Policy and Cultural Relations, 1938–1950* (New York: Cambridge University Press, 1981); Emily Rosenberg, *Spreading the American Dream* (New York: Hill and Wang, 1982); and Richard Pells, *Not Like Us: How Europeans Have Loved, Hated, and Transformed American Culture since World War II* (New York: Basic Books, 1997), 31–36.

27. Schatz, *Boom and Bust*,14.

28. Walter Huston, prepared remarks, January 14, 1943, HDCP, WHS, box 1, file 9.

29. HDC to Rep. Brent Spence, May 10, 1945, HDCP, WHS, box 2, file 6.

30. John Morton Blum, *V Was for Victory* (New York: Harcourt Brace Jovanovich, 1976), 131–140.

31. In addition to Blum, for good discussions of Hollywood's wartime film content, see Schatz, *Boom and Bust*; John Dower, *War without Mercy: Race and Power in the Pacific War* (New York: Pantheon, 1986); Lewis A. Erenberg and Susan E. Hirsch, eds., *The War in American Culture: Society and Consciousness during World War II* (Chicago: University of Chicago Press, 1996).

32. Arthur L. Mayer, "Fact into Film," *Public Opinion Quarterly* 8, no. 2. (Summer 1944): 206–225.

33. Dower, *War without Mercy*, 16.

34. Ibid., 15; Schatz, *Boom and Bust*, 3.

35. For a good introduction to wartime censorship practices, see Schatz, *Boom and Bust*, 262–284.

36. Davis quoted in ibid., 269–270.

37. Franklin D. Roosevelt quoted in Blum, *V Was for Victory*, 24.

38. Lowell Mellett quoted in Blum, *V Was for Victory*, 25.

39. Emmett Lavery, "The Reviewing Stand," broadcast by Mutual Radio, September 16, 1945, DSP, WHS, box 26, file 1.

40. Dorothy B. Jones, "Hollywood Goes to War," *The Nation*, January 27, 1945. See Bromley, *Cinema Nation*, 125.

41. See Blum, *V Was for Victory*, 46, and Harold R. Isaacs, *Images of Asia: American Views of China and India* (New York: Harper, 1972).

42. Dower, *War without Mercy*, 11.

43. "How to Tell Your Friends from the Japs," *Time*, December 22, 1941, 33. See also Blum, *V Was for Victory*, 46.

44. Dower, *War without Mercy*, 10.

45. See Iris Chang, *The Rape of Nanking: The Forgotten Holocaust of World War II* (New York: Basic Books, 1997).

46. Jones, "Hollywood Goes to War," 125.

47. Les K. Adler and Thomas G. Paterson, "Red Fascism: The Merger of Nazi Germany and Soviet Russia in the American Image of Totalitarianism, 1930's–1950's," *American Historical Review* 75, no. 4 (April 1970): 1046–1064.

48. David O. Selznick to Philip Berg, May 16, 1942, DOSP, HRC, box 2366, file 1.

49. Philip Berg to David O. Selznick, May 19, 1942; Selznick to Berg, May 20, 1942, DOSP, HRC, box 2366, file 1.

50. Charles Einfield of Warner Bros to David O. Selznick, March 2, 1945, DOSP, HRC, box 2367, file 6.

51. Dr. Norman Salit, Executive Director of Wartime Emergency Commission for Conservative Judaism, to David O. Selznick, December 8, 1944, DOSP, HRC, box 2363, file 2.

52. Dower, *War without Mercy*, chaps. 1 and 2; Blum, *V Was for Victory*, 45–52.

53. That October, FBI director J. Edgar Hoover authorized a secret investigation into Hellman's political activities. See LHP, HRC, box 132.

54. "Russia Acclaimed by Miss Hellman," *New York Times*, March 2, 1945, 5.

55. In the 1960s editors were kept busy with a later release of the film under the title *Armored Attack*. After the Cuban missile crisis in 1962, they felt compelled to include a narrator who reminds postwar audiences that Americans and Soviets had been allies.

56. Melvyn P. Leffler, *The Specter of Communism: The United States and the Origins of the Cold War, 1917–1953* (New York: Hill and Wang, 1994), chap. 2.

57. Blum, *V Was for Victory*, 55.

58. Ibid., 41.

59. Frank Capra, *The Name above the Title: An Autobiography* (New York: Macmillan, 1971), 358–362.

60. Beverly Cram to Albert Maltz, September 14, 1943, Albert Maltz Papers, WHS, box 15, file 3.

61. Schatz, *Boom and Bust*, 244–246.

62. Ibid., 272–274.

63. Ibid., 2, 153.

64. Harry S Truman to David O. Selznick, September 5, 1945, DOSP, HRC, box 2363, file 1.

65. Mayer, "Fact into Film," 212, 224.

66. Jones, "Hollywood Goes to War."

67. Dore Schary, "Our War Effort," DSP, WHS, box 2, file 3.

68. Lary May, "Making the American Consensus: The Narrative of Conversion and Subversion in World War II Films," in Erenberg and Hirsch, *The War in American Culture*, 78.

69. Ceplar and Englund, *Inquisition*, 182.

70. Virginia Wright, drama editor, *Los Angeles Daily News*, April 16, 1945, 13.

71. Maj. Kenneth Mackenna, Director, Morale Films Division, to Albert Maltz, September 10, 1945, Albert Maltz Papers, WHS, box 15, file 3.

72. Dore Schary to David O. Selznick, January 27 and 30, 1945, DSP, WHS, box 113, file 13.

73. David O. Selznick memo to Vanguard Films staff, February 10, 1945, DSP, WHS, box 113, file 13. Robert Penn Warren's *All the King's Men* (1949) would gain critical acclaim a few years later when it was adapted for the screen by writer-director Robert Rossen, an "unfriendly" witness in HUAC's 1947 hearings.

74. Dore Schary to Los Angeles Advertising Club, April 16, 1945, DSP, WHS, box 113, file 13.

75. Schatz, *Boom and Bust*,165.

76. Eric Smoodin, *Animating Culture* (New Brunswick, NJ: Rutgers University Press, 1993), 161.

77. Louis Lighton to David O. Selznick, May 3, 1944, DOSP, HRC, box 2352, file 8.

78. Dore Schary to the Motion Picture Alliance for Preservation of American Ideals, June 17 and 20, 1944, DSP, WHS, box 2, file 3.

2. One World or Two?

1. John Lewis Gaddis, *Strategies of Containment: A Critical Appraisal of Postwar American National Security Policy* (Oxford: Oxford University Press, 1982), 3–9, 11–12.

2. John Morton Blum, *V Was for Victory* (New York: Harcourt Brace Jovanovich, 1976), 8.

3. Luce's article served for years as fodder for commentators wishing to chastise American involvement overseas by employing terms such as "exceptionalism" and even "hegemony." The influential article was even the starting point for a series of articles by some of the most prestigious diplomatic historians, who sought to evaluate American foreign affairs in the twentieth century. See Michael J. Hogan, ed., *The Ambiguous Legacy: U.S. Foreign Relations in the "American Century"* (Cambridge: Cambridge University Press, 1999).

4. Henry Luce, "The American Century," *Life*, February 17, 1941, reprinted in Hogan, *Ambiguous Legacy*, 11–13.

5. Arthur Vandenberg Jr., ed., *The Private Papers of Senator Vandenberg* (Boston: Houghton Mifflin, 1952), 1.

6. Justus D. Doenecke, *Not to the Swift: The Old Isolationists in the Cold War Era* (Lewisburg, PA: Bucknell University Press, 1979). Doenecke goes to great pains to show the noninterventionists' varied and conflicting backgrounds and beliefs. The diversity of internationalist opinion is introduced in Andrew Johnstone, "Americans Disunited: Americans United for World Organization and the Triumph of Internationalism," *Journal of American Studies* (forthcoming, 2009).

7. David O. Selznick to Henry Luce, March 4, 1941, DOSP, HRC, box 2361, file 5.

8. Nicholas Doman, *The Coming Age of World Control: The Transition to an Organized World Society* (New York: Harper, 1942), viii, 223.

9. Akira Iriye, *Global Community: The Role of International Organizations in the Making of the Contemporary World* (Berkeley: University of California Press, 2002), 42–43.

10. Fremont Rider, *The Great Dilemma of World Organization* (New York: Reynal and Hitchcock, 1946), 2.

11. Reinhold Niebuhr, *The Children of Light and the Children of Darkness* (New York: Scribner, 1945), x, 9–10, 32–33, 40–41; Reinhold Niebuhr, *The Nature and Destiny of Man* (New York: Scribner, 1943), 18–23, 99.

12. Arthur M. Schlesinger Jr., *A Life in the Twentieth Century: Innocent Beginnings, 1917–1950* (Boston: Houghton Mifflin, 2000), 511.

13. Reinhold Niebuhr, "The Democratic Elite and American Foreign Policy" in *Walter Lippmann and His Times*, ed. Marquis Childs and James Reston (New York: Harcourt Brace 1959), 188.

14. See Barton Bernstein, "Walter Lippmann and the Early Cold War" in *Cold War Critics: Alternatives to American Foreign Policy in the Truman Years*, ed. Thomas G. Paterson (Chicago: Quadrangle, 1971), 18–53.

15. Ronald Steel, *Walter Lippmann and the American Century* (Boston: Little, Brown, 1980), 404.

16. Walter Lippmann, *U.S. Foreign Policy: Shield of the Republic* (Boston: Little, Brown, 1943); Wendell Willkie, *One World* (New York: Simon and Schuster, 1943); Steel, *Walter Lippmann*, chap. 32.

17. Bernstein, "Walter Lippman," 19.

18. Lippmann, *U.S. Foreign Policy*, 9–10; Steel, *Walter Lippmann*, 410.

19. Elizabeth Borgwardt, *A New Deal for the World: America's Vision for Human Rights* (Cambridge: Harvard University Press, 2005), 158–159.

20. Robert Clark Keough, *Democracy's World* (Boston: Meador, 1944), 13–15, 25.

21. Doman, *Coming Age*, 5–6, 7, 11, 15.

22. Joseph P. Kamp, *We Must Abolish the United States: The Hidden Facts behind the Crusade for World Government* (New York: Hallmark, 1950), xii–xiii, 15; Doman, *Coming Age*, vii–viii; Rider, *Great Dilemma*, 3–4.

23. Willkie, *One World*, 163, 164–165.

24. Ibid., ix.

25. Ibid., 1 (emphasis added), 157.

26. Lillian Hellman FBI file, March 24, 1945, LHP, HRC, box 132, file 7; Reinhold Wagnleitner, *Coca-Colonization and the Cold War: The Cultural Mission of the United States in Austria after the Second World War* (Chapel Hill: University of North Carolina Press, 1994), ix.

27. Willkie, *One World*, 159–160.

28. Keough, *Democracy's World*, 67. Congress even investigated such conspiracies with the famed Nye Committee, which bitterly chastised munitions makers for profiting from the Great War.

29. Willkie, *One World*, 180, 159–160, 173–176, 182.

30. Ibid., 188.

31. Penny Von Eschen, *Race against Empire: Black Americans and Anticolonialism, 1937–1957* (Ithaca: Cornell University Press, 1997).

32. Willkie, *One World*, 183–185, chap. 13, 192, 166–167, 190–191.

33. Dore Schary, prepared remarks for a public forum, May 9, 1944, DSP, WHS, box 2, file 3.

34. Other leaders—Elijah Muhammad, for one—were arrested for publicly identifying racially rather than nationally with the Japanese. See John W. Dower, *War without Mercy: Race and Power in the Pacific War* (New York: Pantheon, 1986), 174–176; Akira Iriye, *Power and Culture: The Japanese-American War, 1941–1945* (Cambridge: Cambridge University Press, 1981); and Gerald Horne, "Race for Power: U.S. Foreign Policy and the General Crisis of 'White Supremacy,'" in Hogan, *Ambiguous Legacy*, 323.

35. Walter White, "Race Relations in the Armed Services of the United States," *Journal of Negro Education* 12, no. 3 (Summer 1943): 350–354. See also the views of the Morehouse College president, Benjamin E. Mays, June 8, 1945, in his commencement address to Howard University, reprinted as "Democratizing and Christianizing America in This Generation," *Journal of Negro Education* 14, no. 4 (Autumn 1945): 527.

36. Mays, "Democratizing," 533.

37. Ellen Schrecker, *Many Are the Crimes: McCarthyism in America* (Boston: Little, Brown, 1998), 103.

38. Willkie, *One World*, 167–168.

39. Emil Lengyel, "International Education as an Aid to World Peace," *Journal of Educational Sociology* 20, no. 9 (May 1947): 562–563.

40. Warren B. Walsh, "What the American People Think of Russia," *Public Opinion Quarterly* 8, no. 4 (Winter 1944–1945): 518.

41. Vandenberg Jr., *Private Papers of Senator Vandenberg*, 29.

42. The Willkie Memorial Building stands at 20 West 40th Street in New York City. The Board of Trustees, including Norman Cousins, Allan Nevins, Dore Schary, Spyros Skouras, and Roy Wilkins, granted the annual Freedom Award to, among others, Walter Lippmann, Sumner Welles, Bernard Baruch, George C. Marshall, David Lilienthal, and Edward R. Murrow.

43. Zanuck reportedly paid $100,000 for the film rights to *One World*.

44. Arthur L. Mayer, "Fact into Film," *Public Opinion Quarterly* 8, no. 2 (Summer 1944): 225; Willkie, *One World*, 187.

45. Dore Schary, notes for speech, June 21, 1945, DSP, WHS, box 26, file 1.

46. Fraser Harbutt, "Churchill, Hopkins, and the 'Other' Americans . . . ," *International History Review* 8 (May 1986): 261, quoted in Walter LaFeber, *The American Age: U.S. Foreign Policy at Home and Abroad, 1750 to the Present*, 2nd ed. (New York: Norton, 1994), 433.

47. HDC *Report*, April 20, 1945, HDCP, WHS, box 1, file 1; box 2, file 6.

48. Henry Morgenthau to Robert Hannegan, chair of the DNC, March 19, 1945, HDCP, WHS, box 2, file 6.

49. George Pepper to Robert Hannegan, March 26, 1945, and George Pepper to Joseph Schenck, April 4, 1945, HDCP, WHS, box 2, file 6.

50. Morgenthau to Hannegan, March 19, 1945.

51. Lillian Hellman FBI file, May 7, 1945, LHP, HRC, box 132, file 7.

52. George Pepper to Hubbel Robinson, April 1945, HDCP, WHS, box 2, file 7.

53. Radio script "The Crew of Model T," April 30, 1945, HDCP, WHS, box 2, file 7.

54. Francis Hes to ABC, June 2, 1945, HDCP, WHS, box 2, file 6.

55. HDC Meeting Minutes, May 22, 1945, HDCP, WHS, box 8, file 12; George Pepper to Gwendolyn Peacher of CBS, March 15, 1945, HDCP, WHS, box 2, file 6.

56. Selznick radio speech, April 14, 1945, DOSP, HRC, box 2367, file 6.

57. Iriye, *Global Community*, 42–43.

58. Bruce Cook, *Dalton Trumbo* (New York: Scribner, 1977), 150–153. "It was a reunion after many, many years," Trumbo remembered. "Wally [Llewellyn Thompson] and I talked at great length. Obviously none of them knew anything about my political tendencies."

59. Dalton Trumbo to Lynch, May 1945, DTP, WHS, box 40, file 1.

60. Dalton Trumbo to Thomas Finletter, May 1945, DTP, WHS, box 40, file 1.

61. Thomas Finletter to Dalton Trumbo, May 25, 1945, DTP, WHS, box 40, file 2; Trumbo to Finletter, May 1945.

62. Finletter to Trumbo, May 25, 1945; Trumbo to Finletter, May 1945.

63. Trumbo to Finletter, May 1945.

64. Cook, *Dalton Trumbo*, 151–152; Trumbo to Lynch, May 1945. The photograph remains part of Trumbo's personal papers at the Wisconsin Historical Society in Madison.

65. Press Release, June 27, 1945, HDCP, WHS, box 5, file 6; radio script, May 1945, HDCP, WHS, box 8, file 12.

66. Paul Boyer points out that the atomic bomb gave the World Government and One World ideals greater prominence. Boyer, *By the Bomb's Early Light: American Thought and Culture at the Dawn of the Atomic Age* (Chapel Hill: University of North Carolina Press, 1985). See Stephen King-Hall, "World Government or World Destruction?" *Reader's Digest*, November 1945, 14, 16; Freda Kirchwey, "One World or None" *The Nation*, August 18, 1945, 150; *New York Herald Tribune*, October 30, 1945, 16.

67. HDC pamphlet, "Crisis Meeting," December 4, 1945, HDCP, WHS, box 2, file 4; Helen Gahagan Douglas speech, December 12, 1945, HDCP, WHS, box 2, file 4 (original emphasis).

68. HDC Press Release, October 28, 1945, HDCP, WHS, box 5, file 6; Pamphlet of the National Committee to Abolish the Poll Tax, "The Poll Tax Fact Sheet," 1946, HDCP, WHS, box 7, file 2; Hollywood Independent Citizens Committee of the Arts, Sciences, and Professions, political broadcast, June 3, 1946, HDCP, WHS, box 4, file 1; Louis Harris, HICCASP Executive Board, to Valley Amusement Corporation, January 26, 1946, HDCP, WHS, box 6, file 1.

69. Schary speech, November 14, 1945, DSP, WHS, box 75, file 1.

70. Thomas Schatz, *Boom and Bust: American Cinema in the 1940s* (Berkeley: University of California Press, 1997), 3.

3. Casting the Iron Curtain

1. Tennessee Williams to Audrey Wood, September 1946, TWP, HRC, box 55, file 2.

2. Thomas Schatz, *Boom and Bust: American Cinema in the 1940s* (Berkeley: University of California Press, 1997), 326.

3. Ibid., 285.

4. Fred Stanley, "Diplomatic Hollywood," *New York Times*, October 7, 1945, 1.

5. Schatz, *Boom and Bust*, 155–160, 298–303.

6. Helen Ashby, "Films vs. Iron Curtains," *PM*, April 14, 1947, 9.

7. Paul Buhle and Dave Wagner, *Radical Hollywood: The Untold Story behind America's Favorite Movies* (New York: New Press, 2002), 328–329.

8. Other participants included the Society of Independent Motion Picture Producers and the Independent Motion Picture Producers Association. See Schatz, *Boom and Bust*, 303–304.

9. "Hollywood Riot Flares in Strike," *New York Times*, October 6, 1945, 3. A thorough discussion of the Hollywood union struggles appears in Gerald Horne, *Class Struggle in Hollywood, 1930–1950: Moguls, Mobsters, Stars, Reds, and Trade Unionists* (Austin: University of Texas Press, 2001).

10. Dalton Trumbo, Olympic Stadium speech, later reprinted as "The Real Facts behind the Motion Picture Lockout" by the United Labor and Citizens Committee, October 13, 1945, DTP, WHS, box 4, file 3.

11. *Anonymous*, "Hollywood Meets Frankenstein," *The Nation*, June 28, 1952. See Carl Bromley, ed., *Cinema Nation: The Best Writing on Film from* The Nation, *1913–2000* (New York: Nation Books, 2000), 173.

12. Information for *Time* article, September 1946, HDCP, WHS, box 8, file 10. Because the HDC changed its name and its association with national organizations, it appears as HICCASP, ICCASP, and ASP-PCA at various times. The WHS consolidates all of them in the HDCP collection.

13. ICCASP bylaws, 1945, DSP, WHS, box 101, file 2.

14. Michael Fanning to George Pepper, June 11, 1945, HDCP, WHS, box 2, file 15.

15. HDC Meeting Minutes, June 6, 1945, HDCP, WHS, box 1, file 11.

16. Bipartisanship was of real concern. Despite its name, the HDC supported both major political parties, albeit typically favoring Democrats over Republicans. HICCASP endorsed a handful of California Republicans in 1944: John Lyons for 64th Assembly, Jonathan Hollibaught for 52nd, Fletcher Bowron for Mayor of Los Angeles in 1945, and out-of-state Senator Wayne Morse in 1944.

17. Statement of Policy, July 10, 1945, HDCP, WHS, box 1, file 1.

18. HICCASP Meeting Minutes, November 30, 1945, HDCP, WHS, box 2, file 3.

19. Lloyd Gardner, "Re-Reading Mr. X," H-DIPLO discussion listserv, August 2000.

20. "New Deal–Red Alliance On: 'People's Front' Plan for Elections," *Los Angeles Examiner*, March 12, 1946.

21. "U.S. Women to Fight for Amity with Soviets—Lillian Hellman," *Daily Worker*, March 8, 1946, 9.

22. "Report from Washington," March 6, 1946, HDCP, WHS, box 5, file 7.

23. Charles Brinley to W. Averell Harriman, March 19, 1946; R. P. Meiklejohn, assistant to Harriman, to Charles Brinley, April 29, 1946, both in W. Averell Harriman Papers, LC, box 14, American Society for Russian Relief, Inc. file.

24. Program script, December 10, 1945; George Pepper to Dore Schary, December 18, 1945; George Pepper to Ronald Reagan, December 18, 1945, HDCP, WHS, box 2, file 4.

25. "Memorandum by the Secretary of War (Henry L. Stimson) to President Truman, September 11, 1945," in *FRUS*, 1945 (Washington, DC: Government Printing Office, 1971), 2:42.

26. Albert Einstein telegram to David O. Selznick, May 22, 1946, DOSP, HRC, box 2357, file 8. Einstein's political activities, especially with respect to atomic energy control and world government, came under the scrutiny of the FBI, which monitored his mail and telephone calls and began a 1,400-page file on the scientist. Whereas the Einstein file was kept secret for years, the case against another atomic scientist, J. Robert Oppenheimer, became an event in the nation's Cold War collective memory.

27. Joseph Rauh, statement of purpose, JRP, LC, box 23, Emergency Conference for Civilian Control of Atomic Energy 1946 subject file.

28. Ibid.

29. HICCASP political broadcast, June 3, 1946, HDCP, WHS, box 4, file 1.

30. Sam Eperson open letter to HICCASP, 1946, HDCP, WHS, box 6, file 1.

31. ICCASP Platform for 1946, February 10, 1946, HDCP, WHS, box 1, file 12.

32. Henry Luce to David O. Selznick, March 3, 1946, and Clare Boothe Luce to David O. Selznick, September 21, 1946, DOSP, HRC, box 2361, file 5 (original emphasis).

33. George F. Kennan, interviewed on *The Cold War*, CNN, May-June 1996.

34. Warren B. Walsh, "What the American People Think of Russia," *Public Opinion Quarterly* 8, no. 4 (Winter 1944–1945): 513–522.

35. Matthews, Kaltenborn, and Luce quoted in Les K. Adler and Thomas G. Paterson, "Red Fascism: The Merger of Nazi Germany and Soviet Russia in the American Image of Totalitarianism, 1930's–1950's," *American Historical Review* 75, no. 4 (April 1970): 1046, 1052–1053.

36. Ellen Schrecker, *Many Are the Crimes: McCarthyism in America* (Boston: Little, Brown, 1998), chap. 4.

37. Joan Neuberger, *Ivan the Terrible* (New York: I. B. Tauris, 2003); James Agee, "Ivan the Terrible," *The Nation*, April 26, 1947. See Bromley, *Cinema Nation*, 32.

38. While the Luces disagreed with Jo Davidson's politics, they certainly appreciated his talent as a sculptor, having commissioned busts of themselves for $5,000 in 1940.

39. "Glamor Pusses," *Time*, September 9, 1946, 23.

40. Ibid.

41. Ring Lardner Jr. oral history, in *Tender Comrades: A Backstory of the Hollywood Blacklist*, ed. Patrick McGilligan and Paul Buhle (New York: St. Martin's, 1997), 413.

42. HICCASP foreign policy program, October 2, 1946, HDCP, WHS, box 1, file 12.

43. Marquis Childs, "Build-Up for Wallace," *Washington Post*, June 19, 1947. See JRP, LC, box 44, Henry Wallace 1945–1947 file.

44. Americans for Democratic Action press material, 1947, JRP, LC, box 44, Henry Wallace 1945–1947 file.

45. HICCASP Standing Committees as ratified by the Executive Council, August 27, 1946, HDCP, WHS, box 1, file 5.

46. Dore Schary to David O. Selznick, DSP, HRC, September 10, 1946, box 114, file 1.

47. Dore Schary speech to *The Nation* dinner, September 22, 1946, DSP, HRC, box 26, file 1. Several victims of Red-baiting attended that night: two lawyers of the future Hollywood Ten, Robert Kenny and Bartley Crum; Helen Gahagan Douglas; director John Cromwell; and Orson Welles. Members of the Committee for the First Amendment also attended: Paul Henreid, Humphrey Bogart, Lauren Bacall.

48. Information for *Time* article, September 1946, HDCP, WHS, box 8, file 10.

49. "Glamor Pusses," 25.

50. "Jimmy on the Sawdust Trail," *Time*, July 29, 1946.

51. Schlesinger quoted in Joseph Rauh speech at James Loeb memorial service, February 1, 1992, JRP, LC, box 283, Miscellaneous Speeches and Texts (1992) file.

52. James Loeb Jr., "Progressives and Communists," *New Republic*, May 13, 1946, 699 (original emphasis).

53. *Do You Know This Man?* Union for Democratic Action pamphlet, 1946, JRP, LC, box 43, UDA file.

54. "The Foreign Policy of the Union for Democratic Action," 1946, JRP, LC, box 43, UDA file.

55. Lillian Hellman led the Theater Division; Howard Koch, the Film Division; John Howard Lawson, the writers; Paul Robeson, music. All were later blacklisted.

56. Organization statement, HDCP, WHS, box 1, file 1. The first PCA convention was held on December 9, 1946.

57. Program Preamble by Lena Horne, January 28, 1947, HDCP, WHS, box 1, file 3.

58. Untitled *California Daily News* clipping, February 4, 1947.

4. Projectors of Power

1. Patricia Bosworth, *Anything Your Little Heart Desires* (New York: Simon and Schuster, 1997), 170–171.

2. Ibid., 202, 167.

3. Dore Schary to David O. Selznick, April 5, 1946, DSP, WHS, box 113, file 14.

4. Donald Bogle, *Toms, Coons, Mulattoes, Mammies, and Bucks: An Interpretive History of Blacks in American Films*, 3rd ed. (New York: Continuum, 1994), 143–147. Just as a homosexual became Jewish in *Crossfire* (1947), two years later the Jewish main character in the original *Home of the Brave* (1949) became an African American GI in the final version.

5. Bogle, *Toms*, 145.

6. Ibid., 147–154.

7. Dalton Trumbo, "Treatment of Minorities in Films" speech, 1947, DTP, WHS, box 40, file 4.

8. Milton Bracker, "Italians Apologetic; U.S. Zone Speeds Succor for Jews," *New York Times*, August 26, 1945, 34; John MacCormac, "Only 6,900 in Austria," *New York Times*, August 26, 1945, 34. See also DSP, WHS, box 113, file 13.

9. Robert Abzug, *America Views the Holocaust, 1933–1945: A Brief Documentary History* (Boston: Bedford/St. Martin's, 1999), 126, 209.

10. David O. Selznick to Dore Schary, October 2, 1945, DSP, WHS, box 113, file 13.

11. Minutes of Executive Council Meeting of HICCASP, August 13, 1946, DSP, WHS, box 101, file 2.

12. Larry Ceplar and Steven Englund, *The Inquisition in Hollywood: Politics in the Film Community, 1930–1960* (Berkeley: University of California Press, 1983), 317.

13. Edward G. Robinson speech at Justice for Palestine Meeting, September 18, 1946, HDCP, WHS, box 6, file 14.

14. Foreign Policy Statement of HICCASP, October 2, 1946, DSP, WHS, box 101, file 2.

15. Ring Lardner Jr., "Goodbye to Mr. Stark," *The Nation*, February 7, 1981. See Carl Bromley, ed., *Cinema Nation: The Best Writing on Film from* The Nation, *1913–2000* (New York: Nation Books, 2000), 101.

16. Harry Bernstein to Dore Schary, May 11, 1945, DSP, WHS, box 126, file 7.

17. Studio synopsis of *The Brick Foxhole* (*Crossfire*) and film rights information, 1946, DSP, WHS, box 112, file 4; Ceplar and Englund, *Inquisition*, 317–318.

18. Bernstein to Schary, May 11, 1945.

19. William Fadiman to Dore Schary, RKO memorandum, April 25, 1947, DSP, WHS, box 126, file 7. Franklin Roosevelt was also characterized in *Yankee Doodle*

Dandy (1942) and other contemporary films. Dore Schary would even write about Roosevelt's inspirational struggle against paralysis in *Sunrise at Campobello* (1960).

20. Neal Gabler, *An Empire of Their Own: How the Jews Invented Hollywood* (New York: Doubleday, 1988), 299–302.

21. The great *film noir* dramas include *Double Indemnity, Laura, Cornered, Scarlet Street, The Big Sleep, The Killers, The Blue Dahlia, The Third Man.* Thomas Schatz explains that "female gothics" such as Alfred Hitchcock's *Rebecca* (1940), *Shadow of a Doubt* (1943), and *Gaslight* (1944) also qualify. Incidentally, *Shadow of a Doubt* combines the homespun innocence of Thornton Wilder's screenplay with Alfred Hitchcock's suspenseful direction (plus a subtle notion of incest) to provide an unsettling portrait of wartime America. See Thomas Schatz, *Boom and Bust: American Cinema in the 1940s* (Berkeley: University of California Press, 1997), 232–239.

22. John Foster Dulles speech to Inland Daily Press Association, Chicago, February 10, 1947, John W. F. Dulles Papers, HRC, box 4, file 14.

23. Although the picture's controversial themes bothered conservative critics, *Crossfire*'s explicit use of terms such as "Jew boy" drew praise from Progressives. Given the film's ultimate use as a weapon for HUAC investigators, it was for *Crossfire*'s use of these taboo terms that the liberal organ *PM* headlined its July 23, 1947, review "*Crossfire* Names Names."

24. Audience Research Inc. confidential report on audience reactions to *Crossfire* for RKO, April 30, 1947, DSP, WHS, box 127, file 1.

25. David M. Levy to Dore Schary, July 8, 1947, DSP, WHS, box 127, file 1.

26. Elliot E. Cohen, "The Film Drama as a Social Force," *Commentary*, August 1947, 114.

27. Preview cards, May 22, 1947, DSP, WHS, box 127, file 1.

28. Max Horkheimer to Dore Schary, April 1947, DSP, WHS, box 127, file 1; Albert Einstein quoted in Jacques Ferrand to Dore Schary, August 15, 1947, DSP, WHS, box 126, file 16; Albert Maltz to Dore Schary, May 9, 1947, DSP, WHS, box 126, file 16.

29. *Crossfire* trailer, April 1947, DSP, WHS, box 126, file 17.

30. Dore Schary to Max Horkheimer, April 28, 1947, DSP, WHS, box 127, file 1.

31. Paul Buhle and Dave Wagner, *Radical Hollywood: The Untold Story behind America's Favorite Movies* (New York: New Press, 2002), 387.

32. Reprinted in Paul Blanshard, "The Church and the Movies," *The Nation*, May 8, 1948. See Bromley, *Cinema Nation*, 70.

33. Ayn Rand, *Screen Guide for Americans* (Hollywood: Motion Picture Alliance for the Preservation of American Ideals, 1947).

34. Ibid.

35. Ibid.

36. Ibid.

37. Robert Riskin and Emmett Lavery, "The Reviewing Stand," broadcast by Mutual Radio, September 16, 1945, DSP, WHS, box 26, file 1.

38. Trumbo, "Treatment of Minorities in Films" speech.

39. Theodore Geiger, interviewed by CNN in *The Cold War*, November–December 1995.

40. E. K. Gubin, *How to Do Business under the Marshall Plan* (New York: Time-Life, 1948), ii, 24. See NTP, NBC, WHS, box 115, file 18.

41. Schatz, *Boom and Bust*, 159.

42. Untitled, *San Diego Tribune-Sun* clipping, October 14, 1947, DOSP, HRC, box 2353, file 2.

43. Marianne Debouzy, interviewed by CNN in *The Cold War*, April 1996.

44. Emil Lengyel, "International Education as an Aid to World Peace," *Journal of Educational Sociology* 20, no. 9 (May 1947): 562–570.

45. Schatz, *Boom and Bust*, 155–160.

46. Lavery, "Reviewing Stand."

47. HDC Press Release, October 24, 1945, HDCP, WHS, box 5, file 6.

48. Sam O'Neal to George Pepper, July 10, 1945, HDCP, WHS, box 2, file 15; George Pepper to Sam O'Neal, July 16, 1945, HDCP, WHS, box 2, file 14.

49. Jules Dassin oral history, in *Tender Comrades: A Backstory of the Hollywood Blacklist*, ed. Patrick McGilligan and Paul Buhle (New York: St. Martin's, 1997), 204.

50. HUAC, John Charles "Jack" Moffitt testimony, Executive Session Transcripts on Hollywood, 80th Cong., 1st sess., April 11, 1947, RG 233, NA.

51. *Tulsa Tribune*, May 3, 1947.

52. HUAC, Executive Session Transcripts on Hollywood, 80th Cong., 1st sess., May 13–15, 1947, RG 233, NA. The transcripts quoted from include the testimonies of Richard Arlen, Louis B. Mayer, Adolphe Menjou, John Charles "Jack" Moffitt, Robert Taylor, and Jack Warner.

53. HUAC, Moffitt testimony, May 13, 1947.

54. HUAC internal memorandum, January 1948, RG 233, NA.

55. HUAC cited as evidence of "subversion" many clippings, including *New Masses*, May 29, 1945; Westbrook Pegler, *New York Times-Herald*, August 30, 1947; Hedda Hopper's critique of Frank Capra's *Meet John Doe* (1941); *New Masses*, March 24, 1942; Joseph Foster, *New Masses*, April 22, 1947; Sondra Gorney, *Daily Worker*, August 28, 1947; David Platt, *Daily Worker*, August 17, 1946; William Simon, *New Masses*, August 5, 1947; David Platt, *Daily Worker*, October 17, 1947; and Joseph Foster, *New Masses*, April 22, 1947.

56. ASP-PCA pamphlet, July 1947, HDCP, WHS, box 8, file 9.

57. Voice of Freedom press release, June 16, 1947, HDCP, WHS, box 7, file 14.

58. *Variety*, October 29, 1947.

59. Gene Kelly, Lauren Bacall, and William Wyler, quoted in Buhle and Wagner, *Radical Hollywood*, 437–438 (original emphasis).

60. Only Maltz was allowed to read his entire statement, an event that prompted his wife to cable their young son, Peter, "We can all be proud of your daddy today. He spoke to the committee of men we told you about. It is a bad committee and all good Americans should fight it. . . . You know that the way to stop a bully is to fight back." Maltz family telegram, October 28, 1947, Albert Maltz Papers, WHS, box 15, file 15.

61. SISS, Communist Party in Hollywood file, 80th Cong., 1st sess., 1947, RG 46, NA.

62. Eric Johnston pamphlet statement to HUAC, October 27, 1947, Ring Lardner Jr. Papers, WHS, box 1, file 1.

63. HUAC, Executive Session Transcripts on Hollywood, 80th Cong., 1st sess., May 1947, RG 233; NA. Further evidence of congressional pressure is contained in both the Mayer and Warner transcripts.

64. Bosley Crowther, "Light on Film Industry's Anti-Communist Move," *New York Times*, December 7, 1947, 85.

65. Anonymous postcards to Dalton Trumbo, November 26, 1947, and October 31, 1947; William Barnes to Dalton Trumbo, November 1947, DTP, WHS, box 2, file

1. The fact that some of the Hollywood Ten kept even this anonymous correspondence in their files may suggest their pride at the political sacrifices they made.

66. Arthur Miller to Herbert Biberman, November 1, 1950, Herbert Biberman–Gale Sondergaard Papers, WHS, box 26, file 1.

67. Ironically, HUAC's original chairman, Parnell Thomas, provided the only solace for Lester Cole while Cole was serving his term in the Danbury, Connecticut, penitentiary. In the intervening years, Thomas had himself been convicted of padding his congressional payroll, sentenced to Danbury, and assigned to work in the prison farmyard. One morning Cole greeted the sweaty, denim-clad Thomas by saying, "Still handling the chicken shit, I see." Ring Lardner Jr., *I'd Hate Myself in the Morning* (New York: Nation Books, 2000), 131.

68. Tino Balio, ed., *Hollywood in the Age of Television* (Boston: Unwin Hyman, 1990), 12.

69. Arthur Miller, "Why I Wrote 'The Crucible': An Artist's Answer to Politics," *New Yorker*, October 21, 1996, 163.

70. Schlesinger quoted in Dalton Trumbo to Editor, *Saturday Review of Literature*, July 20, 1949, DTP, WHS, box 3, file 2.

71. Dalton Trumbo to Cleo Trumbo, June 14, 1950, DTP, WHS, box 3, file 3.

72. United States Department of Commerce, *United States Exports of Domestic and Foreign Merchandise* (Washington, DC: Government Printing Office, 1960). According to annual records for the years 1947 (Group J, 3–10), 1948 (Group 9, 173–179), and 1949 (Group 9, 194–201), exports of American-made projectors, screens, newsreels, shorts, and feature films to Europe, Asia, Latin America, and the Middle East rose dramatically.

73. See Balio, *Hollywood in the Age of Television*.

74. Quoted in Schatz, *Boom and Bust*, 328.

75. Balio, *Hollywood in the Age of Television*, 8–9, 12.

76. David O. Selznick oral history, June 13, 1958, DOSP, HRC, box 2358, file 6.

77. Miller, "Why I Wrote 'The Crucible,'" 160.

78. Williams's agent responded to news of the great playwright's scripting dialogue for Lana Turner with "ribald laughter," for "it all sounds too much like Hollywood to be true." See Audrey Wood to Tennessee Williams, May 18, 1943, TWP, HRC, box 58, file 3. Later that summer, Williams announced his preference to finish his contract with MGM and then concentrate on better stories. "Let's face it," he told Wood, "I can only write for *love*. . . . But all this effort, all this longing to create something of value—it will be thrown away, gone up the spout, nothing finally gained—if I don't adhere very strictly to the most honest writing, that I am capable of." Williams found relief when he was released from his "Lana Turner horror-play." See Williams to Wood, August 2 and August 11, 1943, TWP, HRC, box 55, file 1.

5. Test Patterns

1. "A New Era: The Secrets of Science," *Newsweek*, August 20, 1945, 37–38; "Stratovision," *Time*, August 20, 1945, 67.

2. "Stratovision," 67.

3. Niles Trammel speech to the FCC, "Television Is Ready to Go," October 11, 1945, NBC, Sound Division of the LC, folder P185.

4. William O'Neill, *American High: The Years of Confidence, 1945–1960* (New York: Free Press, 1986), 77. See also Horace Newcomb and Robert Alley, *The*

Producer's Medium: Conversations with Creators of American Television (New York: Oxford University Press, 1983), 34–35.

5. John Schultheiss, "A Season of Fear: The Blacklisted Teleplays of Abraham Polonsky," *Literature-Film Quarterly* 24, no. 2 (April 1996): 149.

6. Ring Lardner Jr., "My Life on the Blacklist," *Saturday Evening Post*, October 14, 1961, 42; clippings, Communist Party in Hollywood file, 1961, SISS, box 65, RG 46, NA.

7. Wendell Willkie, *One World* (New York: Simon and Schuster, 1943), 187. For a detailed discussion of One World ideology, see chapter 2.

8. Rod Serling to Esther Serling, December 8, 1945, RSP, WHS, box 22, file 1. Esther Serling treasured this handwritten letter and asked, shortly before her death in 1958, that it be returned to her son.

9. Rod Serling, interview by Linda Brevelle, March 4, 1975, http://www.rodser ling.com.

10. Orville Prescott to Gore Vidal, October 28, 1947, Gore Vidal Papers, WHS, box 1, file 2.

11. Rod Serling, "In the Case of the Universe versus War," October 21, 1947, RSP, WHS, box 39, file 6.

12. Ibid.

13. Rod Serling, "Russia and the American Press," c. 1947, RSP, WHS, box 39, file 6.

14. Rod Serling, untitled, c. 1947, RSP, WHS, box 39, file 6.

15. Paddy Chayefsky, untitled, c. 1945–1946, Paddy Chayefsky Papers, WHS, box 1, file 3.

16. Rod Serling speech to Moorpark College, December 3, 1968, RSP, WHS, box 39, file 6.

17. Martin Ritt, Franklin Schaffner, and John Frankenheimer oral histories, in *The Days of Live: Television's Golden Age as Told by 21 Directors Guild of America Members*, ed. Ira Skutch (Los Angeles: Scarecrow, 1998), 4–5, 10–13.

18. Michael Ritchie, *Please Stand By: A Prehistory of Television* (New York: Overlook Press, 1994), 164, 99.

19. Eric Barnouw, *Tube of Plenty: The Evolution of American Television* (New York: Oxford University Press, 1990), 163.

20. For three representative examples, see NBC-CART (all CART reports were authored by Stockton Helffrich), WHS, box 1, file 1. In the CART report for September 30, 1948, Helffrich writes, "We have yet to work out a system with the Television Department paralleling radio practice of indicating on master scripts clocked timings. Television has personnel shortage problems which vitally hold back this kind of thing so much needed by us in our contacts with agencies who run over in their commercial time. We have asked the Television Department to do what they can to get this thing moving along the same lines followed in radio." In the CART report for September 24, 1948, Helffrich referred to Milton Berle's *Texaco Star Theatre*: "Here and there the language has been rough on this program and we have had some difficulty in learning what an MC such as Milton Berle plans to do with adlib spots." The CART report for October 7, 1948, considered allowing a Lucky Strike ad to air during the intermission.

21. Rod Serling, *Patterns: Four Television Plays with the Author's Personal Commentaries* (New York: Simon and Schuster, 1957), 6.

22. Daniel Horowitz, ed., *American Social Classes in the 1950s: Selections from Vance Packard's "The Status Seekers"* (Boston: Bedford/St. Martin's, 1995), 60–61.

23. Joanna R. Jackson, "The Quarter's Polls," *Public Opinion Quarterly* 9, no. 4 (Winter 1945–1946): 510–538; 10, no. 1 (Spring 1946): 110.

24. Ritchie, *Please Stand By*, 197.

25. Tino Balio, ed., *Hollywood in the Age of Television* (Boston: Unwin Hyman, 1990), 15; NBC publication, "What Do We Know about Today's Television Audience?" May 1948, NBC, Sound Division of the LC, folder P507.

26. Mildred Strunk, "The Quarter's Polls," *Public Opinion Quarterly* 13, no. 3 (Fall 1949): 556.

27. Reported percentages of television households vary depending on the source, but according to *Almanac of American Life: Cold War America, 1946–1990*, ed. Richard Balkin and Ross Gregory (New York: Facts on File, 2002), dramatic increases in American television ownership cannot be denied: 9 percent of the population in 1949–1950, 23.5 percent in 1950–1951, 34.2 percent in 1951–1952, 44.7 percent in 1952–1953, 55.7 percent in 1953–1954, 64.5 percent in 1954–1955, 71.8 percent in 1955–1956, 78.6 percent in 1956–1957, 83.2 percent in 1957–1958, 85.9 percent in 1958–1959, 87.1 percent in 1959–1960, and 88.8 percent in 1960–1961. See especially table 17.27 on the number of television households and table 17.28 on the hours of television viewing, both on page 469. See also Balio, *Age of Television*, 15.

28. "Map of TV Cities," October 1, 1951, A. C. Nielsen Company Papers, WHS, box 23, file 2.

29. Strunk, "The Quarter's Polls," 556.

30. Balio, *Hollywood in the Age of Television*, 12.

31. Paddy Chayefsky, *Television Plays* (New York: Simon and Schuster, 1955), 179; Serling, *Patterns*, 15.

32. Horton Foote oral history, in *The Box: An Oral History of Television, 1920–1961*, ed. Jeff Kisselhoff (New York: Viking, 1995), 251.

33. Tom Engelhardt, *The End of Victory Culture: Cold War America and the Disillusioning of a Generation* (New York: Basic Books, 1995), 146.

34. Serling, *Patterns*, 18; Delbert Mann oral history, in *The Box: An Oral History of Television, 1920–1961*, ed. Jeff Kisselhoff (New York: Viking, 1995), 236.

35. Kenneth Jackson, *Crabgrass Frontier: The Suburbanization of the United States* (New York: Oxford University Press, 1985).

36. James L. Baughman, *Same Time, Same Station: Creating American Television, 1948–1961* (Baltimore: Johns Hopkins University Press, 2007), chap. 9.

37. O'Neill, *American High*, 254.

38. "How to Get Better Films from Hollywood," *The Worker*, March 21, 1954, 8. See SISS, box 112, Films (1925–1957) file, RG 46, NA.

39. Barnouw, *Tube of Plenty*, 114; Balio, *Hollywood in the Age of Television*, 24.

40. According to Balkin and Gregory, *Almanac of American Life*, table 17.28, 469, the average hours of television viewing increased from 4 hours, 35 minutes per day in 1949–1950, to 5 hours, 1 minute per day in 1955–1956, to 5 hours, 9 minutes per day the following year. The time spent in front of the set increased, especially as 15-minute programs gave way to 30- and 60-minute blocks of program time.

41. William Boddy, *Fifties Television: The Industry and Its Critics* (Urbana: University of Illinois Press, 1990), 132–154. Boddy shows the swift decline in the number of feature-length releases: from 488 in 1948 to 253 in 1952. See also Christopher Anderson, *Hollywood TV: The Studio System in the Fifties* (Austin: University of Texas Press, 1994). In 1955, RKO pulled out of motion picture production and sold its film

library to an independent television company. Many others, including independents like David O. Selznick, followed this same course.

42. Skutch, *Days of Live*, 27.

43. David Sarnoff speech, "Peace in a Changing World," to Phi Beta Kappa alumni in New York City, December 15, 1948, DOSP, HRC, box 2366, file 3.

44. Committee for the Marshall Plan to Aid European Recovery, *Who Is the Man against the Marshall Plan?* pamphlet, c. 1947–1948, NTP, NBC, WHS, box 115, file 18.

45. Barnouw, *Tube of Plenty*, 112; Balio, *Age of Television*, 15. Even before the Second World War, the two major radio networks both recognized the move toward television but reacted differently. In these first months, Gen. David Sarnoff, head of Radio Corporation of America (RCA), the parent company of NBC, adjusted his mind-set and invested millions of dollars to fund television even to the point of surpassing the radio, the device so prominently mentioned in his company's title. Michael Ritchie quotes David Sarnoff as announcing, "No one can retard TV's advance any more than carriage makers could stop the automobile, the cable the wireless, or silent pictures the talkies." Ritchie, *Please Stand By*, 161–162. One who *had* hoped to retard television in the short term was Sarnoff's rival, William Paley of CBS. As CBS executive Frank Stanton explained later, Paley was ill prepared. Television would hurt his radio enterprise, and the technology proved too expensive. But even Paley recognized its inevitability and simply sought ways to stall. Among the first issues to come before the FCC commissioners were the contests over frequency allocation and color technology. Paley advocated the CBS color wheel system and UHF frequency, where there are more channels available. Sarnoff used his leverage with the FCC to halt development of color technology because his postwar factories were ready to roll black-and-white sets off their assembly lines. Sarnoff assured the FCC that his company would have its own electronic color technology compatible to RCA receivers in the near future. He also urged the commissioners to limit competition by backing VHF frequencies. Based on the recommendations of the National Television Systems Committee (NTSC), composed of technical experts meeting to evaluate the networks' plans in 1941, the FCC favored NBC on both counts and signaled its desire to move methodically in the development of television. Despite the restrictive nature of these two key decisions, the FCC acted more out of a desire to coddle the infant industry than out of a desire to develop a conservative oligopoly akin to the old Hollywood studio system.

46. James L. Baughman, *Television's Guardians: The FCC and the Politics of Programming, 1958–1967* (Knoxville: University of Tennessee Press, 1985), 11: Baughman makes the point that the FCC "never applied the Blue Book to its license renewal procedures, and the violations it had uncovered continued unabated." While certainly true, the perception in 1946 was different. Many believed, the commissioners and broadcasters included, that government would regulate the young television industry with the purpose of "democratizing" the medium in ways it had failed to do with radio.

47. Christopher Sterling and John Kittross, *Stay Tuned: A Concise History of American Broadcasting*, 2nd ed. (Belmont, CA: Wadsworth, 1990), 268, 295–296, 304.

48. General Counsel Frank T. Bow to Repr. Forest A. Harness, chairman, 80th Cong., 2nd sess., House Select Committee to investigate the FCC, box 1, Correspondence with Chair [Forest A. Harness] file, July 23, 1948, RG 233, NA.

49. Sterling and Kittross, *Stay Tuned*, 268, 295–296.

50. House of Representatives, Final Report of Congressional Investigation into FCC, 80th Cong., 2nd sess., box 1, 1948 file, RG 233, NA; Clippings, SISS, box 110, FCC 1945–1948 file, RG 46, NA.

51. *Standards of Practice of the National Association of Broadcasters*, 1947, NTP, NBC, WHS, box 115, file 21.

52. Robert D. Swezey to Harold Fair, October 20, 1947, NTP, NBC, WHS, box 115, file 21.

53. Niles Trammell, "Television's Progress," unpublished article, May 23, 1949, NTP, NBC, WHS, box 106, file 17.

54. *Responsibility: A Working Manual*, 1948, SEP, NBC, WHS, box 156, files 21 and 23.

55. Davidson Taylor to James W. Young of the Ford Foundation, May 2, 1951, SPWP, NBC, WHS, box 120, file 16; Sylvester "Pat" Weaver to Allen Kalmus, October 19, 1949, SPWP, NBC, WHS, box 118, file 6 (emphasis added).

56. Pat Weaver to Advertising Club of New York, March 15, 1950, SPWP, NBC, WHS, box 125, file 37. See also Laurence Bergreen, *Look Now, Pay Later: The Rise of Network Broadcasting* (New York: Doubleday, 1980), 170–171.

57. Pat Weaver to Mr. Canfield, September 16, 1949, SPWP, NBC, WHS, box 118, file 5; Pat Weaver to Fred Coe, October 31, 1949, (original emphasis); Pat Weaver to Fred Wile, November 22, 1949, SPWP, NBC, WHS, box 118, file 6.

58. Pat Weaver to Joseph McConnell, January 11, 1950, SPWP, NBC, WHS, box 125, file 37.

59. CART Report, February 2, 1949, CART, NBC, WHS, box 1, file 2; Joseph McConnell to Niles Trammell, August 10, 1949, SPWP, NBC, WHS, box 118, file 56; Stockton Helffrich to various NBC executives, August 23, 1949, CART, NBC, WHS, box 1, file 2; Pat Weaver to Stockton Helffrich, February 21, 1950, SPWP, NBC, WHS, box 118, file 56.

60. CART Report, November-December 1949, CART, NBC, WHS, box 1, file 2; CART Report, March 23, 1950, CART, NBC, WHS, box 1, file 3; CART Report, January 16, 1951, CART, NBC, WHS, box 1, file 4.

61. Weaver to McConnell, January 11, 1950, SPWP, NBC, WHS, box 125, file 37; CART Report, February 2, 1949, CART, NBC, WHS, box 1, file 2; McConnell to Trammell, August 10, 1949, SPWP, NBC, WHS, box 118, file 56; Helffrich to NBC executives, August 23, 1949, CART, NBC, WHS, box 1, file 2; Weaver to Helffrich, February 21, 1950, SPWP, NBC, WHS, box 118, file 56; CART Report, October 18, 1950, CART, NBC, WHS, box 1, file 3.

62. Audrey Walburger to NBC Hollywood office, August 26, 1946; Sidney Strotz, NBC Hollywood office, to Rowland Angell, public service counselor at NBC New York office, August 29, 1946; Rowland Angell to Walburger, September 9, 1946, all in NBC, Sound Division of the LC, folder 457, A-Z Public Service 1946 file.

63. Jack Gould, "Televising the U.N.," *New York Times*, November 13, 1949, 9. David Sarnoff to NBC President Joseph McConnell, November 14, 1949; Benjamin Cohen, Assistant Secretary-General of the United Nations for Public Information, to Sarnoff, November 21, 1949; Sarnoff to Trammell, November 29, 1949; Trammell to Cohen, November 29, 1949, all in NTP, NBC, WHS, box 115, file 47.

64. CART Report, February 15, 1950, CART, NBC, WHS, box 1, file 3; CART Report, November 10, 1948, CART, NBC, WHS, box 1, file 1; "The NBC and the Negro National Community (a Roundtable)," broadcast transcript, October 25, 1950, WBP,

NBC, WHS, box 129, file 28; CART Report, September 15, 1950, CART, NBC, WHS, box 1, file 3.

65. Lester Ganger, "NBC and the Negro National Community," October 25, 1950.

66. Ibid.

67. CART Report, June 27, 1950, CART, NBC, WHS, box 1, file 3.

68. Granger, "NBC and the Negro."

69. CART Report, May 5, 1949, CART, NBC, WHS, box 1, file 2; CART Report, November 10, 1948; CART Report, November 16, 1948, CART, NBC, WHS, box 1, file 1.

70. CART Report, October 27, 1950; CART Report, March 28, 1950, CART, NBC, WHS, box 1, file 3.

71. CART Report, November 16, 1948.

72. CART Report, March 9, 1949, CART, NBC, WHS, box 1, file 2.

6. Guardians of the Golden Age

1. Arthur Miller, "Why I Wrote 'The Crucible': An Artist's Answer to Politics," *New Yorker*, October 21, 1996, 159.

2. John Lewis Gaddis, *Strategies of Containment: A Critical Appraisal of Postwar American National Security Policy* (Oxford: Oxford University Press, 1982), 92 (original emphasis).

3. Theodore C. Achilles, director of the Office of Western European Affairs, "Future World Must See Close Association of Free Nations," *DOSB* 22, no. 549 (January 9, 1950): 52–53.

4. Edward W. Barrett, Assistant Secretary of State for Public Affairs, "The American People's Part in United States Foreign Policy," *DOSB* 22, no. 564 (April 24, 1950): 646–649.

5. Paul Nitze to Harry Truman, December 15, 1950, PNP, LC, box 136, NSC Meeting Summaries file 5.

6. George Kennan, *Memoirs* (Boston: Little Brown, 1972), 90–92 (original emphasis).

7. Steven Rearden, *The Evolution of American Strategic Doctrine: Paul H. Nitze and the Soviet Challenge* (Boulder, CO: Westview, 1984), 7. See also Ernest R. May, ed., *American Cold War Strategy: Interpreting NSC 68* (Boston: St. Martin's, 1993), 15–16; Warren I. Cohen, *The Cambridge History of American Foreign Relations*, 4 vols. (Cambridge: Cambridge University Press, 1993), 4:69; Gaddis, *Strategies of Containment*, 89–126. The belief that NSC 68 marked some noteworthy change in American foreign policy by redefining the terms of containment is a view not shared by some diplomatic historians. For an alternative view, see Melvyn Leffler, *A Preponderance of Power: National Security, the Truman Administration, and the Cold War* (Stanford, CA: Stanford University Press, 1991), 355–360.

8. May, *American Cold War Strategy*, 17.

9. Ibid.

10. "United States Objectives and Programs for National Security" (NSC 68), April 14, 1950, *FRUS, 1950* (Washington, DC: Government Printing Office, 1977), 1:234–292.

11. Quoted in Gaddis, *Strategies of Containment*, 92.

12. NSC 68, *FRUS 1950*, 1:259, 286.

13. Barrett, "American People's Part," 646–649.

14. NSC 68, *FRUS 1950*, 1:286.

15. For a discussion of cultivation theory, see Richard Jackson Harris and Joseph Andrew Karafa, "A Cultivation Theory Perspective of Worldwide National Impressions of the United States," in *Images of the U.S. around the World: A Multicultural Perspective*, ed. Yahya R. Kamalipour (Albany: State University of New York Press, 1999), 3–5; George Gerbner, "Growing Up with Television: The Cultivation Perspective," in *Media Effects: Advances in Theory and Research*, ed. Jennings. Bryant and Dolf Zillmann (Hillsdale, NJ: Lawrence Erlbaum, 1984), 17–41.

16. NSC 68, *FRUS 1950*, 1:254.

17. Ibid., 240–241.

18. Ibid., 238, 241, 264.

19. Ibid., 241, 254.

20. Penny Von Eschen, "Who's the Real Ambassador? Exploding Cold War Racial Ideology," in *Cold War Constructions: The Political Culture of United States Imperialism, 1945–1966*, ed. Christian G. Appy (Amherst: University of Massachusetts Press, 2000), 115.

21. NSC 68, *FRUS 1950*, 1:241, 242, 247.

22. See Gaddis, *Strategies of Containment*, 127–197, which explains that Eisenhower was satisfied with Truman's foreign policy even more than with the views of some of his fellow Republicans, including Robert Taft. Specifics of Eisenhower's "New Look" foreign policy and cultural diplomacy are explored in the next chapter.

23. NSC 68, *FRUS 1950*, 1:252. See also *DOSB* 22, no. 564 (April 24, 1950): 646–649.

24. Paul Nitze to Harry Truman, July 27, 1950, PNP, LC, box 136, NSC Meeting Summaries file 5.

25. See Walter L. Hixson, *Parting the Curtain: Propaganda, Culture, and the Cold War* (New York: St. Martin's, 1996). This subject is addressed in greater detail in the next chapter.

26. George Kennan, "Where Do You Stand on Communism?" *New York Times Magazine*, May 27, 1951, 53. The extent to which an American garrison state existed is an issue explored in Michael J. Hogan, *Cross of Iron: Harry S Truman and the Origins of the National Security State, 1945–1954* (Cambridge: Cambridge University Press, 1998).

27. NSC 68, *FRUS 1950*, 1:279.

28. Ambassador George V. Allen, quoted in Eric Barnouw, *Tube of Plenty: The Evolution of American Television* (New York: Oxford University Press, 1990), 240–241.

29. Annual Report of the Committee on Un-American Activities for the year 1951, House Internal Security Committee (formerly HUAC), 82nd Cong., 1st sess., SISS, box 129, 1948–1959 file (February 17, 1952), 7–9, RG 46, NA.

30. Broadcasters' perceptions of FCC power outdistanced the commissioners' real regulatory power, but given the environment of the times, perceptions mattered more. And proof that this perception existed rests on the repeated improprieties revealed to the public: alleged misdeeds related to the granting of licenses in Boston, Miami, and St. Louis; the majority-Republican panel favoring Republican applicants; commissioners fraternizing with applicants; commissioners accepting gifts and loans. Such incidents led President Eisenhower to demand the resignation of John Doerfer. See James L. Baughman, *Television's Guardians: The FCC and the Politics*

of Programming, 1958–1967 (Knoxville: University of Tennessee Press, 1985), 13–14, 44–45, 75–76. For Cold War rhetoric, see Robert E. Lee speech, March 30, 1954, and Lee speech to Tennessee Association of Broadcasters in Nashville, March 28, 1955, Robert E. Lee Papers, WHS, box 1, file 1; Edward Webster speech to Lions Club of Miami, August 13, 1951, SEP, NBC, WHS, box 162, file 37; John C. Doerfer speech, October 22, 1953, John C. Doerfer Papers, WHS, box 1, file 1; *Counterattack* quoted in Christopher Sterling and John M. Kittross, *Stay Tuned: A Concise History of American Broadcasting*, 2nd ed. (Belmont, CA: Wadsworth, 1990), 307.

31. Tom Engelhardt, *The End of Victory Culture: Cold War America and the Disillusioning of a Generation* (New York: Basic Books, 1995), 89.

32. Among those named were Lee J. Cobb, Aaron Copland, Jose Ferrer, John Garfield, Ruth Gordon, Garson Kanin, Dashiell Hammett, Judy Holiday, Lena Horne, Langston Hughes, Burl Ives, Howard Koch, Burgess Meredith, Zero Mostel, Dorothy Parker, Edward G. Robinson, Artie Shaw, William L. Shirer, Howard K. Smith, and Orson Welles.

33. Rod Serling, *Patterns: Four Television Plays with the Author's Personal Commentaries* (New York: Simon and Schuster, 1957), 7, 19; Paddy Chayefsky, *Television Plays* (New York: Simon and Schuster, 1955), xii.

34. Delbert Mann oral history, in *The Box: An Oral History of Television, 1920–1961*, ed. Jeff Kisselhoff (New York: Viking, 1995), 260.

35. David Sarnoff, quoted in Michael Ritchie, *Please Stand By: A Prehistory of Television* (New York: Overlook Press, 1994), 167.

36. Arthur Penn oral history, in Kisselhoff, *The Box*, 260.

37. JRP, LC, box 38, Joseph McCarthy file.

38. Chayefsky, *Television Plays*, ix; Serling, *Patterns*, 38–39; Reginald Rose oral history, in Kisselhoff, *The Box*, 248.

39. Wellington Miner oral history, in *Worthington Miner: A Director's Guild Oral History*, ed. Franklin J. Schaffner (London: Scarecrow, 1985), 200–204; David Sarnoff speech to Veterans of Foreign Wars, Chicago, August 28, 1950, NTP, NBC, WHS, box 115, file 51 (emphasis added); Rod Serling, "Television's Sacred Cows," c. 1958–1959, RSP, WHS, box 40, file 1.

40. Stockton Helffrich, broadcast of *The Open Mind*, January 23, 1957, *The Open Mind* files, NBC, WHS, box 247, file 42.

41. Chayefsky, *Television Plays*, ix; Serling, *Patterns*, 38–39; Rose oral history, 248.

42. Elaine Tyler May, *Homeward Bound: American Families in the Cold War Era* (New York: Basic Books, 1988).

43. Charles Wilson's confirmation hearings were recalled in "Harriman Cites Job Need," *New York Times*, October 8, 1954, 17. The pro-business view was shared, notably, by another Eisenhower appointee, one who formulated broadcasting policy: FCC commissioner Robert E. Lee, who stated in a speech to the Minnesota Employers Association in St. Paul, Minnesota, February 2, 1955: "I have never been—and never will be—a business baiter. In fact, I have rarely found any conflict between public interest and business interest. Any governmental action favorable to the one is, generally speaking, favorable to the other." Robert E. Lee Papers, WHS, box 1, file 1.

44. Reginald Rose, *The Atrocity* script, November 16, 1959; Rose, *The Cruel Day* script, February 24, 1960, broadcast by CBS on *Playhouse 90*, Reginald Rose Papers, WHS, box 9, file 1.

45. "The Tension of Change," *Time*, September 19, 1955, 23. For further discussion of the links between domestic civil rights, decolonization, and the Cold War, see Penny Von Eschen, *Race against Empire: Black Americans and Anticolonialism, 1937–1957* (Ithaca: Cornell University Press, 1997).

46. The recollection is from director Delbert Mann's oral history, 250–251; Serling, *Patterns*, 10, 20–23. Rose's teleplay earned an award from the Anti-Defamation League of B'nai B'rith, an organization in which Dore Schary actively participated.

47. Paul Boyer, *By the Bomb's Early Light: American Thought and Culture at the Dawn of the Atomic Age* (Chapel Hill: University of North Carolina Press, 1985), 114. Brian Balogh observes that most Americans feared the atomic bomb in terms of its initial strike, not its aftereffects. He cites one poll from September 1945 showing that 83 percent of Americans surveyed believed the world would eventually be destroyed in an atomic war. Later, he writes that press reports on the Bikini tests created the impression that the atomic bomb was like other weapons, only stronger. AEC experts continued to downplay the radiation hazard into the 1950s. See Balogh, *Chain Reaction* (Cambridge: Cambridge University Press, 1991), 30, 34. See also Paul Boyer, *Fallout: A Historian Reflects on America's Half-Century Encounter with Nuclear Weapons* (Columbus: Ohio State University Press, 1998); Allan M. Winkler, *Life under a Cloud: American Anxiety about the Atom* (New York: Oxford University Press, 1993); Dee Garrison, *Bracing for Armageddon: Why Civil Defense Never Worked* (Oxford: Oxford University Press, 2006); Kenneth D. Rose, *One Nation Underground: The Fallout Shelter in American Culture* (New York: New York University Press, 2001); and Lawrence Wittner, *One World or None: A History of the World Nuclear Disarmament Movement through 1953* (Stanford, CA: Stanford University Press, 1995); and Wittner, *Resisting the Bomb: A History of the World Nuclear Disarmament Movement, 1954–1970* (Stanford, CA: Stanford University Press, 1997).

48. "Guarded Tests," *Time*, April 2, 1951, 40; "Largest Ever," *Time*, June 25, 1951, 20; "Atomic-Power Men," *Time*, March 2, 1953, 80.

49. "H-Bomb," *Time*, November 17, 1952, 28.

50. "Trial Cruise," *Time*, January 25, 1954, 17. While Serling looked at life among atomic tests, *Playhouse 90* made plans to broadcast its version of Pat Frank's novel *Alas, Babylon!* the story of a Florida community that awakens one day to a second sunrise: a nuclear blast. Although many survive, they soon realize that all measures of civilization and order have vanished steadily. It is an inspiring story of persistence but also a bleak tale of destruction caused by humanity. In the end, *Alas, Babylon!* was not used. See Fred Coe Papers, WHS, box 20, file 3.

51. Rod Serling to Alvin Rakoff, March 14, 1960, RSP, WHS, box 5, file 8 (original emphasis).

52. "The New Shows," *Time*, November 30, 1953, 59.

53. "Man in the Mid-Passage," *Time*, June 2, 1952, 23; "Coming Up Slowly," *Time*, May 4, 1953, 32–33.

54. Serling, *Patterns*, 136; Rose oral history, 248. For other examples, see Rose's *The Bus to Nowhere* (1951).

55. Reinhold Wagnleitner, *Coca-Colonization and the Cold War: The Cultural Mission of the United States in Austria after the Second World War* (Chapel Hill: University of North Carolina Press, 1994), 167.

56. "Electrified Utopia," *Time*, March 2, 1953, 80.

57. Reginald Rose, *Thunder on Sycamore Street* script, March 1, 1954, Reginald Rose Papers, WHS, box 18, file 2.

58. CBS producer Wellington Miner oral history, 229.

59. Hixson, *Parting the Curtain*, 124, 155; Wagnleitner, *Coca-Colonization*, 225; Chayefsky, *Television Plays*, 174, 178.

60. Chayefsky, *Television Plays*, 173–174.

61. Barnouw, *Tube of Plenty*, 160–161.

62. Susan Hayward, *Key Concepts in Cinema Studies* (London: Routledge, 1996), 216; Rod Steiger oral history, in Kisselhoff, *The Box*, 258.

63. Mann oral history, 256; Barnouw, *Tube of Plenty*, 160.

64. Vince Hartnett to Richard Arens, August 4, 1959, HUAC, Name Files, box 129, Paddy Chayefsky file, RG 233, NA. According to documents of June 3, 1957 (HUAC, File and Reference box 43, Paddy Chayefsky file, RG 233, NA), both HUAC and the SISS of the Senate Judiciary Committee cited Chayefsky for attaching his name on March 25, 1950, to a leaflet for the New York Council of the Arts, Sciences, and Professions, a group the attorney general labeled as "subversive."

65. Such controversial themes included familial disharmony in Serling's *The Comedian* (1957), directed by John Frankenheimer; juvenile delinquency in Rose's *Crime in the Street*; implied teenage pregnancy in *The Adolescent* (1954), starring Ida Lupino; alcoholism in J. P. Miller's *Days of Wine and Roses* (1958), also directed by Frankenheimer; and mental illness in Rose's *The Incredible World of Horace Ford*, starring Art Carney.

66. Vance Kepley Jr., "From 'Frontal Lobes' to the 'Bob-and-Bob' Show: NBC Management and Programming Strategies, 1949–65," in Tino Balio, ed., *Hollywood in the Age of Television* (Boston: Unwin Hyman, 1990), 51–52.

67. Balio, *Hollywood in the Age of Television*, 19.

68. Ibid., 20.

69. Martin Ritt oral history, in *Tender Comrades: A Backstory of the Hollywood Blacklist*, ed. Patrick McGilligan and Paul Buhle (New York: St. Martin's, 1997), 560; Fred Coe oral history, in Kisselhoff, *The Box* 231.

70. David O. Selznick to Henry Luce, October 30, 1954, DOSP, HRC, box 2357, files 5 and 8.

71. David O. Selznick to Henry Luce, October 30, 1954, DOSP, HRC, box 2361, files 5 and 6.

72. Sterling and Kittross, *Stay Tuned*, 341–343.

73. On the illusion behind the so-called Eisenhower Walden, see David Halberstam, *The Fifties* (New York: Villard, 1993), 515–516; Kisselhoff, *The Box*, 339; Engelhardt, *End of Victory*, 146; May, *Homeward Bound*, 146, 171–172.

74. Nina C. Leibman, *Living Room Lectures: The Fifties Family in Film and Television* (Austin: University of Texas Press, 1995), 7.

75. David Halberstam, *Fifties*, 199–201.

76. James L. Brooks, quoted in Horace Newcomb and Robert Alley, *The Producer's Medium: Conversations with Creators of American Television* (New York: Oxford University Press, 1983), 207. Robert Young recalled his days on *Father Knows Best* this way: "I wasn't Jim Anderson, but it was hard for the public to accept that, and it got to be a pain in the ass." Strangers would ask him "about social conduct and raising a family and I'd say, 'Why are you asking me?' "

77. In the final season, Vito Scotti replaced Irish American actor J. Carrol Naish as Luigi, but none of the other principal players were Italian.

78. George Lipsitz, quoted in May, *Homeward Bound,* 172.

79. Art Buchwald, quoted in *Exploring Media Culture: Communication and Human Values* (Thousand Oaks, CA: Sage Publications, 1996), 222; Barnouw, *Tube of Plenty,* 182; May, *Homeward Bound,* 153.

80. Michelle Hilmes, *Hollywood and Broadcasting: From Radio to Cable* (Champaign: University of Illinois Press, 1999), 142–143.

81. Aubrey Cash to Fred Coe, September 5, 1955, Fred Coe Papers, WHS, box 42, file 5; clipping, *Weekly Television Digest* 16, no. 16 (April 18, 1960), Fred Coe Papers, WHS, box 42, file 8.

82. Akira Iriye explores the role played by those outside of official positions, including artists. See Iriye, *Cultural Internationalism and World Order* (Baltimore: John Hopkins University Press, 1997).

83. As Harris and Karafa have shown in Kamalipour, *Images of the United States,* 4–5, people who watch more violent television programs may or may not be more violent themselves, but they certainly tend to believe the world is a more dangerous place than do those who watch such programs less. Likewise, viewers who watch more television tend to hold more traditional gender-role conceptions and more moderate political views. In "Cultivation Theory," Harris and Karafa have thus concluded, "These findings support the idea that the messages offered by TV affect a person's world view or sense of reality."

7. The Cultural Battlefield in Europe

1. William B. Barnes to Dalton Trumbo, postcard, November 1947, DTP, WHS, box 2, file 1.

2. "Blacklist Fadeout," *Time,* January 26, 1959.

3. Although Martin Ritt, the director, and Walter Bernstein, the writer, had both been blacklisted, they admitted that their script for *The Front* was overly sentimental and light, though entertaining. Ritt said later, "I would like to make another picture that deals more seriously with that time and that subject. It might have a chance to be a better film." See Ritt oral history, in *Tender Comrades: A Backstory of the Hollywood Blacklist,* ed. Patrick McGilligan and Paul Buhle (New York: St. Martin's, 1997), 564–565.

4. Walter L. Hixson, *Parting the Curtain: Propaganda, Culture, and the Cold War, 1945–1961* (New York: St. Martin's, 1997), 230; Reinhold Wagnleitner, *Coca-Colonization and the Cold War: The Cultural Mission of the United States in Austria after the Second World War* (Chapel Hill: University of North Carolina Press, 1994), 270; Kenneth Osgood, *Total Cold War: Eisenhower's Secret Propaganda Battle at Home and Abroad* (Lawrence: University Press of Kansas, 2006), 15.

5. Martin Gang, Trumbo's Hollywood lawyer, to Elsie McKeogh, Trumbo's agent, April 8 and 13, 1949, DTP, WHS, box 2, file 9.

6. Ring Lardner Jr., "My Life on the Blacklist," *Saturday Evening Post,* October 14, 1961, 38–44. Investigators filed a copy of this article in SISS, box 65, Communist Party in Hollywood file, RG 46, NA.

7. Dalton Trumbo to George Willner, January 13, 1950, DTP, WHS, box 3, file 3; Trumbo to Larry Parks, October 6, 1949, and Trumbo to McKeogh, November 8, 1949, DTP, WHS, box 3, file 1.

8. Dalton Trumbo to Sally Deutsch, *Theatre Arts Magazine* editor, October 8, 1949, DTP, WHS, box 3, file 1.

9. McKeogh to Trumbo, September 23, 1949; Trumbo to McKeogh, October 8, 1949; *New Yorker* editor to McKeogh, October 21, 1949; Eleanor Stierhem, *Today's Woman* editor, to Trumbo, December 7, 1949, DTP, WHS, box 2, file 9.

10. Bob Meskill to Dalton Trumbo, January 4, 1950, and Trumbo to McKeogh, October 11, 1949, DTP, WHS, box 2, file 9; Trumbo to McKeogh, March 2, 1950, DTP, WHS, box 3, file 3.

11. Audrey Wood and William Liebling to Dalton Trumbo, March 30, 1949; Albert Maltz to Trumbo, April 5, 1949; Trumbo to Barrett Clark, April 11, 1949; McKeogh to Trumbo, April 13, 1949, DTP, WHS, box 2, file 9.

12. Cecil Madden to Dalton Trumbo, April 21, 1949; McKeogh to Trumbo, May 2, 1949; Trumbo to McKeogh, September 17, 1949; Maltz to Trumbo, November 14, 1949, DTP, WHS, box 2, file 9.

13. Norma Barzman oral history, in McGilligan and Buhle, *Tender Comrades*, 28.

14. Ibid., 9–11.

15. Ibid., 12.

16. Jean Rouverol Butler oral history, in McGilligan and Buhle, *Tender Comrades*, 171.

17. Ibid., 168.

18. For another discussion of Dalton Trumbo's experiences in Mexico, see Bruce Cook, *Dalton Trumbo* (New York: Scribner, 1977), 225–227.

19. Ring Lardner Jr. oral history, in McGilligan and Buhle, *Tender Comrades*, 413.

20. *The Children's Hour* was originally produced in 1934, but Hellman recut it, so to speak, to fit the fashions of 1952. Harry Gilroy, "The Bigger the Lie," *New York Times*, December 14, 1952, 4; see also William Wright, *Lillian Hellman: The Image, the Woman* (New York: Simon and Schuster, 1986), 257–260.

21. Arthur Miller, "Why I Wrote 'The Crucible': An Artist's Answer to Politics," *New Yorker*, October 21, 1996, 164.

22. Brooks Atkinson, "At the Theatre," *New York Times*, January 23, 1953, 15; Walter Kerr, "The Crucible," *New York Herald Tribune*, January 23, 1953, 12.

23. Barzman oral history, 14.

24. Allen Boretz oral history, in McGilligan and Buhle, *Tender Comrades*, 127.

25. Richard Pells, *Not Like Us: How Europeans Have Loved, Hated, and Transformed American Culture since World War II* (New York: Basic Books, 1997), 50. For a good study of the German case, see Uta Poiger, *Jazz, Rock, and Rebels: Cold War Politics and American Culture in a Divided Germany* (Berkeley: University of California Press, 2000).

26. Wagnleitner, *Coca-Colonization*, 150, 295, 140–141, 149.

27. *Picturegoer*, July 15, 1950, 13.

28. Poiger, *Jazz*, 39–40; David O. Selznick memorandum, September 29, 1950, and Emily Sanchez to Selznick, September 30, 1950, DOSP, HRC, box 2357, file 8.

29. Hixson, *Parting the Curtain*, 11–27.

30. *DOSB* 26, no. 664 (March 17, 1952): 421–422; *DOSB* 26, no. 666 (March 31, 1952): 489.

31. John Lewis Gaddis, *Strategies of Containment: A Critical Appraisal of Postwar American National Security Policy* (Oxford: Oxford University Press, 1982), 127–197.

32. Melvyn Leffler, *A Preponderance of Power: National Security, the Truman Administration, and the Cold War* (Stanford, CA: Stanford University Press, 1991).

33. Dwight D. Eisenhower, quoted in Gaddis, *Strategies of Containment*, 154–155, from Memorandum, Eisenhower-Bridges telephone conversation, May 21, 1957, DDEL, Ann Whitman file, box 13, "May 57 Misc (2)." On psychological warfare and information campaigns of the 1950s, see Osgood, *Total Cold War*.

34. Summary Report, President's Committee on International Information Activities (Jackson Committee), 1953, DDEL. For USIA funding and statistics for overseas libraries, see Hixson, *Parting the Curtain*, 123–126.

35. Arthur Kaufman to David O. Selznick, November 20, 1951; Hyman Daab to Selznick, November 21, 1951; Selznick memorandum, November 28, 1951; Selznick memorandum, November 29, 1951; Daab to Selznick, December 5, 1951; Kaufman to Selznick, December 18, 1951, DOSP, HRC, box 2367, file 6.

36. David O. Selznick to William Jackson, July 21, 1953, DOSP, HRC, box 2360, file 2.

37. David O. Selznick to Clare Boothe Luce, November 6, December 8 and 27, 1956, DOSP, HRC, box 2361, file 5, and box 2365, file 6; *Los Angeles Times*, November 15, 1957.

38. USIS Country Plan for Italy, April 19, 1956, CBLP, LC, Ambassadorial files, box 633, Missions, Investigations, Country Plan 1956 file.

39. "Venice Sees 'Oklahoma!'" *New York Times*, August 15, 1955, 19.

40. Ruth Montgomery, *New York Daily News*, April 11, 1955; statement for *Congressional Record*, July 14, 1955, CBLP, LC, Ambassadorial files, box 633, *Congressional Record* Inserts, 1953–1956 file.

41. Stephen Gundle, *Between Hollywood and Moscow: The Italian Communists and the Challenge of Mass Culture, 1943–1991* (Durham: Duke University Press, 2000), 50, 75.

42. Statement for *Congressional Record*, May 23, 1956; statement for *Congressional Record*, May 3, 1954, CBLP, LC, Ambassadorial files, box 633, *Congressional Record* Inserts, 1953–1956 file.

43. Stephen Shadegg, *Clare Boothe Luce: A Biography* (New York: Simon and Schuster, 1970), 253–254.

44. This view is consistent with Hixson, *Parting the Curtain*, 122–124, and Wagnleitner, *Coca-Colonization*, 225.

45. Penny Von Eschen, "Who's the Real Ambassador? Exploding Cold War Racial Ideology," in *Cold War Constructions: The Political Culture of United States Imperialism, 1945–1966*, ed. Christian G. Appy (Amherst: University of Massachusetts Press, 2000), 117. See also Hixson, *Parting the Curtain*, 130–131.

46. Lillian Hellman to Lois Fritsch, Summer 1953; Hellman to Fritsch, 1952, LHP, HRC, box 122, file 2.

47. Wagnleitner, *Coca-Colonization*, 136–138.

48. Dwight D. Eisenhower, commencement address to Dartmouth College, June 14, 1953, in *Public Papers of the Presidents of the United States: Dwight D. Eisenhower*, 8 vols. (Washington, DC: Government Printing Office, 1960), 1:415; Eisenhower, press conference, June 17, 1953, *Public Papers of the Presidents*, 1:429–430.

49. Eisenhower, press conference, July 1, 1953, *Public Papers of the Presidents*, 1:463–467.

50. Arthur Miller to Pascal "Pat" Covici, March 15, 1954, Arthur Miller Papers, HRC, Letters file.

51. Miller, "Why I Wrote 'The Crucible,'" 164.

52. Butler oral history, 174.

53. Barzman oral history, 16.

54. Julian Zimet oral history, in McGilligan and Buhle, *Tender Comrades*, 727–728.

55. Jules Dassin oral history, in McGilligan and Buhle, *Tender Comrades*, 217.

56. "US Film Dropped at Fete in Venice," *New York Times*, August 27, 1955, 9.

57. Bosley Crowther, "Festival Frustration," *New York Times*, September 4, 1955, 1.

58. "'Jungle Fever,'" *New York Times*, September 11, 1955, 7.

59. Dassin oral history, 219–220.

60. House Committee on Un-American Activities Supplement, *Testimony of Arthur Miller, Accompanied by Counsel, Joseph L. Rauh Jr., Investigation of the Unauthorized Use of United States Passports*, 85th Cong., 1st sess., 1956, 4689–4690.

61. Lillian Hellman used a clipping service to provide her with the news of Miller's hearings. Her papers at the University of Texas also contain Miller's complete testimony. See LHP, HRC, box 124, file 2.

62. Tennessee Williams to Audrey Wood, April 1, 1954, Tennessee Williams Papers, HRC, box 55, file 6.

63. Arthur Miller, public statement, August 7, 1958, JRP, LC, box 85, Arthur Miller file.

64. Wagnleitner, *Coca-Colonization*, 160–161, 194–195, 202, 219–220, 269.

65. Ibid., 139.

66. This view is consistent with ibid., 268, and with Hixson, *Parting the Curtain*, 110. Hixson writes, "The shift from an aggressive psychological approach to a gradualist approach remained the consistent focus of policy throughout Eisenhower's second term." What I want to emphasize, though, is that progressive ideology played a role in changing American foreign policy in the area of public diplomacy by seeking outlets for free expression in Europe at the same time that the government deployed its cultural weapon.

67. George Kennan, "Where Do You Stand on Communism?" *New York Times Magazine*, May 27, 1951, 53.

68. USIA, Office of Research and Analysis, "Overseas Television Developments" report for 1959, February 3, 1959, President's Committee on Information Activities Abroad (Sprague Committee), DDEL, box 1. According to the Sprague report, the number of television sets in Europe increased from just over 1 million in 1951 to more than 32 million in 1959. See also Kerry Segrave, *American Television Abroad: Hollywood's Attempt to Dominate World Television* (London: McFarland, 1998), 19.

69. Segrave, *American Television Abroad*, 3.

70. USIA, "Overseas Television Developments," February 3, 1959.

71. Segrave, *American Television Abroad*, 49.

72. Ibid., 9–10.

73. "British TV Goes U.S.," *U.S. News & World Report*, July 20, 1956, 110–111, quoted in Segrave, *American Television Abroad*, 50.

74. Segrave, *American Television Abroad*, 10, 34.

75. Barzman oral history, 16; Robert Lee oral history, in McGilligan and Buhle, *Tender Comrades*, 437.

76. Reginald Rose to Lars Schmidt, November 10, 1958, Reginald Rose Papers, WHS, box 6, file 4; Alvin Rakoff to Blanche Gaines, February 18, 1957, RSP, WHS, box 7, file 2; Rod Serling to Rakoff, April 23, 1959, RSP, WHS, box 5, file 8. As one might

expect, MGM wanted to film *The Rack* in Technicolor during the 1950s, but soon gave up on the project.

77. Rakoff to Serling, November 27, 1959, RSP, WHS, box 5, file 8. On the critical component of audience reception Europe, see Pells, *Not Like Us*; Poiger, *Jazz*; Hixson, *Parting the Curtain*; and Wagnleitner, *Coca-Colonization*.

78. "When a Teddy Bear Really Falls in Love," *London Daily Mail*, June 3, 1955; Dilys Powell, "Seeing Plain," *London Sunday Times*, June 5, 1955; Gavin Lambert, "Two's Company," *London Observer*, June 5, 1955; Gerald Bowman, "Plain Folk in Love," *London Evening News*, June 2, 1955; Robert Manning, "A New Era for Playwrights," *Life International*, July 25, 1955, 34.

79. James O. Eastland, interviewed by CBS, *Face the Nation*, February 27, 1955.

80. Sprague Committee, 1959, DDEL, box 9, People to People file.

81. Sprague Committee, Committee Summary Highlights, "The Image of America in Western Europe," 1959, DDEL, box 4, European View of America file.

82. Ibid.; USIA Memorandum, March 16, 1960, DDEL, box 1, Radio and Television file. See also Sprague Committee report, May 23, 1960, DDEL, box 21, International Television file 3.

83. Von Eschen, "Who's the Real Ambassador?" 110–131.

84. Hixson, *Parting the Curtain*, 115.

85. Quoted in Shaun Considine, *Mad as Hell: The Life and Work of Paddy Chayefsky* (New York: Random House, 1994), 179–181.

86. "The Two Worlds: A Day-Long Debate," *New York Times*, July 25, 1959, 3.

87. Robert H. Haddow, *Pavilions of Plenty: Exhibiting American Culture Abroad in the 1950s* (Washington, DC: Smithsonian Institution Press, 1997), 213.

88. USIA Memorandum, March 16, 1960, DDEL, boxes 12–13.

89. *Hollywood Reporter*, December 30, 1959. Investigators filed a copy of this article in SISS, box 113, Films and Plays file, RG 46, NA.

Afterword

1. George F. Kennan, *Memoirs: 1925–1950* (Boston: Little, Brown, 1967), 300–301.

2. George F. Kennan, *At a Century's Ending: Reflections, 1982–1995* (New York: Norton, 1996), 98–99.

Index

Andrew J. Falk is assistant professor of history at Christopher Newport University in Newport News, Virginia, where he teaches courses in American politics, culture, and foreign relations. He earned his Ph.D. in history at the University of Texas at Austin, and lives in Yorktown, Virginia, with his wife and two children.